BUSINESS AT BAY
Critics and Heretics of American Business

Also by Irving S. Michelman

CONSUMER FINANCE: A CASE HISTORY
IN AMERICAN BUSINESS

BUSINESS AT BAY

Critics and Heretics
of
American Business

by
IRVING S. MICHELMAN

With Introduction by
NEIL H. JACOBY

AUGUSTUS M. KELLEY • *PUBLISHERS*
New York 1969

First Published 1969

Second printing, 1970

AUGUSTUS M. KELLEY • *PUBLISHERS*

New York • New York 10010

ISBN 0 678 00473 0

Library of Congress Catalogue Card Number 69-18160

PRINTED IN THE UNITED STATES OF AMERICA
by SENTRY PRESS, NEW YORK, N. Y. 10019

35,350

To Nancy, John and Ted

My father always told me that all businessmen were sons-of-bitches, but I never realized it till now.

John F. Kennedy

Wherein I'll catch the conscience of the King.

Hamlet, Act II, Scene II.

Contents

ix

Illustrations

(following page 172.)

THORSTEIN VEBLEN by Edward B. Child. About the time he was at the University of Chicago, 1892-1907. The painting is in Sterling Hall at Yale University.

SINCLAIR LEWIS. With his first wife, Grace Hegger Lewis, 1916. They travelled from Sauk Centre, Minnesota to Carmel, California in their Model-T Ford.

MARRINER ECCLES. About 1938. He stands between Carter Glass and Congressman Henry Steagall. Note the father-son resemblance between the adversaries.

T. K. QUINN. As author and business critic, 1953.

CYRUS EATON. Hosting a lunch for Soviet Premier Khrushchev at New York's Hotel Biltmore, September 26, 1960.

ADOLF BERLE. With President John F. Kennedy, July 7, 1961.

MICHAEL HARRINGTON, 1968.

HERBERT MARCUSE. At San Diego campus of University of California, August 1968.

Foreword

Is business at bay? Business holds the fort and is waving the banner of the coming trillion dollar Gross National Product. The old injunction about mankind living its days "getting and spending" has been confirmed. Gross National Product means money *spent* on goods and services. Critics and heretics are dazzled by this immense production and consumption.

We live in a business civilization. There is no escaping from it and all the self-deprecating about the meanness of the business spirit will hardly alter this essential fact. Anyone who regrets living in a business civilization was born about two hundred years too late. That would be the time of Thomas Jefferson's ideal America of yeoman farmers and craftsmen. The ideal was already a lost cause. Jefferson must have suspected that the great sweep of nationalism and capitalism, evolving from a prior civilization of feudalism and theocracy, would find its archetype in late-starting America.

Every institution carries the seed of its own destruction. Time insures that it either withers away, suffers violent extinction or transforms into a new institution. Businessmen are by their calling more sensitive to the forces of change than ordinary men. They worship progress and progress does not stand still.

Yet the rites of businessmen are traditionally turned inward, toward a better mousetrap but not toward interference and regulation from the state. The state, however, cannot keep its hands off the very essence of its civilization. Business is too important to be left to business. In twentieth century America, the history of business is largely the history of the intervention and triumph of the state over business. It is a reasonably happy story. Business survived and flourished. The state met its responsibilities to its citizens. All bitter struggles should end so constructively.

This book is related primarily to what happened to big business in the twentieth century, since big business, with due respect to small business, dominates the American scene. The giant corporation impinges on our consciousness during every waking hour, as we incessantly use its products and are exhorted to use even more. We no longer identify the corporation with the individuals who run it. The day of the larger-than-life business personality is over. On the other hand, each decade of history has seen the normal adversary of the corporation — the federal government — personified by the Presidents, who generally reflect the needs and temper of the times when addressing themselves to business problems. By and large, the Presidents are the major critics of business.

To the Presidents another force can be added, the seminal thinkers, men whose ideas and actions, either on target or far wide of the mark, accelerate change by the force of their ideas or the strength of their personalities. I have deliberately selected eight such men, some of whom would raise their eyebrows at "seminal," although all would be pleased to be called "thinkers."

They have been chosen and presented in approximate chronological order, from the turn-of-the-century to the present. Any number of other choices, no doubt some better ones, could have been made. Part of the charm of writing social history, which is what business history must be, lies in the multiplicity of choice, as color is often as important as fact.

The protagonists each appealed to me, and, I suppose, to my

prejudices. They provided a convenient framework on which to hang the exciting tale of property rights, trust-busting, securities speculation, depression-breaking, labor-baiting, business-worshipping, business-hating and social responsibility in a century of exaggeration. My hope is that seeing some of these events through their eyes, while they carried on, as all of us do, their private ambitions and personal sorrows, may make the dry stuff of economics come to life.

The eight comprise an unlikely group. One is an economist who was trained in philosophy. Another a philosopher who became a political hero to rebellious youth. Two are public servants with backgrounds of wealth. Two are maverick businessmen. One is a novelist who wrote social criticism and one is a social critic with a novelist's eye. Their common qualities are for the reader to perceive.

Equally distinguished is Neil H. Jacoby who has graciously provided the Introduction to this book. Mr. Jacoby has spent a fruitful lifetime guiding government, business and students of business in the ways of economics and finance. Just a few of his accomplishments will suffice: Vice-president of the University of Chicago, member of President Eisenhower's Council of Economic Advisers, U. S. representative to the European Organization for Economic Cooperation and Development, U. S. representative in the Economic and Social Council of the United Nations, economic adviser on government missions to India, Laos and Taiwan, co-organizer of the Committee for Economic Development, and for twenty years Dean and developer of the flourishing Graduate School of Business Administration at UCLA.

My deep thanks are expressed to my wife for her encouragement and interest and to Ella Stoloff, her mother, for much delving into the records for the inevitable footnotes.

IRVING S. MICHELMAN

November, 1968
Los Angeles, California

Introduction

by

NEIL H. JACOBY

Irving S. Michelman's delightful book reminds us of a good deal of American economic history that is easily forgotten. It has lessons to teach that are applicable to the problems of today.

Each of the "critics and heretics" mentioned in this volume has a primary intellectual thrust in relation to business. Thorstein Veblen was disturbingly original in his role of economic iconoclast and social critic. One might say that Michael Harrington and Herbert Marcuse are basically philosophical critics, concerned with large visions for change and impatient with pragmatic reforms. On the other hand, Marriner Eccles, T. K. Quinn, Cyrus Eaton and Adolf Berle are very practical men, socio-economic critics anxious to make the system work through continual reforms and a good measure of common sense. Sinclair Lewis is a fascinating critic from the world of literature who made the American businessman look at himself with a new awareness after reading Lewis's best-selling novels, especially the classic *Babbitt*.

The thoughtful reader of this book will, no doubt, come to ask himself some fundamental questions. Why have there been during the past century so many articulate fault-finders with businessmen and the American business system? Has the social performance of our business system, and of its prime movers — the entrepreneurs and managers — been so poor as to warrant the disapproval of many American writers? Why does criticism continue, even though governments of both socialistic and capitalistic countries have of late been making greater use of autonomous, profit-motivated enterprises in their search for greater economic welfare for their peoples?

Misunderstanding of the respective roles of private enterprise and of the government in the operation of the American economy has been a major source of business criticism. Ever since this nation began to transform itself from an agrarian to an industrial society there has existed the problem of defining, in specific terms, the separate responsibilities of government and business for producing satisfactory economic results. Today, when the U.S. economy has become a "service" economy, this problem persists in the form of an intensive search for a definition of the "social responsibilities" of business. Because there has been no clear operational theory of the economic functions of government, businessmen and government officials have often blamed each other unfairly over their respective roles.

One basic function of government, it is now generally agreed, is to *maintain an adequate but not excessive level of monetary demand* for goods and services at all times. The most dramatic example of government's failure to carry out this task was the disastrous deflation and unemployment during the Great Depression of 1929-1932. The causes of this catastrophe included the misguided budget-balancing efforts of the federal government during the Hoover Administration and the failure of the Federal Reserve System to counteract a deep shrinkage in the money supply. Mr. Michelman's interpretation of the intellectual progress in the economic ideas of Marriner Eccles, an enlightened businessman who went to work for Roosevelt, is an excellent case in point.

Another basic responsibility of government, in a country whose economy operates principally through private enterprises competing in open markets, is to *maintain effective competition* and to keep undue monopoly power from private hands. Much of the business criticism in the United States at the beginning of the century made business monopoly its target. Businessmen were tagged as villains for seeking or using monopoly power. Equal criticism, however, could have been addressed to the government for failing to eliminate business subsidies and to create countervailing bargaining power in the hands of the individual farmer or worker, or to enforce the new antitrust legislation.

A third inescapable responsibility of government under any economic system is to *supply a basic income to all citizens unable to earn it for themselves and to equalize opportunities,* educational and otherwise, for personal development. A considerable segment of the American literature of economic dissent in the early twentieth century decried the great inequalities of wealth and income and deplored the miseries of the poor and handicapped that arose under a *laissez-faire* governmental policy. Government intervention in the form of labor legislation and encouragement of unions solved much of this problem. Equally helpful was development of welfare programs financed by progressive taxation. Today, when many conservative business leaders endorse the principle of the "negative income tax," the existence of this essential task of government is no longer a subject of debate.

Mr. Michelman has written perceptively that "the history of business in America is largely the history of the struggle between the advocates of business freedom and the advocates of government intervention." May we not expand this proposition and assert: The history of business in America is largely the history of a search for a satisfactory theory of the relationship between the role of private enterprise and the role of the state. Stated more precisely, it is the history of a continuing effort to find an optimal form of economic organization — one in which the public and the private sectors each complement the other's functions, jointly maximizing the public welfare. This search has been the crux of domestic political battles from the Civil War to the present. Readers of this book will find Mr. Michelman's exploration of "seminal" thoughts in this respect to be particularly enlightening. Time has brought agreement on the proper resolution of many of these issues. As the economic literacy of Americans has risen, a clearer popular conception has emerged of the best division of labor between business and government. On this subject Americans seem closer to a national consensus today than at any time during the past century.

One reason for continuing criticism of business, for which my fellow economists and I must accept responsibility, is the lack of a generally accepted theory of business entrepreneurship. As Professor William Baumol of Princeton University pointed out recently before the American Economic Association, the "models" of business enterprises generally used in teaching economics unrealistically assume that a business confronts certain cost and demand conditions, and that the businessman reacts to them simply as a price and output "adjuster." The creative and enormously important initiative taken by the enterpriser are completely ignored. Small wonder that many students leave college with the fixed idea that business is dull and non-creative! For the true entrepreneur, success in the game of creating and building business enterprises is the key incentive and reward. Money is merely a set of counters by which success is measured. Profit is subject to a new interpretation, as Mr. Michelman clearly sets forth.

It must be conceded, as this lively book well documents, that the rank and file of businessmen have not usually been allied with the forces of change and improvement during the past century. Although one can point to individual exceptions, such as Henry Ford with his five-dollar daily pay for the factory worker in 1914, or Marriner Eccles with his proposals for revising American banking and fiscal practises, the National Association of Manufacturers and the U. S. Chamber of Commerce have usually been opposed to current proposals for social and economic change. Indeed, it was only with the founding of the Committee for Economic Development in 1942, at the initiative of Paul G. Hoffman, that a union of business leaders and intellectuals was formed, and a group of prominent businessmen began to put their substantial political weight behind economic reforms. CED was the first American effort to bridge the gap between the "two worlds" of the scholar and the businessman. During the past quarter-century, it has written a magnificent record of achievement. It has put businessmen into the action of making progressive economic and social policy. Perhaps, in another quarter of a century, business will not so often be "at bay" as it has been in the past.

Mr. Michelman's discerning history is a call for businessmen to be open-minded and tolerant of change. It is a valuable addition to business history.

THORSTEIN VEBLEN:
Disturber of the Intellectual Peace

PART I

The time is 1929. The setting is the stage version of J. P. Marquand's novel about business success, *Point of No Return*. Malcolm Bryant, anthropologist, speaks to his friend, Charles Gray, on the subject of Charles's marrying into the leisure class:

MALCOLM

When I was in Papua I lived in a nice clear tribe. There was a nice young fellow there — warrior class, not chief class . . . He fell in love with the Chief's third daughter. They made him produce six pigs and a canoe for the marriage rites. Then they made him wear the double nose ring and they tatooed the omoo bird insignia on

1

his right buttock. You don't get those tatoos off when
once they're on. Poor fella. He was out of his group. He
was very unhappy. He began to lose weight. He wasn't
mobile.

CHARLES
Okay, Malcolm, I get it.

Delighted audiences who also got the point may have recalled
1929 as the year of the death of Professor Thorstein Veblen, author of *The Theory of the Leisure Class* in 1899 and merciless
critic of the business system ever since. Alone, improvident and despairing, he was cremated and his ashes were scattered in the Pacific
ocean near his isolated California mountain cabin. The Norwegian
farm boy who had so brilliantly satirized American businessmen as
a tribe of leisure-loving "predatory barbarians," hopelessly conditioned by the forces of anthropology and evolution to "getting something for nothing" through the use of "force and fraud," was finally
silenced at age seventy-two. In his pencilled death note, he characteristically mimicked the language of the lawyers whom he had
consigned to the "kept classes" of his private universe by stipulating
that:

> . . . no tombstone, slab, epitaph, tablet, inscription or
> monument of any nature or posture, be set up in my mem-
> ory or name in any place or at any time; that no obituary,
> memorial, portrait or biography of me, nor any letters
> written to or by me be printed or published, or in any way
> reproduced, copied or circulated.[1]

History has a strange way of coming to the defense of its neglected
geniuses — Veblen's last wishes have been magnificently breached
by the American intellectuals who have installed him in their gal-
lery of great thinkers and creative minds. In so doing, one suspects
they are making amends for the paucity of rewards and recognition
Veblen was tendered in his day, although no one could have courted

failure or incited lack of friendship more ardently than this disturbing, ambivalent and remote personality.

Actually, events themselves wrote a startling epitaph for Veblen immediately after his death. On September 3, 1929, the stock market reached its giddiest peak; on Black Tuesday, October 29, the Big Bull Market was dead beyond belief and the Great Depression, which would see thirteen million people unemployed, was about to settle upon the land. The image of the American businessman sunk to an all time low as President Roosevelt, in his inaugural address on March 4, 1933, asserted that:

> The rulers of the exchange of mankind's goods have failed, through their own stubbornness and their own incompetence . . . Practises of the unscrupulous money-changers stand indicted . . . in the hearts and minds of men . . .

The irreverent scoldings of an eccentric professor of economics who had, incidentally, predicted a major depression could no longer be dismissed as nonsense by a nation soberly reconsidering the merits of its business system under Presidents Harding, Coolidge and Hoover. Thus, in the span of his lifetime, Veblen not only participated in the reaction against the business excesses of the Gilded Age in which he matured but was also an unwelcome guest at the great success celebrations of the twenties. He died as business was about to experience the traumatic convulsions of the depression. Our probings of the business conscience can well start with the education and background of Thorstein Veblen.

II

He was born in 1857 to immigrant Norwegian parents on a Wisconsin frontier farm. Ten years earlier, his father, a stoical master carpenter, had left poverty-stricken Norway for a new life and had suffered the usual hardships in reaching the promised land. Arriving in Milwaukee penniless and sick after a dismal voyage, Thomas Veblen walked twenty-eight miles the next day to a friend's factory in Port Washington and commenced work. If Veblen bore strong affection for any man, it was for this primordial father-figure whom he later said possessed the finest mind he had ever known.

In his quest for the masterless technician independent of all authority (a curiously conservative vision to be incorporated in much of his writings), Veblen's devotion to his father can easily be recognized. At the same time, the mechanically-minded father, who was among the first to use a tractor, was a dominant and unyielding man. This has moved one of the numerous high-level Veblen fans, David Riesman, author of *The Lonely Crowd*, to speculate on the resulting "constraints" in Veblen's subconscious. Yielding to the temptation to psychoanalyze a man who was surely a candidate for the couch, Riesman surmises that Veblen's scheme of contrasting the strong, aggressively male businessmen and warriors with the dominated, peaceable, guileless workers and farmers reflects conflicting memories of his parents.[2] So much for the temptation.

Remarkably self-reliant though he was, Thomas Veblen never learned to speak English, partially because of the fanatic clannishness the Norwegians imposed upon themselves in the midwest communities. Their feuding neighbors were the Yankee traders and townsmen who extended new world hospitality to their less sophisticated fellow Americans by contemptuously dubbing them "Norskies" and "Scandihoofians." The Norwegians in turn felt that those Yankees who farmed were more interested in the speculative value of their real estate than in tilling the soil while those who ran the stores and practised the law in the town itself were to be avoided like the plague. Unable to shake off these childhood memories, Thorstein Veblen later paid a score to his old adversaries in a famous essay which begins with:

> The country town of the Great American farming region is the perfect flower of self-help and cupidity standardised on the American plan.[3]

These Yankee traders and lawyers, at least, endowed the man who would be hailed as America's greatest social critic with the dead-pan humor and tongue-in-cheek exaggerations that are among his saving graces.

In 1865, while many Norwegians were facing service in the Civil War after barely escaping slaughter at the hands of the Sioux Indians only a few years back, Thomas Veblen moved his expanding family to another prairie farm in Wheeling township in Minnesota. Here young Thorstein, growing up with ten brothers and sisters, gained distinction as a tease, a fighter and a precociously brilliant young man. With greatness comes legends, and it is said the odd child who still spoke no English but was excellent in German, Latin and antique Norse dialects disposed of his enemies by writing Greek anathemas against them on the walls of barns.

His mother, Kari Thorsteindatter, appears to have possessed the strong maternal and religious instincts of the pioneer women of Ole Rølvaag's novel, *Giants in the Earth*. It was she who introduced her favorite son to the great Norwegian sagas and the Bible, both of which heritages the teenage skeptic would soon assign to the same area of credibility.

Religion was a constant concern of the Norwegian enclaves and the preachers of the township eventually recommended young Thorstein as a candidate for the Lutheran ministry. Thomas Veblen kept his own counsel on the matter. It was his driving ambition to have his sons go to college, although he was the only farmer in his community to do so, and he decided against the proposed Luther College in favor of the less theological Carleton College in nearby Northfield. In an excess of taciturnity, the father called the seventeen year old Thorstein from the field one day, placed him in a buggy wherein his baggage was all packed and informed him for the first time that he was on his way to Carleton Academy where he would learn English and prepare for enrollment in the college.

Veblen thus began in 1874 a tour of American universities that would see him shuttle from one end of the continent to the other, an academic wanderer to the end, underpaid and under-promoted. It started with conservative, highly religious Carleton and ended in

1919 with classes at the New School for Social Research in New York, at the other end of the spectrum. At Carleton he jarred the faculty and students with papers such as "A Plea for Cannibalism" and "An Apology for a Toper." At the New School he was front page news concerning a revolt within the Junior League. It seems that Mrs. Dorothy Whitney Straight, president of the organization and also one of the founders of *The New Republic* magazine, was requiring aspirants for membership to attend lectures at the New School. A rebel faction, led by the daughter of the rector of Trinity Church, thereupon circulated a petition against the indoctrination program for the reason that Thorstein Veblen, Professor Charles A. Beard, recently resigned from Columbia over the issue of free speech, and Dr. James H. Robinson would be giving the lectures:

> It is submitted that these men are not suitable teachers for the members of the League . . . Dr. Veblen has an article in The Dial of January 25, 1919 on "The Vested Interests and the Common Man" in which he says: "A vested interest is a legitimate right to get something for nothing . . ."[4]

From Carleton, Veblen went to Johns Hopkins for a brief spell of graduate work and then to Yale on a fellowship where he earned his Ph.D. in philosophy. A threadbare student in one of the strongholds of Eastern privilege, he was now prepared for a career in college teaching. His sardonic personality and half-concealed agnosticism were poor credentials for the philosophy departments of the denominational universities—most of the department heads were ministers—and no jobs were forthcoming. The future critic of the leisure class spent seven miserable years (1884-1891) of enforced leisure waiting for an appointment. He used the time profitably by reading prodigiously and aimlessly in a variety of fields. One suspects that the detached scholar secretly enjoyed the luxury of so improving his mind, an opportunity most of the businessmen he attacked might equally envy. If his students later marvelled at the erudition of this man who could discourse effortlessly on prehistoric skull measurements, the trading habits of medieval German merchants and the potlatch wealth of the northwest Indians, it was partly because of his unwanted sabbatical.

For his wife, Ellen Rolfe, whom he married in 1888, the seven lean years were an introduction to ordeals yet to come. A spirited, intelligent young woman, she was the niece of the president of Carleton College and came from a prominent family. A talented writer, possessed with imagination, she saw promises of greatness in the skeptical farm boy she had met at Carleton. They moved to her family's farm at Stacyville, Iowa, where she loyally indulged him in his great bout of reading, relieved by occasional puttering in the garden. Together they studied Greek and Latin and ancient sagas. Their idyll was eventually shattered by Veblen's trail of romances in the universities as well as his fear of fatherhood. After several separations they were divorced in 1912, at which time Ellen correctly feared he would not pay the twenty-five dollars monthly alimony. In losing Ellen, he lost the one person who was a match for him and who might have penetrated his cold exterior. His conduct towards her was humiliating and somewhat sadistic. The rather homely Veblen we see pictured in his old age—a mute, bumpkin Socrates— was apparently more dashing in his youth. In fact he was never without female admirers. "What are you going to do," he asked, "if the lady insists on moving in on you?" when the university authorities complained. The presidents of the University of Chicago and Stanford, more embarrassed by his affairs than his radical writings, were relieved to see him move on. In 1918, Veblen returned the compliment by publishing his book, *The Higher Learning in America*, in which he eloquently defended the pursuit of truth as the essence of the good life but passionately denounced the universities for their submission to business control through their boards of trustees. College presidents were "captains of erudition" reporting to "captains of industry":

> Plato's classic scheme of folly, which would have the philosophers take over the management of affairs, has been turned on its head: the men of affairs have taken over direction of the pursuit of knowledge.[5]

III

What were the business conditions in America in the final quarter of the nineteenth century? What conflicts between business and society were churning in the mind of this unemployed doctor of philosophy—the prematurely returned Candide tilling his garden in Stacyville?

There was first of all the conflict between the farmers and the "interests" of the East, between the men of the plains and farms and the men of the sprawling, powerful cities. This conflict arose from the rapid change of America from a predominantly agrarian society to a new type of urban, industrialized life. Worried and threatened by this change, which was greatly accelerated by the technological impetus of the Civil War, the farmers were further exacerbated by the panic of 1873 and the four year depression starting in 1893. Wheat prices, already depressed by vast technical changes in flour production, fell further. Grasshopper plagues swarmed over the plains and farms were foreclosed by the thousands. What they had not lost on their farms, farmers now lost on defaulted railroad securities as the railroad promoters bought, reorganized and resold the lines which had spanned the continent but brought little benefits to the farmers. The technical revolution in farming and transportation also had international aspects as huge new tracts of farm land in Argentina, Canada and Australia joined in competing with the American export market.

The farmer still occupied a venerated place in American thought and culture. He was the truly independent, democratic man, viewed with nostalgia by his sons in the cities and ennobled by the literature and folklore of the age. His virtues were the national virtues of self-reliance and independence, but in fact, the farmer had already yielded to the demands of the mercantile spirit along with the rest of the country.

By the middle of the nineteenth century, the independent, self-sufficient farmer had become a commercial farmer, usually raising one major crop of wheat, cotton or corn which required an extensive investment in land and equipment. Bankers, interest rates, railroad rates, European conditions, the middlemen who sold him the products used on the farm—all these factors now gravely affected his prosperity. He did more business than ever. Farm lands doubled in acreage in the last half of the century and farm families increased from one and one-half million to five million but farm prices were continually dropping. Wheat, for example, dropped from $1.60 a bushel in 1866 to 49¢ in 1894. Land values boomed in spite of this as the population moved West and increased by millions, including a flood of immigrants each year. The farmer often joined in the speculative mania by borrowing at high rates to acquire more land. Plagued by business cycles, recurrent overproduction and completely unprotected as to prices, the farmer felt he was being cheated out of his share of the nation's obvious progress by his admirers outside the farm. To add to his woes, a great drought came upon the plains in 1887, lasting for five parched years. Kansas was particularly hard hit. Fifteen thousand mortgages were foreclosed, mostly by Eastern lenders, and pioneer wagons limped back with the legend: "In God we trusted, in Kansas we busted." In the 1870's the Grangers, originally a farmers' social organization, burst into political activity and succeeded in obtaining precedent-shattering regulation of railroad rates in a few states but the idea of regulation on a national level was beyond comprehension. Striking out at profiteering middlemen, the Grangers also started the first important farm cooperatives. A few smart businessmen received the message and with Granger blessings Montgomery Ward started the great mail order business in 1872. The Granger movement was an omen, pointing to America's first major protest movement, Populism, which emerged from the farmlands in the 1890's.

Veblen and his father often talked about Ignatius Donnelly, the Minnesota firebrand orator whose warped intelligence and fiery warnings appealed to America's well-read, isolated farmers. Donnelly, a veteran of the Granger movement, and author of the enormously popular *Caesar's Column*, an Orwellian prediction of dictatorship by the plutocracy in 1988, electrified the Populist convention of 1892. Charging that there was a vast conspiracy afoot, bringing the nation to the verge of moral, political and material ruin, he sent the Populist Presidential candidate, James B. Weaver, on to poll 1,041,600 votes (8% of the total) in the ensuing election. The Populists then polled 1,400,000 votes in the 1894 Congressional elections, causing a shiver to run through respectable circles until William Jennings Bryan, the Prairie Avenger, absorbed the Populist movement in his platform of 1896 and met solid defeat at the hands of McKinley. In spite of their show of strength, the Populists carried only a few states and found no support in either the urban labor or the middle class. America was simply not ready to accept reform leadership from the shrill voices of radical leaders. The great majority of the people were conservative and optimistic about the resources and destiny of America regardless of the signs of poverty amidst progress. Yet practically all of the Populist platform, including a federal income tax, would be duly enacted into national or state laws, under more acceptable sponsorship, within twenty years.

There were overtones of racism and native demagoguery in Populism that were unattractive. In addition, there was a falsely simplified separation in their creed of America's complex society into two conflicting classes: the producers, such as farmers, workers and small businessmen and the non-producers, such as the trusts, monopolies and banks. While Veblen would not advocate inefficient smallness as a virtue in the new technological age he was attempting to comprehend, he did think in terms of this separation of interests. Agrarian populism, though far too emotional for his highly sophisticated and rational judgment, was clearly a factor in his developing thought. More important, over one million folk-heroes were beating the tom-toms to American business interests to reform.

How shall we describe these nineteenth century businessmen who were being cast in the villain's role by their outraged and frustrated cousins on the farm? Labels are unfair but the one most likely to survive is "The Robber Barons." Here a leap in time is in order.

The book of that title was published in 1934 by Matthew Josephson. It was dedicated to Charles and Mary Beard, the distinguished historians who were so eloquently reminding surprised Americans that their history—even their Constitution—had both the virtues and *defects* of being conditioned, perhaps primarily, by economic and business considerations. In *The Robber Barons*, Josephson clearly reflects his debt to Veblen, who had often drolly compared the power of business with feudal power. Veblen, however, rarely mentioned names, preferring abstraction to journalism.

In the same year, incidentally, the young Lewis Mumford, who was to become a towering genius in American social analysis, published *Technics and Civilization*, in which he traced the influence of the machine on modern life, again with due acknowledgment to the stimulus of Veblen. Like Veblen, Mumford crosses at will into several disciplines such as sociology, psychology, aesthetics and anthropology. Both men are academic generalists compared with today's typical specialists. Their admirers are likely to term each as "the last man to know everything."

And finally in 1934, Veblen's last book, like his others a poor seller, trickled into print. *Essays in Our Changing Order* was edited posthumously by Leon Ardzrooni, a former student who appears to have played the unlikely role of intellectual groom to Veblen's rueful knight as well as nursemaid and guardian of his final years. Such devotion provokes again the desire to explore the riddle of Veblen's personality and postpone the examination of his tilt—quixotic as it was—with America's overpowering business civilization. In this search, Robert L. Duffus, another of Veblen's admirers, is a friendly witness. An engaging and humane editorial staff member of the *New York Times* for many years, Duffus introduces a more responsive Veblen in his review of the *Essays*:

> He never had, in fact, or needed to have a better friend than Leon Ardzrooni . . . Those who had the good fortune to see the two men together at intervals during the last decade of Veblen's life will never forget the richness of the conversation which almost invariably resulted, or the solicitude and understanding with which Ardzrooni fostered the older man's creative powers.[6]

Duffus had come to know Veblen in a most unusual way. As a young Stanford student in 1907, he and his brother lived in Veblen's cottage in return for doing the household chores after Ellen Rolfe had walked out. Duffus recalls that he could not summon up affection for the "austere, locked-in personality," although there was room for awe and admiration. He feels that the tragic cast of Veblen's life arose from his inability, like Dean Swift's of another century, to believe in any possible reforms for the human folly he exposed:

> I have asked myself whether great men have to be un-
> happy. So many of them seem to be. Perhaps this is
> because they see truth clearly, know what ought to be
> done, and cannot really accept the fact that the mass of
> mankind is so much less wise, so much more ignorant
> than they. But I suppose Veblen was unhappy, as I have
> suggested, because he was sure what ought to be done
> and never sure that it would be done. He was a man out
> of the future, or out of some golden past, and he was not
> at home.[7]

But enough of sentiment, especially for a man who consciously rejected sentimentality as a variant of "animisms"—those super-stitions impeding society's progress. Back to the robber barons.

They came to power in the "Gilded Age," Mark Twain's name for one of the sleaziest, most corrupt, ostentatious and money-lusting periods in American history—the decades after the Civil War. It was a period of boodle and greed, but also one of heroic accom-plishments when business giants forged and consolidated the white-hot industrial machine on private anvils of free, unregulated enterprise. Longfellow's village blacksmith must have settled be-neath his chestnut tree in disbelief. The barefoot boy with cheek of tan reached for the latest Horatio Alger.

It was an age that cast up crass and vulgar business heroes who were admired by the majority of the people as "smart men" in spite of their appalling lack of ethics. It produced a system of big busi-ness as the most distinctive and permanent feature of the American landscape in an incredibly short period. In turn this system survived a series of bloody strikes in the 1890's that seem unbelievable to the businessman of today, weathered the moral indignation of the turn-of-the-century Progressive reform movement, smarted under the chidings of Theodore Roosevelt and Woodrow Wilson, surged triumphantly through the twenties and finally succumbed to domestication at the hands of the federal government as a result of the Great Depression.

It is easy to concentrate on the depredations of the robber barons. There is a perverse pleasure in tracing the beginnings of the great dynastic fortunes such as those of Vanderbilt, Astor, Carnegie, Morgan, Rockefeller, Mellon and Harriman and discovering the flaws in their founders' characters, their arrogance, cunning, rapaciousness and "public be damned" attitude. If we are inclined to forgive by acknowledging their immense productive feats—their creation of industry, transportation and employment for a nation doubling in population from 1879 to 1900—then we can certainly deplore the next level of barons, the completely unprincipled, unproductive speculators like Jim Fisk, Jay Gould, Daniel Drew, Russell Sage and similar assorted scoundrels.

Gould's Goldfinger scheme to corner the nation's gold supply in 1869, involving the corruption of President Grant's brother-in-law in the process, was typical of the insolence of the financial speculators. Young Henry Adams, the disillusioned descendant of incorruptible Presidents, wrote about the gold conspiracy to advance his own brief career as a Washington journalist. Years later he bitterly recalled the incident:

> The worst scandals of the eighteenth century were relatively harmless by the side of this, which smirched executive, judiciary, banks, corporate systems . . . in one dirty cesspool of vulgar corruption.[8]

In the Gilded Age, big business was dominated by individual owners, captains of industry and finance known to all the nation, the reverse of today's condition when few can name the heads of any of our great corporations. If you were a suffering farmer, a striking laborer or a dissenting college professor, you could hardly fail to regard your opposition as individuals rather than impersonal corporations. An extreme example of this personification would be the attempted assassination of the steel magnate Henry C. Frick by the anarchist Alexander Berkman during the Homestead strike of 1892, a strategy hardly conceivable today.

These individuals, it must be admitted, conducted themselves with an infuriating smugness and with touches of divine right that *were* feudal. Old Cornelius Vanderbilt, unlettered and uncouth, might be laughed off for his "What do I care about the law? Hain't I got the power?" but today's most conservative business spokesman must gag over the words of George F. Baer, president of the Philadelphia and Reading Coal & Iron Company, during the anthracite strike of 1902:

> The rights and interests of the laboring man will be protected and cared for by the Christian men to whom God in his infinite wisdom has given control of the property interests of the country.[9]

John D. Rockefeller in all innocence had stated "God gave me my money" as he began to part with it, including millions for the University of Chicago which was soon to shelter Thorstein Veblen. Rockefeller also found it possible to construct a theological bridge to a convenient Darwinism as he explained to his Sunday school class that the development of the Standard Oil Trust was "merely a survival of the fittest . . . This is not an evil tendency in business, it is merely the working out of a law of nature and God."

Andrew Carnegie, Frick's overlord, was more articulate and complex than his fellow barons. The poor immigrant Scottish boy who became the master of steel and one of the richest men in the world possessed an active conscience and a nagging desire to justify his life of ruthless acquisition and exploitation of labor. A religious skeptic, he was refreshingly of this earth as he outlined his thoughts in his book *The Gospel of Wealth*, published in 1900.

In brief, he approved of the fierce competitive rule in life and the economic law of individual self-seeking because these natural forces had produced great wealth and progress for the country. On the other hand, they brought inordinate wealth to the skillful capitalists like himself who had performed their functions so well. "The man who dies thus rich thus dies disgraced," was his startling conclusion.[10] His solution was to advocate confiscatory estate taxes, or to leave nothing to heirs, to give away all of one's money as a return to the social pool, which he did in the amount of $350,000,000.

But Carnegie's compulsion for writing books that would legitimatize his fortune called further attention to one of the great provocations of the Gilded Age, the vast discrepancy in incomes. His personal share in his Carnegie empire's profits in 1900 alone was over $20,000,000, with no income tax to pay and the purchasing value of the dollar equal to four dollars today. Meanwhile the hours were long (twelve hours at Homestead before and after the strike) and the average earnings of American factory workers were about $500 per year, when they worked. The familiar story of child labor, sweatshop labor, bloody repression of unions and strikers, industrial accidents, city slums, water pollution and widespread poverty amidst progress has often been told. The businessman's conscience was not of stone. These were the standards of the times, the price of fantastic, untamed growth. Yet it was a system accepted in good faith by a broad consensus of optimistic people, including the hopeful immigrants whose supply of manpower guaranteed wages at the lowest level.

One of the greatest strains on this public acceptance must surely have been the conduct of the gaudy rich, a display of waste and wealth that gnawed at the ascetic Veblen's viscera and spilled over into some of his most satirical and exaggerated social comment. The social historians have impaled these magnificos in our chronicles, creating a hot-house cast of characters to contrast with another mythology of a purer, antique America, the country of Paul Bunyan, Mike Fink, Leatherstocking, Daniel Boone, Davy Crockett . . .

There was the imperious Morgan with the fierce eyes and bulbous red nose which none of his courtiers could acknowledge they saw, sailing away in a yacht named *Corsair* to raid Europe for first editions and fabulous paintings. When the country faced a financial panic because of a gold reserve drain in 1895, President Cleveland went to Morgan for help and the flow of gold was checked. When Theodore Roosevelt moved against Morgan's Northern Securities Company in 1901 under the recent Sherman Antitrust Act, Morgan told the President, "If we have done anything wrong, send your man to my man and they can fix it up." In 1912, the House's Pujo Investigating Committee revealed that the Morgan interests held control or directorships in corporations involving over twenty-two billion dollars. As with all kingdoms, Morgan's would decline and by the time the midget climbed on the knee of J. P. Morgan the Younger at the Senate Banking Committee investigation in 1933, the fears of banker control were abated. The Senate probe revealed that Morgan and his nineteen partners had paid no income taxes for 1931 and 1932 and kept a list of insiders for stock purchases below market price. Yet Morgan lectured the Senate Committee with words that must have been of supreme irony to the ghost of Thorstein Veblen: "If you destroy the leisure class," Morgan said, "you destroy civilization."[11]

The Vanderbilts as their contribution built seven great mansions on Fifth Avenue in the 1880's. Some of them duplicated fifteenth century castles and the total expense exceeded twelve million dollars. In addition there were mansions by the sea in Newport, the most dazzling of which was William K. Vanderbilt's Marble House, at a cost of eleven millions. George W. Vanderbilt's ducal residence in Asheville, North Carolina, reputed to top them all in cost and splendor, may have caught the fancy of the academic world with its library of 250,000 volumes. The construction of these palatial homes from Long Island Sound to Nob Hill in San Francisco provided a tidy contribution to the gross national product of the day, even if it injured the sensibilities of those out-of-tune Americans like Henry Adams who wistfully remembered a plainer and more virtuous aristocracy based on land, culture and patriotism. It was a case of capitalists running rampant in a style never to be repeated in American history—not in our Southwest or elsewhere.

The mansions were filled to overflowing with the clutter of art objects and bric-a-brac characteristic of the overblown age, great emphasis being placed on treasures from Europe, the only model available for such grandeur. Even the titles of Europe were imported, as the great families married their daughters into the British nobility, often with a written contract documenting the consideration.

It was something of a strenuous life for the business giants of those days. Even among the more circumspect American-Jewish banking dynasties which were just beginning to flourish, "our crowd," as this élite called themselves, were on a continual schedule of trips from one seasonal home to another or on ritual travels abroad that required great planning for their accomplishment.

Others were less circumspect. It was routine for the great houses to serve dinner for a hundred guests at a time, since money was no object and a genuine servant class existed, but inevitably someone would go too far, beyond the limits permitted by a daydreaming public which followed the rich as it followed movie stars and celebrities in a later day. The Bradley Martin ball, given in 1897 as the country emerged from a long and bitter depression, managed to consume $369,000 of expenses in one evening, or at least so it was reported. The James Hazen Hyde ball a few years later, which transformed Sherry's into a miniature Versailles, was equally offensive, especially when Hyde was later found to be looting his own Equitable Life Assurance Society. Both the Bradley Martins and the Hydes eventually moved to Europe. They sensed a reaction to their pursuit of happiness quite different from the popular reception extended, for example, to the drawings of Charles Dana Gibson of the rich at play.

IV

The rich at play! Perhaps here we are given an insight into the tolerance shown for the great capitalists and the newly rich, an explanation of why the indignant Bryan was overwhelmed by the conservative McKinley in the most decisive Presidential defeat since Greeley by Grant. True enough the forces of reform would soon prevail but they would arrive through patrician figures like Theodore Roosevelt and Woodrow Wilson, not through the populist Bryan, the socialist Debs, or the sideline critic Veblen, though the importance of these probers and prodders should never be underestimated. The American character has always had a secret affection for the tall story, the gambling instinct, the big venture, the big money—for success itself. Trade was the Yankee's natural bent, and speculation a matter of second nature in a country possessing an unlimited frontier for close to one hundred years. Nor was the government itself the passive spectator one would associate with the official doctrine of *laissez-faire*. It distributed *largesse* on a grand scale. There were reckless grants of land and funds to the railroad promoters who would risk spanning the continent, a long history of fabulous homestead grants to encourage the pioneers, tariffs to protect the home industries and occasionally the militia to quell the strikers. The original dour New Englanders had exchanged much of their Puritanism for an exuberant self-confidence as they wrested the wilderness with their own hands and won the west. The immigrants who came to the New World could only remember worse conditions, both spiritually and physically, in their Old World. No doubt the rich were recognized by all for what they were, a spurious nobility playing with their toys and smart enough to put away their crowns and robes when the game was over. Their mighty wars for railroads and oil fields and steel mills were gigantic games to be read about with an apparent good humor by the average voter who was proud in any case of the incontrovertible statistics of economic growth. In the final fifty years of the nineteenth century America not only caught up with the mother

country England but also passed her in terms of national wealth
by one-third! Confident that they would some day get their share,
most people were not particularly interested in levelling down the
rich. Yet let a man by the name of Morgan or Rockefeller run for
President and the whistle would be blown soon enough. These men
were not even to be compared with the great democratic hero Lincoln, who was a failure as a storekeeper.

But many of the great businessmen had something in common
with Lincoln—their humble origins. If Carnegie could begin at
thirteen as a $1.20 a week bobbin boy in a Pittsburgh cotton mill,
John D. Rockefeller as a $4.00 a week clerk in Cleveland and
Edward H. Harriman as an office boy in a New York broker's office
at $5.00 a week, why could not anyone become a tycoon and
philanthropist to boot? While thoughtful Americans more concerned with moral problems than material interests were reading
Edward Bellamy's Utopian *Looking Backward* ("I believe this was
the turning point of our lives," exclaimed Ellen Veblen as she and
her husband read the book together in Stacyville[12]), others read
Horatio Alger. Bellamy's sales were sensational, over one million
copies in the 1890's and national fan clubs as well, but Alger's
books on rags-to-riches sold *twenty million copies* between the
Civil War and World War I. Since they were written as boys'
books, preaching industry and frugality as the way to success
along with outwitting villains and ingratiating one's self with rich
people, surely the position of the businessman was invulnerable—
that is, if books are weapons and the minds of the young can be
captured.

The Alger books were just one more link in the "steel chain of
ideas" that existed at the turn of the century.[13] These ideas supported America's traditional conservatism and would test the mettle
of would-be reformers. There was the doctrine of individualism,
deriving from Christianity's individuality of conscience and im-
planted in the American mind along with the founding doctrine
of equality. It tended to glorify the self-made, self-reliant man who
did not need the interference of the state. Organized religion was

also linked with materialism and the status quo, somehow finding a way to preach a gospel of success derived from the Protestant ethic of laying up wealth for the greater glory of God. Bishop Lawrence proclaimed that "in the long run it is only to the man of morality that wealth comes," equating Godliness with riches. Henry Ward Beecher opposed man-made reforms on the grounds that "God has intended the great to be great and the little to be little." The greatest endorsement from the pulpit came from Russell Conwell who delivered his "Acres of Diamonds" lecture to no less than six thousand audiences, an estimated thirteen million people: "Money is power . . . and for a man to say 'I do not want money' is to say 'I do not wish to do any good for my fellow men'." Granted these spokesmen wanted the money to be spent for good causes, their sentiments were a strong force for non-interference in Caesar's realm. They would be repudiated by ministers preaching the "social gospel" soon enough.

In the field of law, the most formidable barriers were being erected against remedies for what now seem obvious inequalities falling upon laborers, tenants and consumers in the new age of industrialism, big cities and big business. As with the ministers, the judges had willingly submitted to the materialist standards, converting the concept of "natural law," which had loomed so large in the American heritage, into a sanction for the oppressiveness of the industrial order. Natural law, and its "self-evident" corollary, natural rights, were revered democratic catch-words. They now became a legal and philosophical shield for the natural rights of property against all challengers. The fact that this property tended to fall into vastly unequal hands, in relation to capacity to bargain over its use, was conveniently overlooked. The Supreme Court, dominated by Associate Justice Stephen J. Field, made it clear in a series of cases that "liberty" meant more than political liberty. It meant also economic liberty, or more to the point, liberty for businessmen and corporations to be exempt from programs of restraint and reform. The recently passed Fourteenth Amendment, intended to protect the rights of Negroes after the Civil War, was interpreted to include business corporations as "persons." This aid to enterprise accelerated the country's economic progress but it postponed necessary governmental regulations.

It did not help matters that these jurists believed passionately in the morality of their position. When in 1873 Field invoked the Declaration of Independence itself on behalf of property rights, he accepted this version of economic freedom as a primary value of the American system, an end in itself, a necessary adjunct to the great era of capitalism and business power in which he believed.[14] Since his views apparently reflected the triumphant materialist consensus of the day, it can be assumed the country was receiving the law it deserved. If such ideas still prevailed, we would not have our present wages, hours, and workmen's compensation regulations, our powerful unions, or our income tax, regrettable as this may seem. There were, of course, other jurists like Holmes, Brandeis and Pound who did not accept self-evident truths of any kind. Holmes believed his dissent from an anti-picketing decision of his fellow judges of the Massachusetts Supreme Court in 1896 had ended his chances for judicial advancement. Fortunately, Theodore Roosevelt appointed him to the Supreme Court in 1902, where he continued to shape the nation's laws as a continually changing response to what he called "the felt necessities of the times."

V

Roscoe Pound, one of the great Harvard Law School deans, labelled the new experimental approach to law "sociological jurisprudence." It is to the field of sociology that one should turn for a final strand in the nineteenth century America of Thorstein Veblen before examining Veblen's counter-attack. As Veblen languished in Stacyville, brooding, reading books and observing the world from the outside, his thoughts must have turned frequently to one of his teachers at Yale, a giant in the intellectual world, William Graham Sumner.

The history of business in America is largely the history of the struggle between advocates of business freedom and advocates of government intervention. Only government can stand up to business on even terms. Labor, of course, might claim otherwise, but labor gained power through government support; and now that labor has lost a good deal of its ideological impetus, government again becomes the basic counter-force. As the nineteenth century drew to a close, the scales were highly tipped in favor of unregulated capitalism, or true *laissez-faire*. The popular support for such an accommodation can be expected to derive strength from some underlying intellectual structure. In the teaching and influence of William Graham Sumner, economic conservatism found an adequate champion.

A clergyman who had decided to "put his faith away in a drawer" and turn to the tougher-minded sciences of economics and sociology, Sumner came to Yale in 1872. For the next thirty years he held forth as a national figure endowing intellectual authority to the concept of survival of the fittest in the capitalist system and heaping scorn on reformers engaged in "the absurd effort to make the world over." A towering figure, he is not to be compared with the trade association economists or docile professors of a later day —that would hardly have qualified him for the eminence he enjoyed. Businessmen took great pleasure and comfort from his scholarly deductions in their favor but they were also aware of a cold consistency that carried his logic to unyielding ends. He was, for example, as ruthlessly against their protective tariffs as he was against state authority in matters of public education and child labor. When the entire country revelled in America's first burst of irresponsible imperialism in the Spanish-American War of 1898, Sumner denounced the arguments for America's "manifest destiny" as "national vanity" and a "thirst for glory." His rejection of the doctrine that "those who oppose war are responsible for the lives lost in it, or that a citizen may criticize any action of his government except a war" has a timeless echo.[15]

Perhaps it was for these intransigent qualities that Veblen would later attack practically everything Sumner represented while expressing for him, as for no one else, deep and unqualified admiration.[16] When Veblen arrived at Yale, Sumner had just met defeat in a two year running battle with Yale's president, Reverend Noah Porter. The issue was over Sumner's use of Herbert Spencer's *Study of Sociology* in his classes. Spencer was the renowned English philosopher who had become the great messenger of Darwinism to other branches of learning. Porter, clinging to traditional theology, assailed the book's evolutionary principles as a threat against "good taste and decency" but he was already defending a lost cause. Spencer meanwhile made a triumphant lecture tour of America in 1882, during which he warned Americans that their freedom was being threatened, a condition always certain to rally support. Socialism was the threat but he reassured the leaders of public opinion that society was just another expression of Darwin's evolution of the fittest and that poverty and corruption, while highly regrettable, must evolve away through the centuries rather than be submitted to unworkable social legislation.

At a farewell dinner for Spencer at Delmonico's in New York, Henry Ward Beecher, less rigid than Porter, predicted a reunion in heaven for those fittest to become immortal. Sumner was there and delivered a toast to Spencer in front of the glittering audience on behalf of sociology, praising the master for having given the social sciences a "powerful and correct method." It should be noted that both Sumner and Spencer at that time were considered to be in the vanguard rather than rear guard of economic thought. The steelmasters and financiers of the new industrial age were deriving from these advanced thinkers a made-to-order, modern rationalisation for their economic interests. A scientific age could use above all scientific justification. This the Social Darwinists, as such men are now called, supplied on the evidence of inexorable, concrete facts and findings, implying great material progress if only businessmen were left alone. Looked at from this point of view, the dinner at Delmonico's would be the equivalent today of, for example, Reinhold Niebuhr, one of America's most eminent yet advanced theologians and Lord Bertrand Russell, England's world famous philosopher, toasting the president of the National Association of Manufacturers on nationwide television.

Most of the economics textbooks in use in the colleges at the time of Spencer's visit were grounded in the distant "classical" theories of Adam Smith, the benevolent founder of the "dismal science." They were now heavily augmented by sanctifications of property and prohibitions against interference by the state. Many of the professors and textbook authors were recruited from the ministry since "political economy," as it was then called, was generally a branch of the department of moral philosophy. At Carleton, Veblen's economics textbook was written by Bishop Francis Wayland and revised by Reverend A. L. Chapin, the president of the nearby Congregationalist Beloit College. It followed the usual nineteenth century procedure of an assumed order of perfect competition wherein a quaint "economic man," responding to his own selfish, competitive, acquisitive instincts (often measured in terms of "pleasure" or "pain") plays a role in a self-regulating design that automatically establishes the correct flow of goods, prices and wages. The book adds a few improvements over Adam Smith: Strikes are a violation of man's sacred right "to do what he will with himself, his time, his strength and skill" and philanthropy or other aid to the poor is a violation of the laws of God and property.[17]

The maxims and laws of these economists were immutable and unerring. The entire process was thus only dimly related to the real world of monopolies, cutthroat competition, labor antagonism and the new kind of property which was incorporated and concentrated. These official texts had progressed little beyond Adam Smith's concept of an "invisible hand" which coordinated a mass of hedonistic, competitive decisions into one benign result. Yet Smith's theories were at least reasonably relevant to eighteenth century conditions in England, including a valid political message of "hands-off" to a restricting, mercantilist state. Now *laissez-faire* economics was being used as a defense against newly sensed threats to the present business order. The most popular textbook of all was *Elements of Political Economy* by Reverend A. L. Perry of Williams College. It labels proposed wages and hours legislation an "economic abomination" which would interfere with the "wage-fund theory," namely that wages are determined by simple mathematics—the amount of capital available for wages divided by the number of workers. "This principle determines the current rate of wages in any country," is the weighty conclusion.[18] Lest today's businessman take undue satisfaction that his son's tuition is being spent on more enduring thought, a comment by Robert Lekachman, the able author of *The Age of Keynes*, is in order. Lekachman notes that the Garver and Hansen textbook, published in 1937 and encountered by him as a student in 1939, was considered a leading textbook as late as 1947. Yet its references to the causes and cure of unemployment, that shattering social problem of the 1930's, center on two pages devoted to the recently passed Social Security Act of 1935 and little else. Conversely, the present popular Samuelson text, published recently during our long cycle of prosperity, is thoroughly engaged in this subject. In addition 10% of the Samuelson book is devoted to the new economic growth measurements and techniques ushered in by Keynes and his interpreters including Hansen.[19] What will be the texts for the year 2000?

No doubt Veblen saw in Sumner a kindred rebel in attitudes toward orthodoxy. Yet where his sociology touched on economics, Sumner differed little from the "received traditions" which Veblen would denounce. With Veblen, evolution created a demand that economics be treated as an evolutionary, inductive science—like Holmes's law — instead of a fixed set of truths. Sumner simply grafted evolution's "survival of the fittest" terminology to his tooth and fang analysis of society. High-minded though he was and professing to abhor the political threat of the plutocracy,[20] Sumner did not flinch from following through his line of reasoning to its logical conclusions. These would include great aggregations of capital in a few rugged hands and inevitably some abject poverty and misery. It was part of the price to be paid for the ultimate benefits that would flow from the all important accumulation of capital. "Get capital!" he urged upon his Yale students, including the penurious Veblen. For homework, they might read in Sumner's fiercely titled *Earth-Hunger* that "the savings bank depositor is a hero of civilization."[21]

As might be expected, Sumner's—and for that matter Herbert Spencer's—writings are now museum pieces. Though portions of Sumner's creed live on in the conservative ideology, he is rarely quoted *verbatim*. His uncompromising candor and materialistic consistency are too much for contemporary conservatives either in politics or in business. Ironically, he is immortalised in the phrase "the forgotten man," like Veblen's independent mechanic a wistful reincarnation of his father. Sumner coined the phrase in an 1884 essay devoted against the business interests whose protective tariff of 1883 he thought was achieved at the expense of the lower middle-class. Its revival in the New Deal can be traced to Franklin D. Roosevelt, the most un-doctrinaire of Presidents, whose cheerful turn to state intervention would have terminated Yale's relations with Harvard in Sumner's era. Yet Sumner's cold determinism —glorifying selfishness and without pity—was the dominant economic and sociological theory of his time. In its emphasis on industry, frugality and self-sufficiency, along with the naïve optimism of its appropriated scientific clothing, "Sumnerology," as William Lyons Phelps called it, influenced generations of impressionable undergraduates.

VI

"I am Thorstein Veblen."

Professor J. Laurence Laughlin looked up from his desk at Cornell University one afternoon in 1891 to see an anaemic looking graduate student of thirty-four dressed in a coonskin cap and corduroy trousers.

As Laughlin later related the tale, Veblen described his enforced idleness culminating in a sudden decision to register as a graduate student in Cornell's history department. Now he wanted to switch to economics if he could get a fellowship. To his everlasting credit, Laughlin sensed something remarkable in Veblen, placed him under his wing and a year later took him along to the University of

Chicago. Laughlin had gladly responded to the academic raids of Chicago's bustling young president, William Rainey Harper, who had left the ministry and teaching at Yale to build the great new university founded by John D. Rockefeller. As head professor of the economics department, Laughlin was a power among the conventional economists, always ready to add his weight in the fight against Bryanism, socialism and unionism. Although he was surrounded by a galaxy of innovating philosophers and scientists netted by the ambitious and well-financed Harper, Laughlin still refused to join the American Economic Association because he thought it was too inclined towards socialism.[22] The association had been founded in 1885 by a group of restless young professors including Richard P. Ely, who would become famous at Wisconsin, Simon Patten of the University of Pennsylvania and strangely, Woodrow Wilson of Princeton.

Veblen started at $500 a year and made painfully slow progress along the lower rungs of the academic ladder. But he was given the managing editorship of Chicago's *Journal of Political Economy* and soon was energetically involved in writing articles for learned journals and planning his first book. In addition to the stimulation of the fine minds assembled at Chicago (John Dewey the philosopher, Franz Boas the anthropologist, Jacques Loeb the physiologist and Albert Michelson the physicist), Veblen was exposed to first hand observation of the great business and political currents of America's second largest city.

This was the Chicago of industrial titans like Charles Yerkes, the corrupter of city councils and legislatures, whose trolley nickels had just paid for the new Yerkes Observatory at Veblen's university. It was the home of a harvest of millionaires which had emerged from the great expansion following the Civil War. These new meat-packing, farm equipment, publishing and merchant princes held court in opulent mansions on the shores of Lake Michigan, topped by a fantastic Gothic castle built by Potter Palmer in 1882. All this was grist for Veblen's searching, satirical eye, providing the final touch of sophistication he needed for his role of social critic.

It was also the Chicago of the Columbian World's Fair of 1893, which attracted twenty-seven million visitors to the sprawling, smog-covered railway center of the nation. The city's population had just raced to one million, of which 70% were immigrants. Most of them lived in slums and worked in the giant industrial complexes.

It was a city marked by bloody labor unrest. In 1886 a bomb went off in the Haymarket section and four of the accused anarchists were summarily executed for throwing it. John Peter Altgeld, a foreign-born Civil War veteran and self-made millionaire who had abandoned business to become a judge, watched the funeral cortège and vowed to do something about this miscarriage of justice. Elected Democratic Governor of Illinois with Populist support, he pardoned the three surviving anarchists in 1893 and further invited the wrath of respectable people by refusing to call out the state militia, as Pennsylvania had done for the Homestead employers, to quell the Pullman strike in 1894. Over Altgeld's strident protests, President Cleveland ordered 2,000 United States troops into Chicago and the strike was broken. The railway union leader, Eugene V. Debs, was then imprisoned, causing him to emerge a confirmed socialist. Chicago became the American Socialist Party headquarters.

As the dominant figure in the Democratic convention of 1896 (both parties met in Chicago, the door to the key farm states), Altgeld exceeded Bryan in vilification by the country's press. He was overwhelmingly defeated for reelection as Governor and went into political eclipse, penniless and one of the most reviled men in public life. Later praised as "the eagle forgotten" by the poet Vachel Lindsay and celebrated as an authentic American hero by Edgar Lee Masters in *Spoon River Anthology*, Altgeld spent his few remaining years in the office of a young admirer, Clarence Darrow. America tends to make up to its uncompromising men. A suitable public monument to Altgeld now graces Chicago and even Veblen's portrait was hung in Yale's Sterling Hall, by popular subscription, in 1947.

VII

For seven years Veblen taught his courses in socialism and economic history to bewildered Chicago students who suffered through his deliberate mumblings and casual lack of interest in their grades, though some testified later to the genuine intellectual excitement he could provide. The century was rushing to a close and Veblen, ambitious as any creative man, was determined to make his bid for what the philosopher William James would soon acknowledge as the American "bitch-goddess Success." The only national forum for a little-known social scientist was a book. In spite of his impressive credentials, Veblen had to subsidize *The Theory of the Leisure Class* with a good part of his year's salary when it appeared in 1899.

Every age generates its own reaction and Veblen's time was ready for him. The philosopher Charles Peirce, like William James an apostle of the new philosophical method of "pragmatism"—of testing by experience rather than yielding to dogma—had sounded the clarion call in 1893: "Soon a flash and a quick peal will shake economists out of their complacency."[23] Veblen, who had studied briefly under Peirce at Johns Hopkins, was chafing to sound the trumpet.

Old ideas die hard and it was not so much a matter of the established economists changing their time-honored concepts as it was the appearance of a new school of thought to challenge the old conservatisms. The thinkers, mostly university people in the halls of institutions being cheerfully endowed by the objects of their wrath, were in turn encouraged by a new type of President. Theodore Roosevelt and Woodrow Wilson were patricians in the Roman or Churchillian sense, men who not only read books but wrote books, who felt, like Oliver Wendell Holmes, a devotion above all to duty and a thinly veiled disdain for powerful men of business. Soon a massive force of public opinion—muckrakers writing in mass circulation magazines, novelists of social protest, Progressives like William Allen White of Emporia, Kansas and Governor La Follette of Wisconsin, reform mayors, irreverent newspaper wits like

Mr. Dooley, even the Congress beginning with its Antitrust bill of 1890, had turned upon the beleaguered businessman in a wave of investigations, scorn and regulation. The historian Richard Hofstadter feels that no period, including the New Deal, was as anti-big-business as the first decade at the start of the new century.[24] This popular sentiment against business exceeded the basically conservative positions of Roosevelt and Wilson, who wished to regulate rather than decapitate American industry.

Roosevelt became America's forty-three year old President upon McKinley's assassination in 1901 and introduced a completely different version of the Presidency with his strong emphasis on executive power and action. Although he was a reluctant reformer with no patience for "wild radicals," he was responsive enough to his times to lash out at "the malefactors of great wealth" on the one hand while discreetly praising the results of industry and the benefits of "good" large-scale organizations on the other. His target was J. P. Morgan, symbol of the most impersonal and massive absentee control of industry. The young President brought Morgan to bay in both the Northern Securities trust case and the coal strike of 1902, which Roosevelt personally arbitrated. With a politician's realism, he then allowed the Republicans to accept a $150,000 campaign contribution from Morgan in 1904. Yet Roosevelt was more independent of the monied interests than any President since the Civil War and he irrevocably set the stage for government intervention in the domain of business, which was one of the basic demands of the new school of economists and sociologists working in the less realistic world of theory. The industrialists for their part did not feel particularly threatened. They concentrated on developing the holding company as a quite satisfactory substitute for the outlawed trust device and on the "scientific management" of production first introduced at Bethlehem Steel by Frederick W. Taylor in the 1890's. The unabashed Morgan remarked to a friend upon Roosevelt's premature retirement from office to hunt lions in Africa, "I hope the first lion he meets does his duty." Morgan looked forward with pleasure to the conservatism of Taft little realizing that the stern, moralizing Woodrow Wilson would reverse the trend in 1912.

VIII

Woodrow Wilson was a teacher and a preacher in the White House. As such he brought the Progressive reform movement to its peak before it expired under the exigencies of World War I and the subsequent "return to normalcy." As Veblen recognized the impact of evolution on traditional economics, so Wilson recognized it on political science. Both men were involved in reform but only one with morality. Veblen continually insisted that morality had no place in his views. He simply was dispassionately pointing out how things really were, how they got that way and where they might end if left unchecked. Veblen in spite of himself was moralising, but Wilson, the minister's son, made virtue crack in the air like a whip. Responding to the fervent temper of his contemporary America, Wilson flailed the nation's conscience as spokesman for its élite citizens. Veblen probed the nation's conscience from behind the mask of the outsider. Veblen the critic remained a scholar to the end, neither joining a party nor voting regularly.[25] Wilson easily made the transition from political scholar to political leader. Both men left their marks on the national character, adding to the richness of the American experience.

Wilson lost little time in demonstrating the power of executive leadership in initiating reform. "The nation has been deeply stirred . . . by the knowledge of wrong, of ideals lost, of government too often debauched and made an instrument of evil," he stated passionately in his inaugural address. Within eight months he had driven through Congress the Federal Reserve Bill. The Bill, which remains the bulwark of our financial structure, was opposed almost to a man by the banking fraternity. They produced college professors and presidents to back up their predictions of ruin and inflation if the Bill were passed. The public generally regarded this legislation as an effort to break up the "money trust." In fact it was an overdue installation of a central banking system, the need for which had been sharply brought home in the "Rich Man's Panic" of 1907. Within four months of Wilson's inauguration, enough states had ratified amendments to the Constitution to provide for direct election of United States Senators and to permit a federal income tax. The new century saw reform sweep through the nation, reaching down to the state and national levels, flourishing in the churches and settlement houses, screaming in the press of Pulitzer, Hearst and Scripps—even creating a new profession, the social workers.

The size and power of American business was a subject of more lively debate in this period than at any other time in our history, rising above the previous regional controversies over currency reform, railroad rates and tariffs. Although Roosevelt had inveighed against the plutocracy and demonstrated the government's potential equality of strength, he also acknowledged the inevitability of great industrial combinations and their merits if properly regulated. His reputation as a "trust-buster" was politically expedient but undeserved. Wilson attacked Roosevelt's stand on trusts as "regulation of monopoly" instead of "regulation of competition" which was Wilson's counter-offer. Thus in the campaign of 1912 we have the curious record of the liberal Wilson eulogizing certain frontier values later associated with the campaign of Barry Goldwater. In his 1913 book *The New Freedom* Wilson repeated these victorious themes, although he had the defection of T. R.'s Bull Moose party to thank most of all for his election. Wilson's hero was the entrepreneurial hero, "the man on the make," the "new entry" in the "race of life," "the man with only a little capital," who would seek success through energy, ambition and frugality but who was being thwarted by the monopolistic tendencies of big business. "Anything that depresses, anything that makes the organization greater than the man, anything that blocks, discourages, dismays the humble man is against all the principles of progress,"[26] stated Wilson, using terms now reserved for attacks on big government rather than big business.

"Rural toryism," bellowed Roosevelt, describing the attack on his "New Nationalism" program as the exploitation of old agrarian fears of corporations and government power of any kind. Roosevelt had more than Wilson to reckon with. The braintruster behind much of Wilson's "New Freedom" economics was Louis D. Brandeis, the Boston corporation lawyer who made a fortune in his practise and then retired to become a "people's lawyer," serving the cause of reform. To Brandeis, bigness was a curse, destroying the moral values of individualism. Economic bigness was not an inevitable product of the new technology. It was the result of the manipulation of "other people's money" by J. P. Morgan and similar financiers who were eager to float securities and water stocks, as demonstrated by the revelations of the House's Pujo Committee. Competition, Brandeis advised Wilson, should be maintained in every branch of private industry. Rather than allow monopoly, certain industries should be owned by the people and not by the capitalists. Government regulation of monopoly was a delusion. The great combinations should be broken up or taken over. This was not socialism; it was the way to avoid the socialism that would surely follow as a reaction to the mania for consolidation.

Meanwhile the powerful men of business sat back and waited for the storm to blow over as they had done so many times before. In fact neither party had the desire to carry out its platform in regard to business. Roosevelt never intended to encourage monopoly and when Wilson defeated him, Wilson stopped far short of any attempts to implement the Brandeis theories. Both men were really more interested in a strong government capable of regulating and influencing business than in a showdown between monopoly and competition. In a sense, the Roosevelt approach won out and became the basic tradition to the present day. Antitrust has had a fitful history and big business is tacitly accepted. Small business is affectionately hailed and supported by Congress and the public, joining the farmers as a special interest in our economic mythology.

As for Brandeis, Wilson appointed him to join his friend Holmes on the Supreme Court in 1916, creating a wave of protest from the business and legal establishment that rocked the nation. Typical of those who testified against Senate confirmation of the appointment was Clarence Barron, publisher of the *Wall Street Journal*, who editorialized in his Boston News Service:

> The nomination by President Wilson of Louis D. Brandeis to the United States Supreme Court is an insult to New England and the business interests of the country. There is only one redeeming feature in the nomination and that is that it will assist to bury Mr. Wilson in the next Presidential election.[27]

IX

Such was the broad background of the new century in which Veblen would begin to present his books to the public. As might be expected, the established journals and reviewers hardly acknowledged or enjoyed *The Theory of the Leisure Class*. William Dean Howells, the dean of American letters, who had been cultivating a sharp anti-business sentiment of his own, was an exception. His reviews were highly enthusiastic, bringing immediate national acclaim to the author. To Veblen's chagrin, Howells treated the book as social satire of a high literary style rather than serious economics. Still the sudden acclaim must have been heady wine for the parched Veblen. Edward A. Ross, a heretic sociologist whose *Sin and Society* bore an introduction written by the unpredictable Theodore Roosevelt himself, was particularly impressed. Ross was the nephew of the great sociologist Lester Ward, whose ground-breaking *Dynamic Sociology*, published in 1895, inspired a generation of scholars and reformers including Veblen. To Lester Ward, the nephew wrote:

> I am looking forward to your review of Veblen's book. How it fluttered the dovecotes of the East! All the reviews I have seen of it so far are shocked and angry. Clearly their household gods have been assailed by this iconoclast.[28]

PART II

I

In *The Theory of the Leisure Class*, Veblen examines the motivations of the "real" man behind the puppet-like "economic man" of the classical economists. The exposé, supported by his mock-serious excursions into anthropology and psychology, hardly shocks today's reader. In common with the rest of America, Veblen was still unfamiliar with his contemporary Sigmund Freud. Today there is hardly a farm boy alive who cannot recognize the barrage of Freudian messages contained in our incessant advertising and other forms of entertainment. We accept the so-called "irrational" drives of conspicuous display, of desire for power and of keeping up with the Joneses as standard procedure in the moving of goods and services. We are not surprised that the Federal Reserve Board hires the University of Michigan Survey Research Center to chart the current psychological responses of consumers as a valid barometer of next season's business expectations. Indeed the cynical

35

manipulation of our vanities by the motivational researchers of Madison Avenue would cry for a new Veblen were it not for the recent gratifying discovery that our five year olds quickly learn to identify all sales messages as "commercials."

Still in our surrender to quantity in place of quality, we are not much wiser than our grandfathers after all. A review of Veblen's thought, disproved and diluted though it is by time and events, is always in order. He reminds us that "what is" is not necessarily right; it is more likely to be wrong. We don't quote Darwin any longer as authority for this position, because there is a general consensus about the inevitability of change in human institutions. Moreover, we readily admit the effectiveness of government responsibility for our economic affairs, which the noted historian of the American mind, Henry Steele Commager, regards as the most notable development in twentieth century America.[29] To Veblen's probing, we owe a debt for this train of events.

For Veblen, however, the pragmatic, experimental reforms that brought about our present type of capitalism had little appeal. His ray of hope for the most part resided in man's capacity to change his institutional framework—which included in Veblen's view business, the dynastic state, the church and education—by ridding himself of archaic traditions and preconceptions. This was a tall order, involving a change in human nature rather than the effective use of reform. Small wonder that Veblen chose to attack these institutions under cover of satire, at least for the time being, as he would say.

Thus *The Theory of the Leisure Class* can be read for its amusement value alone, since it avoids controversial remedies. In its polysyllabic profundities, its circumlocution and deadpan innocence, the *Theory* disarmingly guides us on a tour of society stripped of all pretensions. The leisure class people are the upper crust of wealth and power in turn-of-the-century America. We are not surprised to find that they are ostentatious and wasteful—what else would you expect of the idle rich? They are not even consistently idle, Veblen points out, especially their captains of industry who are furiously engaged in the pursuit of money. What does surprise us is the ancestry of these businessmen. They go back to the barbarians who succeeded a more peaceful and amiable lot we might call noble savages. These barbarians discovered pride of possession, first by capturing females as the booty of conquest, next by assigning menial and domestic work to females as their part of the ingenious device of marriage. Somewhere along the line, the dominant male began to glorify "honorific" instead of "workmanlike" pursuits. Ritual, pomp and ceremony, hunting and warfare were the admired activities of the chiefs, headmen, priests and potentates who coursed through the stream of history. When these strong men acquired private property, they did so through "force and fraud," since their activities were now predatory by second nature. As might be expected, those in power took care to protect the interests of the propertied classes, by laws and contracts and privileges, thus legitimatizing the use of "force and fraud" up to and including America of 1899. The captains of industry, Veblen would later point out, were adventurous and constructive in the pre-industrial period when they worked side by side with their employees. Now in the era of absentee ownership and finance capitalism, they were predatory to the core, exceeded in irresponsibility only by their new masters, the captains of finance.[30] Both groups were modern robber barons, collecting a toll from "the underlying population." A fable, yes, but many a harried clerk thought twice as he greeted his employer as "chief" thereafter.

Veblen did not push his anti-business sentiment to its logical conclusions in this book. As a result, sturdy capitalists read it with the same good humor granted to Mark Twain's tales of business rascality, or to the great political cartoons of the era, providing these did not strike too close to home. Besides, it was not just the rich who were being satirized by this lowly professor in Mr. Rockefeller's university. The "underlying population" itself did not come out much better. It too was caught in the "pecuniary standard of living" because its mind had become "habituated" to venerate money and to "emulate" its betters. The surrender extends even to Veblen's colleagues:

> In any modern community where there is no priestly
> monopoly of these occupations, the people of scholarly
> pursuits are unavoidably thrown into contact with classes
> that are pecuniarily their superiors. The high standard
> of pecuniary decency in force among these superior
> classes is transfused among the scholarly classes with
> but little mitigation of its rigour; and as a consequence
> there is no class of the community that spends a larger
> proportion of its substance in conspicuous waste than
> these.[31]

It was for the leisure class that Veblen reserved his special
barbs, however, for life at the bottom of the pyramid was somewhat beyond humor. Take the consumption habits of the leisure
class. It not only consumed conspicuously to prove its status by
"invidious comparison," but also wasted conspicuously. In addition
it was heavily engaged in "vicarious consumption." In this activity
the fashionable, servant-ridden wife becomes a "ceremonial consumer" rather than stay "the drudge and the chattel" Veblen
unkindly infers she might once have been.

For a man who would become the despair of two wives, Veblen
expressed a lively interest in their problems. The tyranny of the
corset is treated at length and joins the barbarism of Chinese
foot-binding as a case in point. The full length dresses of the day
are an insignia of leisure because they hamper the wearer at
every turn and incapacitate her from any useful exertion.

As soon as we let our guard down, however, Veblen strikes
hard. Under "devout observances," he lists religion and sports,
both concerned with archaic rituals, anthropomorphic cults and
appeals to luck. Shall we take him seriously when he solemnly
concludes that these institutions stress mastery and subservience
and thus are a lag holding back "the industrial evolution of society
in its later stages"?[32] Certainly there is more cutting edge to Marx's
dogma about religion being the opiate of the masses.

Yet who would not chuckle over the preposterous story of the
king of France who burned himself beyond repair because his
standards of aristocratic leisure prevented him from moving his

own chair away from the fire? Consider why the upper class man prefers dogs to cats. The dog servilely accepts the complete domination of his master and, never chasing mice, cannot be accused of performing menial functions, thus making him the natural favorite of the leisure class.

> At the same time the cat's temperament does not fit her for the honorific purpose. She lives with men on terms of equality, knows nothing of that relation of status which is the ancient basis of all distinctions of worth, honor, and repute, and she does not lend herself with facility to an invidious comparison between her owner and his neighbors. The exception to this last rule occurs in the case of such scarce and fanciful products as the Angora cat, which have some slight honorific value on the ground of expensiveness . . .[33]

No detail of dress or habit fails to receive new importance in the eye of this strange beholder. Observe what he has to say about the use of the walking stick (after all, it did disappear shortly thereafter):

> The walking-stick serves the purpose of an advertisement that the bearer's hands are employed otherwise than in useful effort, and it therefore has utility as an evidence of leisure. But it is also a weapon, and it meets a felt need of barbarian man on that ground. The handling of so tangible and primitive a means of offense is very comforting to any one who is gifted with even a moderate share of ferocity.[34]

Gifted with ferocity! There is a portrait of Veblen in this phrase, lurking below the humor, angry and frustrated at the world about him. These leisure class people are dangerous. Wherever they are, among the rich or for that matter, the non-rich, they are *holding up progress* by the weight of their archaic traditions and superstitions. In Veblen's total work, they will appear again and again as the purveyors of meretricious taste, corrupters of education,

causers of depressions, agents of wasteful production and wasteful
consumption—in short, something shouting for replacement. Logically the situation would seem to call for some kind of class
struggle, but Veblen was not a Marxist. Besides, the fault of the
leisure class was in its cast of mind, not in its control of the means
of production. As we shall see, what bothered Veblen most of all
about America's productive system was his personal concept of its
inevitable inefficiency in the hands of money-minded rather than
production-minded capitalists. In an economy of scarcity, Veblen
could not stand waste. He had uncovered an innate conflict between
industry and the business spirit which he would never be able
to resolve.

II

Shortly before *Leisure Class* appeared, Veblen was turned down
by President Harper for a raise on the grounds that he did not
advertise the university. The story goes that Veblen would have
marched off the campus had not the patient Laughlin interceded
for him and obtained the raise, thus giving Harper quite a bargain
for his money, if he cared to look at it that way. Veblen's next book,
The Theory of Business Enterprise, appeared in 1904. Here
Veblen analyzes the economic system rather than the economic man.
In doing so, he draws a formal line of battle between the "machine
process" and the "pecuniary businessman" from which he was never
to retreat in a series of books ending with *Absentee Ownership* in
1923. The businessman might wonder if his eyes were deceiving
him when he read Veblen's *Enterprise*. After all, weren't modern
technology and business enterprise one and the same? If not, what
were executives doing in their own plants and factories, many of
which they had more or less built up with their own hands? Not so,
Veblen would answer, modern technology has grown to the point
where it now has an independent life of its own. Master technicians,
foremen and engineers may be compatible with industry but the
businessman is like some ghostly incubus clinging to industry's
back, parasitically enjoying a free ride. "Subversion!" is about all

the businessman might answer to this charge but he should hear Veblen out.

Within the terms of Veblen's hypothesis and definitions, his theories are not so far-fetched. This grants a latitude which would justify the wildest of theories but one should start by recognizing the seriousness and importance of Veblen's thought. When in the *Leisure Class* Veblen showed that businessmen were descended from barbarians, he had in mind a deeper purpose than satire. His real interest lay in the paradox of men with money on their minds being in control of an institution—modern industry— which simply would run more efficiently if operated by men more harmoniously related to the machine process. As a disinterested observer, Veblen probably viewed modern capitalism, meaning mass production for profit, as a recent invention (succeeding medieval guilds and Renaissance mercantilism) without special claims to permanence in a world of change. At the same time the machine for the first time had become the dominant institution in society and (here Veblen was prophetic) would become tremendously more dominant in a short time. With a fanatical faith in the machine process, to which he assigned the same kind of mystical awe he derided in the thinking of others, Veblen undoubtedly saw in modern industry the horn of plenty for a happy and just society of contented workers. The machine process, or way of life, is about the only virtuous institution in Veblen's universe, calling into play the most virtuous instinct of man, the instinct of workmanship. This instinct, in contrast with the predatory conniving instinct, seeks to provide for and perpetuate the race. At home in the factory, the modern technician apparently would be efficient and productive, surrounded by rationally coordinated processes and measurable, factual duties.

As with all Utopias, Veblen's can quickly be demolished. One need only recall visions of man dominated by his machine, pathetically as in Charlie Chaplin's *Modern Times*, or monstrously, as with Hitler's Adolf Eichmann. Veblen was unwilling to face the decision of who would replace the hapless businessman, let alone the problem of the machine turning on its master, and so he concentrated on indicting the business system itself.

III

There was much to criticize. There was also a body of facts—nineteen volumes in all—which the United States Industrial Commission had published in 1902, the first great production of government economic statistics, testimony and analysis. Veblen pored over the report, which critically reviewed the tremendous consolidations in industry that had taken place through the trust and holding company devices. In most cases, the report stated, the resulting combination had exercised control over prices, choosing to increase profits rather than pass on the benefits of reduced production costs to the public. Veblen referred specifically to the report in relating in *Enterprise* how the "excessive competition" of Andrew Carnegie had forced the J. P. Morgan interests to buy him out and establish the country's first billion dollar corporation, U.S. Steel, in 1901.[35] Veblen theorized that the overcapitalization of these giant industries through "watering" of the stock for good-will created a requirement for high profits and dividends that could only be maintained by increasing prices at the expense of labor and consumers. In fact, U.S. Steel was indeed a classic exploit of investment banking. The good-will and other intangible assets amounted to $720 million of the $1,402 million capitalization — a tremendous "watering" ratio — including as it did Carnegie's premium on his $447 million sale and a hefty $65 million fee for Morgan. It should be noted in retrospect that this mammoth corporation was so successful that its stockholders prospered greatly and dividends have been omitted for only two years to date. As a war arsenal, Steel of course came into its own in 1917, justifying its size in that respect. Although monopolistic pricing cannot be proved the reason, the cost of living did go up about 35% from 1897 to 1913, creating a ready market for Veblen's theories. From today's point of view, this increase appears to be similar to our own post World War II experience with inflation, wherein the productivity, or production per man-hour, of our fabulous industrial system and the growing purchasing power of our increasing "middle-class" surpassed the gradual price increases, thus improving our overall standard of living. Now as in the early 1900's, a typically unplanned and unexpected economic solution, based primarily on our great resources, technology and increased payrolls, has carried the day for capitalism—at least so far, as Veblen would say.

Veblen was realistic enough to admit that America's industrial machine was so dynamic it worked reasonably well in spite of the profit-seeking of businessmen and the manipulations of financiers. He also found little unrest among the working class because of its propensity to emulate the standards of the Establishment and its satisfaction with the relative progress on hand. His harsh attacks on stock market transactions for the benefit of "insiders" were completely on target although he would have been surprised to see a friend of business such as Joseph P. Kennedy become the first chairman of the Securities & Exchange Commission in the early days of the New Deal. Piecemeal reforms were of little interest to Veblen. He was a theorist in the grand, comprehensive tradition of his predecessors Auguste Comte, the French philosopher of social reform and Marx, and of his contemporaries, Spencer and Sumner. In the end we must examine some of his intuitive, unproved assertions in this tradition.

IV

Sabotage! Of all the unlikely words to hurl at the hard-working businessman, this is the cruellest. Perhaps it fits when applied to the financiers whose stock-rigging, pools and rumor-spreading would now earn prison sentences. There is a charming story of what happened in 1881, when a great blizzard tore down the telegraph lines and forced Jay Gould to send his orders to his brokers by messenger. His enemies kidnapped the messenger, substituted a facsimile and thus were privy to Gould's moves in advance for several weeks. Today we have industrial espionage in an electronic age, but not, we hope, sabotage. Veblen made it very clear that he meant what he said: The businessman was throwing sand into the gears, deliberately banking down the great industrial machine to create scarcity and maintain prices. With icy aplomb, Veblen ac-

knowledged that the best definition of sabotage came from the
I.W.W.—the International Workers of the World—who had called
it "conscientious withdrawal of efficiency" in their fight against
unfair employers.[36] Now Veblen placed the strategy of the despised
"Wobblies" square in the laps of the employers themselves, maintaining his reputation for grim and outrageous humor:

> This line of least resistance and greatest present gain
> runs in the main by way of a vigilant sabotage on pro-
> duction. So true is this and so impassively binding is
> this duty of businesslike sabotage, that even in a crisis
> of unexampled privation, such as these years since the
> War, the captains of Big Business have been unable to
> break away and let the forces of production take their
> course: and this in spite of their being notably humane
> persons, imbued with the most benevolent sentiments.
> With an eye single to the net gain, business strategy
> still continues impartially to dictate a conscientious with-
> drawal of efficiency.[37]

Like so many of Veblen's broadsides, this one contains a grain of
truth. At the risk of giving him more credit than he deserves for
his malicious gibes, we might speculate on thoughts Veblen provokes as gadfly of the business conscience. Take the price control
which he continually deplores. In fact the "price system" is his
favorite description of predatory capitalism. For one thing it reminds
us that for all the veneration paid to the law of competition, even
in Veblen's time when the philosophy was fresh and newly minted,
businessmen were not really interested in price competition unless
it provided a chance to eliminate competitors. It was a kind of
Sunday observance, similar to free tariffs. Today we note that the
role of government in relation to pricing has increasingly come to
mean surveillance of an administered price system, meaning prices
reflecting other forces than supply and demand. If not that, the
government may even find itself involved in preventing cutthroat
pricing that would eliminate competition altogether, under laws
such as the Robinson-Patman Act. Yet there has always been

an active fear of monopoly because of monopoly pricing powers. The opposition to the price-fixing in the NRA of the early New Deal, the hearings of the Temporary National Economic Committee (TNEC) in 1938, the periodic resurgences of antitrust prosecutions and Senator Kefauver's hearings in 1957 are all cases in point. Ironically we recognize the need for price stability, especially for the planning and solvency of our giant corporate industry, as J. K. Galbraith emphasizes in *The New Industrial State*.[38] Yet we send corporation executives to jail for certain types of price collusion which are illegal. All of which bears on Veblen's reminder that there are no immutable rules, that our economic system is still evolving.

Or consider whether or not Veblen strikes home when he criticizes the under-use of our industrial system. Granted his concept of sabotage is tendentious and unproved. With or without sabotage, underproduction was always a definite possibility before America unleashed the tremendous purchasing power of a constantly growing middle-class. The formula for this "effective demand" is now reasonably well established—productivity, government spending (with occasional deficits), strong unions and, unfortunately—wars. Advertising, salesmanship and consumer credit, considered "chicanery" by the austere Veblen, are also part of the mixture. Yet the problem of unused industrial capacity still sticks, as each era meets a new level of needs. In spite of our sophistication in creating purchasing power, major criticism is in order. Assuming non-war conditions, we are greatly under-utilizing our vast productive capacity in our effort to bring about a greater society at home and abroad. Thurman Arnold, who exorcised symbols and folklore in a way that would have delighted Veblen but who applied his genius to practical reforms in a way that would have annoyed Veblen, is a competent authority on this subject:

> The actual cost in terms of goods and services resulting from our failure to utilize our full industrial capacity has been estimated by Leon Keyserling to amount to the stupendous sum of $387 billion from 1953 to the middle

of 1962. This enormous wealth was available to us but we could not use it because there was not enough purchasing power in the United States economy to absorb the products which our industrial plant was able to produce.

And thus under the same economic symbols and rituals that we had during the great depression we are developing today the same symptoms that prolonged that depression. The only time we were free from the tyranny of these nineteenth-century economic images was during the Second World War. Then, for the first time since the depression began, we were able to use and to expand our production to the full limit of our industrial ability. As a result we came out of that war richer in our productive capacity than at any time before. But after the Second World War the old religion took over. Since 1953 we have been progressively slowing down and increasingly unable to sustain the economic growth necessary for full employment.

Today we write about ourselves as an affluent society. But in 1960 there were almost 10½ million families (households of two or more persons) with annual incomes of under $4,000 before taxes. This means that one family in every four was living in poverty in the United States in 1960.[39]

V

What conclusions did Veblen draw for his grand design? They were not even the optimistic ones of Karl Marx who envisioned the workers in highly industrialized countries like England throwing off their chains and finding time for "fishing in the afternoon" as peaceable men did somewhere in the past.[40] Veblen was pessimistic. No revolt was in the offing and neither the machine process nor the business system seemed sure to triumph. He speculates that the business system might drain off so much production that a fast-growing population would fall below the biological subsistence level—much as Marx had predicted the "immiseration" of the

masses prior to revolt—but he was too shrewd an observer of the
American scene to pursue the point. Besides, as he corrected Marx:
"The experience of history teaches that abject misery carries with
it deterioration and abject subjection."[41]

Actually Veblen was always careful to sidestep identification
with Marx, although businessmen and professors discussed Marx
with less passion and more light before the Russian Revolution
changed the sound of Marxism. Veblen taught about Marx as
part of his courses in socialism. He respected Marx as a great
intellect worthy of his own professional criticism but he shied away
from Marx's propaganda and crusader's approach. He took exception to Marx's theory of the surplus value of labor, contending it
was a "natural rights" approach to claim that laborers had a natural right to the increment of value they added. Veblen dogmatically
rejected natural rights philosophy at every point, having in mind
court decisions, for example, that maintained employers had the
natural right to contract with bakers to work ten hours a day
and similar contractual fantasies that had caused Holmes and
Brandeis to register dissent.

For America, Veblen found the struggle to be highly unpredictable. In both *Enterprise* and *Absentee Ownership*, spanning
twenty years of brooding thought, Veblen came to the same conclusion—that the tide, or "drift" as he called it, seemed to favor
the triumph of "archaic principles of conduct" after all, thus insuring a shaky business triumph. As he had reluctantly admitted in
The Instinct of Workmanship, published in 1914:

> History records more frequent and more spectacular in-
> stances of the triumph of imbecile institutions over life
> and culture than of peoples who have by force of instinc-
> tive insight saved themselves alive out of a desperately
> precarious institutional situation . . .[42]

Among the imbecile institutions, Veblen was particularly apprehensive about the renewed militarism that had appeared in World

War I. In his valedictory *Absentee Ownership*, he satirically refers to "the growth and value of the national integrity" as the factor that will probably tip the scales in favor of the business interests. He notes that as industry becomes more and more concentrated in the hands of absentee owners there is a "drift into retardation and industrial paralysis." At the same time technology has become more dynamic than ever, producing a "continued run of discoveries, inventions, adaptations and short-cuts in the industrial arts." It would seem that the machine process would be preparing to ease out the unwelcome, sluggish business process, were it not for the resurgence of war-like attitudes that bind the underlying population to nationalism and imperial adventures instead of domestic progress. In short, Veblen suggests that the threat of war can be used by capitalist countries to gain popular support for a sinister alliance of the vested interests, which is what did happen in Germany, Italy and Japan not so many years later. To warn against the excesses of patriotism requires moral stamina in any age, even for an iconoclast like Veblen. The following quotation is strangely parallel to Veblen's thought:

> We annually spend on military security more than the net income of all United States corporations. This conjunction of an immense military establishment and a large arms industry is something new in the American experience. The total influence—economic, political, even spiritual—is felt in every city, every state house, every office of the federal government . . .
>
> In the councils of government we must guard against the acquisition of unwarranted influence, whether sought or unsought, by the military-industrial complex. The potential for the disastrous rise of misplaced power exists and will persist.
>
> We must never let the weight of this combination endanger our liberties or democratic processes. We should take nothing for granted. Only an alert and knowledge-

able citizenry can compel the proper meshing of the huge
industrial and military machinery of defense with our
peaceful methods and goals, so that security and liberty
may prosper together.[43]

It would be whimsical to suppose that Dwight D. Eisenhower's
farewell warning to his countrymen reflected a brushing up on his
Veblen. He could not have marched to such a distant drummer.
Veblen himself did not predict a military-industrial alliance for
America, although he quite amazingly predicted the same for the
Japan and Germany of World War II, as far back as 1917.[44] His
conclusion for America is contained in the final sentence of his
last book, *Absentee Ownership.* In his involved way he tells us
we are heading for a major depression:

> The outlook should accordingly be that the businesslike
> control of the industrial system in detail should presently
> reach . . . and should speedily pass beyond that critical
> point of chronic derangement in the aggregate beyond
> which a continued pursuit of the same strategy on the
> same businesslike principles will result in a progressively
> widening margin of deficiency in the aggregate material
> output and a progressive shrinking of the available means
> of life.[45]

VI

By 1907, Veblen had worn out his welcome at Chicago and had
moved on to Stanford. There he taught the usual courses and fought
with his wife Ellen who finally abandoned the cottage at Cedro
where the Duffus brothers were to earn their residence. By December
1909 he had been invited to leave Stanford and it was not
until a year later that he secured a position at the University of
Missouri through the help of a former student, Herbert J. Davenport, who headed its economics department. For a while he lived
in Davenport's cellar where he produced *The Instinct of Work-*

manship and other distinguished works even though he found Columbia, Missouri to be the oppressive prototype of the "country town" whose values he had ridiculed. In 1914 he married his second wife, Anne F. Bradley. Characteristically he equipped their household with rough, self-made furniture and refused to admit those triumphs of technology, the telephone and the typewriter. His unfortunate wife was committed to a mental sanitarium soon after Veblen moved to New York in June 1918 and died shortly thereafter.

Veblen had come to New York to become an editor of *The Dial* magazine, which was to have a brief post-war success as a left-of-center intellectual publication. He had spent the previous six months in Washington in a minor administrative position, unable to attract the confidence or the attention of the Wilsonian liberals such as Brandeis, Newton D. Baker and Walter Lippmann with whom he wished to associate. Although he had published in 1917 a brilliant but controversial book, *The Nature of Peace*, which brought him charges of being both pro-German[46] and anti-German, he was not invited into the peace-making councils and no doubt felt the rejection deeply. At *The Dial*, he wrote a series of fiery articles which were published in 1921 in book form as *The Engineers and the Price System*.

The noted sociologist Daniel Bell, a Veblen expert, conjectures that "a woman spurned in love turns to reform as a second choice; a man scorned by power often turns to revolution." Veblen certainly was subversive enough verbally to become a revolutionary; and he also possessed the Puritanical streak encountered in such men from Cromwell to Castro. At any rate, for once he offered a prescription and a program rather than plead non-involvement and watchful waiting. The familiar story of sabotage as the cause of under-production and depression is unfolded, this time with special emphasis on the retarding influence of the investment banker. Then we are told that if a revolution comes to America it will not be politically based. Instead it will be an uprising of the only strategic group capable of organizing and running a great industrial system —the engineers.

Caught up as always with his unconscious urge to promote and demote militarily, Veblen proposes:

> It follows that the material welfare of all the advanced industrial peoples rests in the hands of these technicians, if they will only see it that way, take counsel together, constitute themselves the self-directing General Staff of the country's industry, and dispense with the interference of the lieutenants of the absentee owners. Already they are strategically in a position to take the lead and impose their own terms of leadership, so soon as they, or a decisive number of them, shall reach a common understanding to that effect and agree on a plan of action.[47]

These engineers would constitute a "Soviet of technicians"— about as tactless a title as anyone could advance for a native-born revolt. Out on a limb, Veblen retreats just far enough to avoid prosecution for sedition. *The Dial* essays, after all, were written during the "red scare" raids of Attorney General A. Mitchell Palmer, a period of reaction unmatched in our history. With typical tongue-in-cheek humor, Veblen states categorically that there is no hope for any action that would bring about a revolutionary overthrow since the engineers are too unorganized, the trade unions are interested only in the full dinner-pail and the underlying population are uninformed and uninterested. "There is nothing in the situation," Veblen assures us, "that should reasonably flutter the sensibilities of the Guardians or of that massive body of well-to-do citizens who make up the rank and file of absentee owners, just yet."[48]

Yet there was considerable unrest among businessmen when Veblen wrote these lines. In 1919 over 4,000,000 workers were on strike, reflecting a drive towards unionism and a reluctance to give up wage increases gained during the War. U.S. Steel met the challenge by firing all union members and charging Communist leadership. Strikebreakers ran the plants at three-quarters capacity. The strikers were starved out and Steel remained unorganized for another fifteen years. At the Carnegie works, half the employees worked a twelve-hour day and one-quarter worked seven days a week. Semi-skilled workers earned less than $2,000 a year and unskilled workers less than $1,500, which was the subsistence level income required for a family of five in 1919. The lack of purchasing power would inevitably lead to depression.

The hysteria typified by Palmer's raids resulted in one-third of the states passing anti-radical laws by 1920. The New York State law specifically prohibited aiding, abetting or committing sabotage in industrial plants. From the safe vantage point of history, can reasonable businessmen fail to acknowledge the devilish humor of the old professor's charge of sabotage by *them*?

An interesting by-product of the "technicians" proposal was the emergence of an amiable band of crackpots known as the "Technocrats" in the dark days of the 1930's when any straw was clutched for relief from the great depression. This group, under the leadership of Howard Scott, preached production for use rather than profit, payment in energy units called "ergs," and the virtues of technicians and engineers over businessmen. Veblen died in 1929 and many of his admirers have attempted to detach him from Technocracy, which was more or less laughed out of existence after enjoying immense publicity and hopeful interest. Though the similarity of positions is obvious, Veblen probably would have avoided personal involvement as he detested cults.

In *Engineers*, Veblen not only revealed a weakness in his role of dispassionate observer but also chose a curious group for a power struggle with the vested interests. True enough, industrial engineers like Frederick W. Taylor and his disciples Morris L. Cooke and Henry L. Gantt were articulate prophets of scientific management in Veblen's time. They were devoted to efficiency and possessed a high-minded desire to improve the employee's lot as well as the employer's conscience, but within the present framework.[49] The man whom Cooke regarded as the "engineering method personified" was Herbert Hoover, former engineer and then an aspiring Republican politician, who was hardly a candidate for the Soviet of technicians. In fact, the engineers can be counted on to vote for the business party more readily than any other segment in American life. There is nothing they presently like better than incorporating with former university professors to engage in production for profit and capital gains. Often their chief customer is the military-industrial complex, which gives added glamor to their high-flying issues of stock.

VII

The Dial editorship came to an end in the fall of 1919. It was followed by a few years of uninspired teaching at the New School. Tired and disillusioned, Veblen left New York in 1926 to live out his days in California, barely supported by a few investments and royalties as well as the contributions of former students. His only writing was the completion of some Norse sagas which he had started thirty-seven years before.

Yet he had the satisfaction of knowing he was a national figure, that he had made an impression on his times after all. In 1925, at the insistence of men like ex-Senator Paul Douglas, who was a noted professor of economics at the University of Chicago himself, the American Economic Association tendered its presidency to Veblen. He refused: "They didn't offer it to me when I needed it." He could at least console himself with memories of *The Dial* days when he was the sudden hero of the sophisticates and intellectuals, those bright spirits who were disillusioned with the post-war world but vigorously interested in anything revolutionary in politics and the arts. H. L. Mencken, the equal to Veblen in savage humor but a tough-minded enemy of the left, gave Veblen his due in a *Smart Set* essay in 1919:

> Overnight . . . the nihilistic dethronement of Professor Dewey—and rah, rah, rah for Professor Dr. Veblen!
>
> In a few months—almost it seemed a few days—he was all over *The Nation*, *The Dial*, *The New Republic* and the rest of them, and his bookstand pamphlets began to

pour from the presses, and newspapers reported his every
wink and whisper . . . everyone of intellectual pretensions
read his works. Veblenianism was shining in full bril-
liance. There were Veblenists, Veblen clubs, Veblen
remedies, for all the sorrows of the world. There were
even in Chicago, Veblen Girls—perhaps Gibson Girls
grown middle-aged and despairing.[50]

How shall we estimate this strange, paradoxical man? In simplest terms he was against production for profit and against businessmen as the agents of production. He was not a Marxist since
he rejected the class struggle and had too much stubborn pride of
authorship to share another's theory anyway. (In fact he was
rather ungenerous in failing to acknowledge his intellectual debts
—Carlyle for "captain of industry," Proudhon for "force and fraud,"
Fourier and Saint-Simon for lining up the parasitic merchants,
soldiers, bureaucrats and lawyers who were not "producers.") Yet
in his anti-business animus this citizen of the world's greatest
business nation probably exceeded Marx. His claims for a shiny
new world of machines and technocracy are hardly consistent with
his yearnings for craftsmen with an instinct for workmanship.
Such men would be crushed in the mass production of big cities.
They belong to the imaginary past of the agrarian populists whom
Veblen spiritually never left, or to the world of small enterprise
which beguiled Brandeis's keen mind. His anthropological approach
is outmoded for economic interpretation and his instinctual psychology is barely acknowledged in the social sciences. He ignored
Freud's existence but he can lay claim to being the first Freudian
economist.

In his griping and grousing about business, Veblen is quite in
keeping with American traditions—if we can overlook his one
feeble call to the barricades. Certainly in his preoccupation with
the waste and inefficiency of our system, rather than the European
concern with class exploitation, Veblen is in the American tradition.
One wonders how he might have felt about another American
original, Henry Ford. Businessmen may be surprised to learn that
for a while Henry Ford was about as unpopular in business circles

as Veblen himself. Ford was a master of efficiency and workmanship. He had an absolute dread of bankers of any kind and would
have subscribed wholeheartedly to Veblen's warnings against
finance capitalism. He shared Veblen's functional aesthetics and
would have bankrupted his company with all-black vehicles of
Model T vintage had not his associates sabotaged such styling.
What really irritated his fellow businessmen was his inspired
raising of wages in 1914 from a minimum of $2.40 to $5.00 for
a nine-hour day, thus bringing the price of automobiles within the
reach of the laborers who made them. But consider his statement
on profits when his stockholders demanded more dividends:

> Business and industry are first and foremost a public
> service.

> We are organized to do as much good as we can, every-
> where, for everybody concerned.

> I do not believe we should make such an awful profit on
> our cars. A reasonable profit is right but not too much.

> So it has been my policy to force the price of the car
> down as fast as production would permit and give the
> benefits to the users and laborers with resulting sur-
> prisingly enormous benefits to ourselves.[51]

Since Ford was conscious enough of profits to become one of
the world's richest men, the comparison with Veblen must not be
stretched too far. Ford's dark side, expressed in "history is bunk,"
anti-Semitism and a preference for private bullies like Harry Ben-
nett, emphasizes their differences. Ironically it was Ford rather
than Veblen who captivated the Russians of the period in their
revolutionists' quest for the machine society of the future.

Ford ignored Veblen's existence but Edgar Monsanto Queeny,
head of Monsanto Chemical Company, responded to the challenge.
In 1943 Queeny published a book entitled *The Spirit of Enterprise*
in which he attributed just about everything wrong with American
life to the New Deal, whose "characteristics can be traced in sub-

stantial measure to the incubation of the teachings of the late Thorstein Veblen."[52] Through the eyes of Queeny, we get a fresh view of Veblen.

For Queeny, a man who is against dogs, horses, the Y.M.C.A. and college athletics cannot be all bad but is close to it. Veblen's sense of inferiority, his origin, his difficulty in finding employment and his own poverty are given as reasons for his "bitter and sarcastic attitude toward the American economic system out of which the riches came." In addition Veblen "as a student was a failure in mathematics but excelled in philosophy and economics." As for the latter:

> Both sciences provide opportunities for armchair mental gymnastics, individual dogmas, palaver and gush. They are not even a prelude to adventure, risk or physical exertion.[53]

Queeny gives Veblen too much credit for shaping the New Deal. He also reveals the standard business antagonism towards the meddling, impractical "brain-trust" professors of the political cartoons. No doubt Veblen deserves some punishment for his outrageous and unreal descriptions of business. Still, royalty should show some tolerance and possibly a sense of humor for its jesters and philosophers.

At any rate, the program of the New Deal was largely one of trial and error rather than doctrine. Roosevelt had little patience for grand changes in the system. Some of the early brain-trusters such as Rexford Tugwell and Stuart Chase, both of whom admired Veblen deeply, Adolf Berle and Raymond Moley soon found this out. But the professors, particularly those who could write good reform legislation, were called in as never before. Veblen's spirit of inquiry and disregard for tradition must surely have been pulsating in the atmosphere of adventure and mental exertion which the old New Dealers fondly recall. In fairness to Queeny's bitterness about the anti-business sentiment of the New Deal, it did indeed exist and with a vengeance. Americans are the most self-critical of peoples. A breakdown in the economic system of such appalling magnitude, along with the revelations of dishonesty and irresponsibility on the part of certain business heroes, could hardly result in anything other than a low point in public esteem for the businessman. The patient recovered as always and was somewhat better for the experience.

VIII

In the end how shall we evaluate Veblen? Most of his claims have turned out to rest on foundations of sand but that is the fate of any number of seminal thinkers who still must be recognized. Time changes the relevancy of their positions but the thrust of their ideas and personalities make a selected few become historical figures. In attacking the most powerful institution of all, the business system, Veblen was a failure as most giant-killers are. Yet the daring failure must have contributed in some way to the re-shaping of capitalism which has been such a great—perhaps the greatest—accomplishment of the twentieth century.

George Bernard Shaw states in the Preface to *Man and Superman:* "All the assertions get disproved sooner or later, and so we find the world full of magnificent débris of artistic fossils, with the matter-of-fact credibility gone clean out of them, but the form still splendid." Veblen's most famous work, *The Theory of the Leisure Class,* is now probably such a fossil with its form or style the main reason for its survival. On the other hand, we can add to Veblen's style his prophetic concept of the dominance of our life by technology and his uncompromising lifetime role of social critic.

It is in this role that Veblen shows best. He is one of the critics we not only tolerate but shake our heads at in rueful admiration. Like the prophets of old, he refuses to accommodate or to be compromised. With just a touch of reasonableness, good-will and sociability he could today join the ranks of best-selling social critics like William H. Whyte, Jr. (*The Organization Man*), Vance Packard (*The Hidden Persuaders*) and J. K. Galbraith. They are Veblenians all in their concern with institutions and the quality of our life—but for Veblen to conform would be out of character.

A comparison of Veblen with Galbraith is intriguing. They span the twentieth century, Veblen at the start breaking away from economics textbooks written by ministers about imaginary economic men, Galbraith at his end walking in and out of the White House where economists are now palace advisers to the Presidents. Both are satirists with an eye for the telling phrase. With Veblen it might be "conspicuous consumption" or the "received tradition" of orthodoxy; with Galbraith, the "affluent society" or the "conventional wisdom." Both are generalists looking askance at their specialist colleagues who can't see the forest for the trees. Both are highly critical of their sheltering universities for subservience to business, and they are equally concerned with the vulgar and cheap aspects of a business civilization. Both acknowledge the rationale of big business, mass production and the disturbing effects of too much competition. Veblen's engineers were to be the non-owning technocrats of industry. Galbraith has identified the new managerial class, combining technical and administrative skills, as the non-owning technostructure of industry. Both condemn American industry for underproduction or for emphasizing the wrong products, particularly weapons. They share a fear of the garrison state.

There are of course more differences than similarities. Veblen was an economist of scarcity, unable to comprehend that conspicuous consumption by a gadget-ridden middle-class would soon become an economic necessity and an achievement in its own way. Veblen distrusted the profit motive completely. Galbraith, more sophisticated politically, is weary of socialist claims and has no objection to profits. He is more concerned with priorities. Who will tell the technostructure which way to go? An American Keynes, Galbraith is energetically and happily involved in the social, cultural and political life of our times. The morose Veblen was always an outsider. By his own thinly-veiled definition, he is "a disturber of the intellectual peace . . . a wanderer in the intellectual no-man's land, seeking another place to rest, farther along the road, somewhere over the horizon."[54]

Footnotes

CHAPTER 1

Thorstein Veblen:

Disturber of the Intellectual Peace

No research into the life of Veblen can proceed without gratefully encountering Joseph Dorfman's definitive biography *Thorstein Veblen and His America*. Professor Dorfman, still active at Columbia, wrote the biography on a fellowship from the New School for Social Research in 1930-31, shortly after Veblen's death, and thus was in touch with a host of Veblen's friends, students and colleagues. Published in 1934, the book had been out of print but was reprinted in 1966 with new appendices and corrections by Augustus M. Kelley, New York, as part of its *Reprints of Economic Classics*, which include all of Veblen's major works.

Veblen fans have been abundant in intellectual circles. They include Leonard Silk, economist and government official, who saw enough drama in the lives of Veblen, Ellen, Professor Laughlin and some of the others mentioned herein to create *Veblen, A Play in Three Acts* (Kelley, 1966), still awaiting production. David Riesman's psychoanalytic approach, *Thorstein Veblen, A Critical Interpretation* (New York, 1953), illustrates the fascination always emanating from Veblen and has additional interest since Riesman considers him over-rated. Of particular value are recent paperbacks reflecting a current Veblen boom and prefaced by a most distinguished group, each of whom chose to evaluate Veblen in terms of his specialty. Thus, C. Wright Mills (*The Theory of The Leisure Class*, Mentor, 1953) emphasizes that Veblen somewhat missed the point by not evaluating the "power élite" of his time, since "leisure-class people" do not really make history. Daniel Bell, in the preface to *The Engineers and the Price System* (Harbinger, 1963), points out how the vast increase in our engineering and scientific work force makes Veblen prophetic in spite of his political unrealism.

Robert Lekachman has contributed engaging and insightful prefaces for *Absentee Ownership* (Beacon, 1967) and *The Theory of the Leisure Class* (Viking, 1967), which seem to suggest that Veblen was a great iconoclastic spirit but hardly the intellectual giant and social seer others have claimed.

A most valuable and closely reasoned analysis of Veblen is Max Lerner's brilliant introduction to *The Portable Veblen* (New York, 1948). Lerner describes Veblen as "the most creative mind American social thought has produced." In Lerner's *America As a Civilization* (New York, 1957), he frequently measures American institutions and values against Veblen's criteria and in every case finds Veblen in error of exaggeration or fact, which may mean creative minds have a great deal of leeway denied to others. At any rate, all agree Veblen was prober and stimulator *par excellence*.

[1] Joseph Dorfman, *Thorstein Veblen and His America* (New York, 1966), p. 504.

[2] David Riesman, *Thorstein Veblen, A Critical Interpretation* (New York, 1953), pp. 6-7.

[3] Thorstein Veblen, *Absentee Ownership* (New York, 1923), p. 142.

[4] *New York Times*, February 17, 1919, p. 1.

[5] Thorstein Veblen, *The Higher Learning in America* (New York, 1918), p. 57.

[6] *New York Times*, September 30, 1934, Book Review, p. 4.

[7] R. L. Duffus, "Veblen at Cedro," *American Scholar* (October, 1946), p. 464.

[8] Henry Adams, *The Education of Henry Adams* (Boston, 1918), pp. 271-272, Sentry Edition, 1961.

⁹ Robert L. Heilbroner, "The View from the Top," in Earl F. Cheit, ed., *The Business Establishment* (New York, 1964), p. 5.

¹⁰ Andrew Carnegie, *The Gospel of Wealth* (New York, 1900), p. 19.

¹¹ Senate Committee Investigating the Munitions Industry, *Hearings*, 74 Cong., 2 Sess. (Part 29, February 4, 1936).

¹² Dorfman, *op. cit.*, p. 68.

¹³ The phrase is aptly used in Eric F. Goldman, *Rendezvous with Destiny* (New York, 1952), Chapter 5.

¹⁴ Robert G. McCloskey, *American Conservatism in the Age of Enterprise 1865-1910* (Cambridge, 1951), pp. 8-9.

¹⁵ Emmet John Hughes, "The Pest of Glory," *Newsweek* (August 21, 1967), p. 13.

¹⁶ Dorfman, *op. cit.*, p. 311.

¹⁷ *Ibid.*, pp. 24-25.

¹⁸ Henry Steele Commager, *The American Mind* (New Haven, 1950), p. 231.

¹⁹ Robert Lekachman, *The Age of Keynes* (New York, 1966), pp. 78-81.

²⁰ William G. Sumner, *Earth-Hunger and Other Essays* (New Haven, 1913), p. 294.

²¹ *Ibid.*, p. 345.

²² Dorfman, *op. cit.*, p. 64.

²³ Commager, *op. cit.*, p. 232.

²⁴ Richard Hofstadter, "What Happened to the Antitrust Movement?" in Earl F. Cheit, *op. cit.*, p. 114.

²⁵ Dorfman, *op. cit.*, p. 57 and p. 39; also Riesman, *op. cit.*, pp. 138-139.

[26] Woodrow Wilson, *The New Freedom* (New York, 1913), pp. 86-87.

[27] A. L. Todd, *Justice on Trial* (New York, 1964), p. 105.

[28] Dorfman, *op. cit.*, p. 194.

[29] Commager, *op. cit.*, pp. 215-216.

[30] Thorstein Veblen, *Absentee Ownership, The Case of America* (New York, 1923), pp. 112-114.

[31] Thorstein Veblen, *The Theory of the Leisure Class* (New York, 1899), pp. 113-114.

[32] *Ibid.*, p. 331.

[33] *Ibid.*, p. 140.

[34] *Ibid.*, p. 265.

[35] Thorstein Veblen, *The Theory of Business Enterprise* (New York, 1904), Ch. 3, fn. 9.

[36] Thorstein Veblen, *The Engineers and the Price System* (New York, 1921), p. 38, Harbinger Edition, 1963.

[37] Thorstein Veblen, *Absentee Ownership, op. cit.*, pp. 217-219.

[38] J. K. Galbraith, *The New Industrial State* (Boston, 1967), pp. 189-197.

[39] Thurman Arnold, in the 1962 Preface to *The Folklore of Capitalism* (New Haven, 1937), p. xi.

[40] Daniel Bell, in the Introduction to Veblen's *The Engineers and the Price System, op. cit.*, p. 34.

[41] Thorstein Veblen, *The Place of Science in Modern Civilization* (New York, 1919), p. 443.

[42] Thorstein Veblen, *The Instinct of Workmanship* (New York, 1914), p. 25.

[43] Farewell message of Dwight D. Eisenhower, broadcast from the White House, January 17, 1961.

[44] Paul W. Sweezy, "Veblen: A Cautionary View," *The New Republic* (February 25, 1946), pp. 287-288.

[45] Thorstein Veblen, *Absentee Ownership, op. cit.*, p. 445.

[46] *New York Times*, March 7, 1918, II, p. 2. Letter from Professor William Herbert Hobbs of University of Michigan.

[47] Thorstein Veblen, *The Engineers and the Price System, op. cit.*, p. 129.

[48] *Ibid.*, p. 151.

[49] Kenneth Trombley, *The Life and Times of a Happy Liberal* (New York, 1954), p. 9.

[50] Dorfman, *op. cit.*, p. 423.

[51] Henry Ford, *My Life and Work* (New York, 1926), p. 162.

[52] Edgar M. Queeny, *The Spirit of Enterprise* (New York, 1943), p. 64.

[53] *Ibid.*, p. 65.

[54] Thorstein Veblen, "The Intellectual Pre-eminence of Jews in Modern Europe," from *Essays in Our Changing Order* (New York, 1934), reprinted in *The Portable Veblen* (New York, 1948), p. 475.

Chapter 2

SINCLAIR LEWIS:
The Search for a Business Hero

Main Street, Sinclair Lewis's tale of Gopher Prairie, was the publishing sensation of 1920. America was never more ready for a particular book and author. In a post-war mood of self-examination and cynicism, it showered fame and fortune on the thirty-five year old author from Sauk Centre, Minnesota who joyously satirized his own birthright. "Hell's sweet bells, here is divine comedy," Lewis gloated as millions read his book, "an earnest young man, Yankee of physical type, comic and therefore the more humorless, writes a long book to slap the bourgeois—the bourgeois love it— eat it!"[1]

An earnest young woman named Carol Kennicott, who reads Thorstein Veblen, is the heroine of *Main Street*. Married to the hopelessly stolid, unromantic Dr. Will Kennicott, she tries to bring art and culture to Gopher Prairie. Bloodied by the grim-lipped morality of bankers' wives, village gossips, inane pastors and other pillars of society, she has the good sense to flee from it all to do war work in Washington. In the end she sulks back to her patient Will and the dull, deadening, conforming, tasteless life of the small town.

A generation of critics have pointed out what most readers must have realized all along, that Sinclair Lewis was as sympathetic to the dependable, midwestern, no-nonsense Will as he was to the flighty Carol. Although Lewis wrote five nearly great novels in the twenties alone, *Main Street, Babbitt, Arrowsmith, Elmer Gantry* and *Dodsworth,* not to mention seventeen other best-sellers through 1951, his reputation as an artist is insecure even though he won the Nobel Prize for literature in 1930. It is said that he lacks depth. Yet no one can deny his reputation as a great satirist, master mimic and walking camera. He is particularly fascinating on the rampant business spirit of the twenties.

Gopher Prairie is a fifty year old frontier town which has missed its chance to become a city. Carol views it with disbelief: "Dyer's Drug Store . . . a greasy marble soda-fountain with an electric lamp of red and green and curdled yellow mosaic shade." "The Minniemashie House . . . in the hotel office she could see a stretch of bare unclean floors, a line of rickety chairs with brass cuspidors between, a writing-desk with advertisements in mother-of-pearl letters upon the glass-covered back. The dining room beyond was a jungle of stained table-cloths and catsup bottles." Only the Ford Garage and the Buick Garage are busy with the roar of testing motors and are housed in competent brick and cement structures, a portent of escape by wheels for future generations.

Gopher Prairie's businessmen, however, are a lively group, blissfully unaware that their town has peaked out and highly devoted to "boosterism." A campaign has been launched under the auspices of the Commercial Club and a newcomer, "Honest Jim" Blausser, delivers the keynote address. A sample from his speech evokes some questions. Could businessmen in any size town ever have been so fatuous? Is it possible for the language, even slang, to be so ephemeral? Close to one-half million hard-cover *Main*

Streets bearing these lines were sold to a population of only 105 million Americans:

> Now, frien's, there's some folks so yellow and small and so few in the pod that they go to work and claim that those of us that have the big vision are off our trolleys. They say we can't make Gopher Prairie, God bless her! just as big as Minneapolis or St. Paul or Duluth. But lemme tell you right here and now that there ain't a town under the blue canopy of heaven that's got a better chance to take a running jump and go scooting right up into the two-hundred-thousand class than little old G.P.! And if there's anybody that's got such cold kismets that he's afraid to tag after Jim Blausser on the Big Going Up, then we don't want him here! Way I figger it, you folks are just patriotic enough so that you ain't going to stand for any guy sneering and knocking his own town, no matter how much of a smart Aleck he is—and just on the side I want to add that this Farmers' Nonpartisan League and the whole bunch of socialists are right in the same category, or, as the fellow says, in the same scategory, meaning This Way Out, Exit, Beat It While the Going's Good, This Means You, for all knockers of prosperity and the rights of property!

II

While *Main Street* swept the nation, Lewis was already planning his next creation, the story of the American businessman. He had written to his publisher, Alfred Harcourt, in 1920:

> He is the Tired Business Man, the man you hear drooling in the Pullman smoker; but having once seen him, I want utterly to develop him so that he will seem just not typical but an individual . . . He is all of us Americans at 46, prosperous but worried, wanting—passionately—to seize something more than motor cars and a house *before it's too late.*[2]

His name is George F. Babbitt and far from being known as an individual, he entered American culture as an archetype of the conforming, middle-class, perspiring businessman. He had practically no saving graces, inspiring at best pity mingled with horror at the contemplation of his narrow horizons. He was the *boobus Americanus* of Lewis's favorite journalist, Henry L. Mencken, the Baltimore newspaperman who had already become a famous common scold of middle-class values while Lewis was still waiting in the wings. Mencken and Lewis were a natural partnership and their friendship, flavored by great drinking bouts, was one of the few relationships the incredibly bad-mannered Lewis was able to sustain through the years. Even before the war, Mencken had launched a superbly vitriolic campaign against the standardized manners and the inhibited morals of the middle-class, both of which he cavalierly attributed to the dominant business culture. In retrospect Mencken's prose and wit are more acceptable to the contemporary ear, which responds more favorably to dry, subtle humor than to corn. (When the news of Coolidge's death was announced, he asked: "How do they know?") Yet there were profound differences. Mencken cordially hated the Babbitts; Lewis was at bottom sentimentally fond of them and part Babbitt himself. Politically Mencken was anti-democratic and élitist. He was soon to become violently anti-Roosevelt and as great an enemy of the New Deal as the most reactionary businessman. Lewis had an incorruptible faith in the people as a whole and though he became sharply critical of causes and do-gooders was staunchly liberal to the end.

At any rate, Lewis went to work on *Babbitt* with the most businesslike zeal. It may come as a surprise to residents of Cincinnati to note that he chose Cincinnati as the model for Zenith, the city in the three-hundred to four-hundred-thousand class in which George Babbitt and the forces of conformity would shine.

Lewis moved into the Queen City Club in Cincinnati, using it as a base for his writing while he restlessly lectured and hopped from city to city, a constitutional weakness that would pursue him all his life. Here he consolidated his prodigious research for the new novel, filling his notebooks with observations. Disordered in his personal life, Lewis was a most orderly writer. He planned his novels like military campaigns, drawing up large maps of Zenith, for example, on which the streets and stores would be laid out and named with precision. Even Babbitt's home in suburban Floral Heights had a floor-plan, on which the standard furniture and glass fruit appeared in scale before entering the manuscript.

As a result, *Babbitt* is staggering in the type of detail called verisimilitude. But Babbitt, the wistful, conniving, harassed little businessman, briefly human in the awareness of his entrapment by his environment, emerges unforgettably from the background detail. The novel has no plot to speak of. It is a calendar of a few months in Babbitt's life, showing what a middle-class real estate broker—a middleman rather than producer and thus quite low on the anti-business scale—does with himself and his thoughts in this brief period.

Babbitt is a good husband and provider who, once he pulls himself together to face another day, draws strength from the distant observation of the towers of downtown Zenith:

> As Babbitt stared, the nervousness was soothed from his face, his slack chin lifted in reverence. All he articulated was "That's one lovely sight!" but he was inspired by the rhythm of the city, his love for it renewed. He beheld the tower as a temple-spire of the religion of business, a faith passionate, exalted, surpassing common men; and as he clumped down to breakfast he whistled the ballad "Oh, by gee, by gosh, by jingo" as though it were a hymn melancholy and noble.

He is losing his grip, however, in spite of the protective habit of reacting to all great and little issues as a Republican, Elk, Presbyterian and member of the Boosters Club. A mixture of boredom, change of life and perhaps some buried residue of daring inherited from his pioneer ancestors impel him first to an affair with a sympathetic widow named Tanis Judique and then to a far more serious revolt—defiance of the thinking of the herd.

Before these crises in the life of George Babbitt take place, noted by Lewis as occurring in the year Warren G. Harding of Marion, Ohio was elected President, he reaches pinnacles of achievement which make his fall all the more incomprehensible to his fellow businessmen. Babbitt has been discovered to be an orator in a land where interminable speech-making by politicians and businessmen has become ingrained in the fabric of the republic. He has appeared on the program of the State Association of Real Estate Boards where he wins acclaim by demanding that "folks call us 'realtors' and not 'real-estate men'. Sounds more like a regular profession." Next he is called upon for a high civic duty. As precinct leader of the Republican party in Floral Heights, he speaks against Seneca Doane who is running for Mayor on an alarming labor ticket. The Democrats themselves have joined the Republicans in nominating Lucas Prout, a mattress manufacturer with a record of perfect sanity, rather than debate their usual differences at such a time. Seneca Doane is the radical lawyer of Zenith. Like Miles Bjornstam, the village atheist of *Main Street*, he is influenced by Veblen and hopelessly non-conformist. Doane is defeated, Zenith is saved and now Lewis calls upon Babbitt for the greatest speech of his career, the principal address at the annual meeting of the Zenith Real Estate Board. Since the speech is too embarrassing to stand the full light of day and since it seriously questions the credibility of Babbitt as a graduate of the State University and Cincinnati-Zenith as any improvement over Gopher Prairie, Babbitt's peroration will suffice:

> Not till that is done will our sons and daughters see that the ideal of American manhood and culture isn't a lot of cranks sitting around chewing the rag about their Rights and their Wrongs, but a God-fearing, hustling, successful, two-fisted Regular Guy, who belongs to some church with pep and piety to it, who belongs to the Boosters or the Rotarians or the Kiwanis, to the Elks or Moose or Red Men or Knights of Columbus or any one of a score of organizations of good, jolly, kidding, laughing, sweating, upstanding, lend-a-handing Royal Good

Fellows, who plays hard and works hard, and whose answer to his critics is a square-toed boot that'll teach the grouches and smart alecks to respect the He-man and get out and root for Uncle Samuel, U.S.A.!

III

A dark and sinister chapter remains in the story of Babbitt that makes all the horseplay seem irrelevant and yet is hardly mentioned in the reams of printed controversy that swept over America about Babbitt the Booster and Babbitt the Philistine. It is Babbitt's confrontation with his friends and peers in the Good Citizens League, an outright anti-labor and anti-crank Vigilante Committee. It seems shocking today but was perhaps more understandable in the 1920's when the Ku Klux Klan grew from practically nothing to over four and one-half million white-sheeted members and Attorney General Palmer was conducting his hysterical invasions of constitutional liberties, all in the name of high causes.

Babbitt's cause was innocent enough. Half-conscious of a rebel streak within himself, fortified by his flings with Tanis Judique and oratory, he chose to be "publicly liberal" over the telephone girls' strike. When the strike expanded to include dairy-product workers and truck drivers, the National Guard was called out and Zenith parted into two belligerent sides, with a puzzled Babbitt wavering towards each. To his dismay Babbitt heard his minister deplore the strikers. His fellow boosters and luncheon club members failed to see the humor of his reluctant admiration for Seneca Doane and the distinguished Professor Brockbank when they marched defiantly in the strikers' parade. The final heresy was to be darkly observed by Vergil Gunch, a leading coal dealer and power in the clubs, as he joshed a self-important citizen-officer in the National Guard for expressing a desire to beat up the strikers. Next he politely declined Vergil Gunch's invitation to join the newly formed Good Citizens League, even though it was allied with the Chamber of Commerce, and the die was cast. The amiable, dim-witted

Zenith of the small businessmen now becomes an ominous camp of whisperings, disapproval and rejection. When his wife begs him to join up, Babbitt is for once eloquent:

> I know what the League stands for! It stands for the suppression of free speech and free thought and everything else! I don't propose to be bullied and rushed into joining anything, and it isn't a question of whether it's a good league or a bad league or what the hell kind of league it is; it's just a question of my refusing to be told I got to—

A committee of three pays him a special visit, Dr. Dilling the surgeon, Charles McKelvey the contractor and Colonel Rutherford Snow, owner of the newspaper. When the amenities are over, they go for Babbitt's jugular, his business life. A shaky Babbitt calls their bluff but in a few days he knows he is defeated as his business associates, employees and bankers withdraw from his touch. The painful drama comes to an end when his wife has an attack of acute appendicitis and he calls in Dr. Dilling. The shock brings him back to his senses. He realizes how much he needs and appreciates the secure world of clubs, conformity and respectability. The novel closes as he advises his son, Theodore Roosevelt Babbitt: "Don't be scared of the family. No, nor all of Zenith. Nor of yourself, the way I've been. Go ahead, old man! The world is yours!"

IV

As might be expected, this novel which lashed the business spirit so unremittingly became a center of controversy as well as a runaway best-seller. The response in the world of opinion was enormous, insuring the word Babbitt as a synonym for an unattractive type of businessman and fulfilling Lewis's prediction to his publishers that the whole country would be talking about "Babbittry" soon enough. Mencken became the book's greatest press-agent. "As an old professor of Babbittry," he wrote, "I welcome him as an almost perfect specimen." The Babbitts are "the palladiums of 100% Americanism, the apostles of Harding politics, the guardians of the Only True Christianity . . . the Rotary Club, the Kiwanis Clubs . . . the Good Citizens Leagues," he continued, endowing the last-named with a reality that existed by that title only in Lewis's novel. "Every American city swarms with his brothers."[3] Lewis, who had spent his struggling years working as a publisher's publicity man, kept the pot boiling. "If I had the power," he announced, "I'd make Henry Mencken the Pope of America. He spreads just the message of sophistication we need so badly."[4]

There were international repercussions as well, as a grateful Europe saw upstart America pilloried by its own author for its mean materialism. C. E. M. Joad, the bearded English critic and future television celebrity, was inspired to write a bitter account of American civilization entitled *The Babbitt Warren*. Rebecca West, one of the ablest English critics, was more discerning and compassionate, although condescending, in a *New Statesman* review in 1922: "It is a bonehead Walt Whitman speaking," she writes, marvellously characterizing the mangled visions in Babbitt's oratory of boosterism; yet:

> Stuffed like a Christmas goose as Babbitt is, with silly films, silly talk, silly oratory, there has yet struck him the majestic creativeness of his own country, its miraculous power to bear and nourish without end countless multitudes of men and women . . . There is in these people a vitality so intense that it must eventually bolt with them and land them willy-nilly into the sphere of intelligence; and this immense commercial machine will become the instrument of their aspirations.[5]

Isaac Marcosson, a noted American correspondent, interviewed Trotsky and found him reading and enjoying the Russian translation of *Babbitt*. When the Nobel prize was awarded in 1930 to Lewis, the first American writer to win it, the Swedes made it clear that it was for *Babbitt*, even though officially the prize is always awarded for an author's total work.

One of the first protests came from George F. Babbitt of Boston who claimed his reputation as a writer was threatened by the caricature in the book. Lewis's publishers (or was it his press-agents?) averted a lawsuit by establishing that there was only one George Follansbee Babbitt. Anne O'Hare McCormick of the *New York Times* interviewed people in the midwest and found a certain pride in Zenith's assignment to that region. Newspapers in Minneapolis, Milwaukee, Duluth, Kansas City and Cincinnati each proudly claimed it served as the model for Zenith. (Cincinnati's present Chamber of Commerce regards the connection with total lack of recall, although it is proud of having served as the locale for Fannie Hurst's *Back Street* in 1931.) Minneapolis actually celebrated a "Babbitt Week," sure at least that Lewis was a native son of Minnesota.

In the beginning the special interest journals of the business world responded temperately, perhaps because they were distracted by the magnificent sales curve of the book that attacked them. The *National Real Estate Journal* in 1922 and the *Rotarian* in 1923 calmly questioned the credibility of Babbitt as a realtor and as a booster. The *Rotarian's* point of view was quite balanced, pointing out that there were many Rotarians like Babbitt, but these were the followers, not the leading citizens. The Babbitts may add nothing to the creative side of life, the article states, but they do add to the material side which needs the standardized alarm clocks they produce if not their standardized ideas.

In time, the business journals rose to the bait with ironical results. The *Kiwanis* magazine exhorted its membership as follows:

> Until the boosters and the Babbitts make the soft voice of Confidence drown the harsher voices of Hate, Selfishness and Suspicion, we cannot slough off the aftermath of the war. Let carping critics fatten their batting average of sarcasm against the boosters of the organizations which boost. It is of such men that substantial citizenship is made.[6]

"I'm proud to be called a Babbitt," announced the president of Lions International in a *Collier's* article. "Back of the effulgence of community patriotism, there is the solid achievement of community betterment . . . If that is Babbittry, make the most of it."[7] The president of the New York Rotary Club made a radio speech charging that Zenith was not typical. Rotarians were not annoyed with Sinclair Lewis, he said, they just think "he is a little bit off his trolley."[8]

Nation's Business, the official journal of the United States Chamber of Commerce and the spokesman for American business, was goaded by the Lewis-Mencken line into a defiant stand. "Dare to be a Babbitt!" editorialized Merle Thorpe. "Why should a man be condemned for his pride in his real estate business, his membership in the Zenith Boosters Club and Zenith Chamber of Commerce, his simple joy in the conveniences of his life and home?" The country "would be better off for more Babbitts."[9] Thorpe then led *Nation's Business* through a pro-Babbitt campaign of cartoons, articles and "Babbitt Ballads." The poetry compares favorably with that of Babbitt's one and only acquaintance in the arts, T. Cholmondoley ("Chum") Frink, the syndicated poet-laureate of Zenith who is modelled on Edgar A. Guest. The letters to the editor of *Nation's Business* justified the apotheosis of Babbitt. "I applaud the Babbitt Revolution which you have so vigorously encouraged in the pages of your splendid magazine," wrote a vice-president of the Illinois Central Railroad. One man wrote that he had not read *Babbitt* when it was a best-seller, but after reading it because it was so controversial he wished to announce, "I want to be a Babbitt and with Babbitt I stand."[10] Still another claimed George Washington and the framers of the Constitution were Babbitts, which should have found agreement from Professor Charles A. Beard who had said more or less the same thing in his famous economic interpretations of the Constitution and democracy. Instead, with the perversity of the intellectual, Beard made a late entry on behalf of the pro-Babbitt forces in 1928 by attacking the "pet notions of the Mencken-Sinclair Lewis school" that Babbitt's case was hopeless. There was no valid historical basis, he declared, for the belief that the American businessman could never be civilized.[11]

As evidence of how long a play the Babbitt episode received, there is the final statement by *Rotarian* editor Vivian Carter in 1929, six years after the dignified initial reaction in 1923. Rotary Clubs in general did not conform to the Babbitt stereotype, he stated, although admittedly a typical meeting might proceed as follows:

> Take this one for instance. It is an interclub meeting . . . over a hundred present. We sit; the song leader bids each of us shake the right hand and "know" our next neighbor. So done. Before we've had time to say "Howdy, Dave" or "Glad to know you Pete," the song leader is at us with instructions to sing "Love's Old Sweet Song." That done, we start to sip our soup, to be interrupted at the second sip with loud instructions to sing "A Long, Long Trail." We start to make a remark to Dave or Pete but before a sentence is through, we are at it again, singing "Sweet Adeline," "Hero Mine," "That Rotary Smile," and so on with barely an interval even to eat, let alone "to cultivate acquaintance with a view to service." When singing and attempting to eat is done with, we are in for "talks." Fifteen visiting Rotarians each say a word— usually it is to tell a tale; the platform says a word apiece; the district governor makes an address, there are more tales, and lastly, the "Speaker of the Evening" comes to the attack . . . and listen we shall for an hour though we faint with heat, shuffle, look at our watches.[12]

It all seems to add up to the fact that businessmen wind up second best in any contest with artists and writers. In passing it is worth noting the comments of a midwestern leader of public opinion who saw Babbitt more clearly than Babbitt's fellow boosters saw him. William Allen White, the Emporia, Kansas editor, almost always sane and wise about everything in American life during his great career, was interviewed on *Babbitt* by the *Rotarian* in 1927. He applauded Lewis for criticizing that which needed to be criticized and for exposing the "garish externals of American life."

On the other hand, though Lewis recognized a more optimistic side of America, its "fundamental and inviolable excellences," White stated, he failed to incorporate them sufficiently in his work.[13] White was of course correct in his analysis of Lewis, who had ambivalent feelings about Main Street and Babbitt. Lewis believed, as Rebecca West did, in the potential of America to be great in spirit as well as in things. As a story-teller and social critic, however, he knew the value of exaggeration.

Professor Perry Miller of Harvard tells a touching story of meeting an older and shattered Lewis on shipboard to Europe in 1949 two years before his death in 1951. Lewis became his friend and Miller invited him to lecture to his class at the University of Leiden the following month. In the lecture Lewis firmly avowed: "I wrote *Babbitt* not out of hatred for him but out of love." Similarly Lewis had insisted to Miller: "I love America. I love it, but I don't like it."[14]

V

From Babbitt Lewis was to progress to other business characters, notably Dodsworth. Before examining Dodsworth, it would be profitable to survey briefly the "real" world (assuming history does not transform all reality into fiction) of government and business in the twenties.

America of the twenties has many provocative names, the Roaring Twenties, the Restless Decade, the Prohibition Decade, the Jazz Age—but not the Business Decade. Yet as far as business is concerned, it was the age of business triumphant, a New Era when for the most part there was a steady rise in prosperity until the watershed year of 1929. Politics, religion and idealism were in low repute in the wake of the post-war disillusionment. It was a time for the "return to normalcy" as Harding so well put it. It was considered abnormal to become excited over European entanglements, to seek inspired Presidents like Woodrow Wilson or to advance lofty civic goals requiring the restraint or downgrading of business such as the Progressive leaders proclaimed before the

War. Almost as if they were type-cast for the mood of the nation, Harding, Coolidge and Hoover presided in the White House somewhat as Chairmen of the Board of the United States.

The reputation of the businessman as the wizard of prosperity was not undeserved. Unlike the post World War II period of affluence, that of the twenties could claim it made it on its own. Government had neither the desire nor the power to share responsibility for the Gross National Product, the accurate measurement of which was not even available until shortly before World War II. Nor was it done with deficit financing, armaments, public works or foreign aid to any extent. The fact that it was a prosperity heading for a cataclysmic depression due to its speculative mania and its poorly distributed purchasing power, both geographically and by classes, does not diminish some of its real accomplishments.

The automobile was the key to the great increase in jobs and payrolls. There were 23 million autos on the road in 1929 compared with 7 million in 1919. It was the most practical and dynamic expression of America's industrial genius, involving not only native inventive ability but also mass production and the new techniques of modern advertising, salesmanship and instalment credit. They all combined miraculously to change the morality, the landscape and the habits of Americans. Henry Ford was the authentic business hero even though the novelists failed to take him on and everything he said or did, crackpot or sensible, was major news. Besides the automobile there were the new gadgets for every home such as the radio. Its total sales approached one billion dollars annually in 1929 although broadcasting had only commenced in 1920. Radio Corporation of America, without ever paying a dividend, roared to a price of $500 in 1929.

Prosperity in that period of primitive economics was also a matter of psychological readiness. Since there had never been a great depression, there could be no particular fear of one. The post-war slump of 1921 had turned around by itself giving further credence to the perfectibility of the business system. Americans as never before wanted to have fun and their share of the possessions the industrialists were so efficiently providing for them. As they drove their automobiles, patronized the glamorous retail stores and marched to the movies and ballrooms once a week, they created more jobs and more purchasing power to keep the great system churning. While they listened to booster oratory in their service clubs, they also heard it from high places. In 1929 John J. Raskob, a top business executive in General Motors and Du Pont, wrote an article for the *Ladies Home Journal* entitled *Everybody Ought to be Rich*, the title faithfully reflecting the national expectations. The fact that Raskob's formula wasn't based on the old virtues of thrift and hard work but on stock market investments on the instalment plan for the common man did not diminish the national acclaim it received. Though Raskob was known as a Republican and a stock market speculator he had been selected by Al Smith to be Chairman of the Democratic National Committee in the recent Presidential election. It was an endorsement of the supremacy of the business spirit for the party of Bryan and Wilson to have made such a choice.

In the White House itself business was given the place of honor and the three Presidents who celebrated this event bring the times into focus.

Harding was unique in being George Babbitt magnified and made President. To complete the illusion, he brought Main Street into the White House with him, having nurtured his roots and personality in a small midwestern city. Although a much handsomer man than Babbitt, he shared his petty tastes, bringing cronies, poker, cigars and bootlegged highballs into the White House. These hail-fellow pursuits and even his Babbitt-like indiscretions would not have prevented him from being a good President. Harding, however, was barely more intelligent than Babbitt and like him unable to withstand the pressures of his friends. The dreary tale of two of them, Attorney General Harry Daugherty, his campaign manager from the Ohio days, and Secretary of the Interior Albert B. Fall, is well known. There was the "Little Green House on K Street" where the "Ohio Gang" surrounding Daugherty peddled influence and solicited bribes, particularly from bootleggers about to face prosecution and from German owners of property sequestered during the war. Daugherty escaped conviction when juries disagreed but Coolidge forced him to resign in 1924. The most famous of the other scandals is known as "Teapot Dome," the name of one of the involved naval oil reserves. Harding's old friend from the Senate, the newly appointed Secretary of the Interior, persuaded him to transfer these naval oil reserve properties from the Navy to the Interior Department on the grounds that they would be in better custody, to which the compliant Harding agreed. Fall immediately leased the two reserves in California to Edward Doheny and the Teapot Dome reserve in Wyoming to Harry Sinclair. The leases were secret, without the competitive bidding the law required and, as later proved, strictly on a bribery basis. It took almost ten years for Senate committees headed by Thomas J. Walsh and Burton K. Wheeler of Montana to uncover all the details—long after Harding's death in 1923—but they revealed the most shocking corruption since the Grant administration. Fall went to prison and Sinclair served a short term for contempt. Eventually the oil leases were declared void. Sinclair returned twelve million dollars to the government as additional royalties and Doheny close to thirty-five million. The investigations by chance brought to light a sideline swindle quite damaging to the business image. Sinclair and a group of other oil executives had set up a private purchasing company, Continental Trading Company, to buy oil to sell to their own companies at a profit without their fellow directors' knowledge and of course at the expense of their own stockholders. An indignant John D. Rockefeller, Jr. forced the ouster of Robert W. Stewart, chairman of the board of Standard Oil of New Jersey, for participating in this ingenious plan.

Of greater significance than these crimes was the apathetic attitude taken by the public. Walsh and Wheeler were generally vilified by the press as scandalmongers and character assassins. John W. Davis, running on what was known at the time of the Harding scandals, was overwhelmed by Coolidge in 1924. A conclusion might be drawn that the predominant public sentiment was in favor of the government keeping its hands off business. The details of the Harding scandals were difficult to follow and their unravelling was spread over a long period of time. Though Harding was obviously too easy with his friendships, his successor appeared to be the soul of probity and the agent of continuing prosperity who had a proper understanding of the roles of government and business.

Coolidge was so disarmingly "New England" in his shrewd silence and cracker-barrel aphorisms that biographers cannot resist the fun of describing his personality before getting on to his philosophy. A study in inertia, a Puritan in Babylon, silent Cal. A nation given to ballyhoo, intolerance and stock market gambling found it comforting to have a man in the White House with the old virtues of quiet dignity and frugality. He was a stand-in for the national conscience.

He had a serenely simple concept of government. The best government is the least government and the most important interest is the business interest. "The chief business of the American people is business," he announced within five months of taking office, an inconceivable remark, even if true, for any President since that time. "Wealth is the chief end of men." "This is a business country . . . and it wants a business government." "Never before," exulted the *Wall Street Journal*, "has a government been so completely fused with business."[15] The federal government justified itself, Coolidge believed, only as it served business. This philosophy allowed him to diminish the office and to work less hours than any man in the history of the Presidency. No doubt he reassured business and accelerated prosperity, just as Eisenhower sustained prosperity in the 1950's by gaining the confidence of business leaders. But Coolidge was the complete servant of business as Eisenhower was not and his hibernation in the White House while the economy was courting disaster condemns him as a second-rate President from the hindsight of history. A few examples will illustrate his sins, which were always of omission. His roots were with farmers and he was aware that the loss of foreign markets, the boll weevil invasions, droughts and increased industrial prices made the farmer a fatality amidst the prosperity of the twenties. When farm

interests advanced a surplus purchase bill that would do what protective tariffs were doing for industry, Washington responded with
measures for self-help rather than government help, such as encouraging the farm cooperative movement. "Farmers have never
made money," Coolidge noted, "I don't believe we can do much
about it."[16] Yet the imbalance in the spreading of the riches of the
twenties obviously threatened the prosperity. A more direct option
for action was given to Coolidge in relation to the tremendous credit
expansion the country was undergoing, which must have alarmed
his innate austerity. Brokers' loans—the source for buying securities
on margin—reached a fantastic four billion dollars by the end of
1927. Relying on his businessmen advisers rather than the few
warning voices that reached the White House, Coolidge announced
in January 1928 that this was only a natural result of expansion
of business in the securities market. He took pleasure in seeing
stock prices shoot up twenty-six points within a day as a direct
result. Unlike Harding, whose brokers voluntarily cancelled
$150,000 of speculative loans after his death, Coolidge personally
had no interest in the market and saved a tidy fortune from his salary.

In fairness, what genius existed who would have headed off the
depression or invented controls in a time of prosperity that were
only to arise from the chaos of depression? Even today the perils
of prosperity seem more difficult to cope with than those of deflation, although in neither case will it ever again be a matter of
inaction in Washington. The Presidents of the twenties can at
least share the blame with the business leaders of the twenties who
dazzled them with their own riches, the temptations of observed
results and the rigidity of their self-interested economics.

Capitalism had in effect been dragged into a new world of
dependent laborers, mass technology, interdependent foreign markets and wild credit gyrations that called either for a new system or
a managed system. The Federal Reserve System, for example, essential for today's monetary control, was only ten years old and
half-understood when Coolidge took office. The whole concept of
federal intervention was too daring for most minds to conceive and
was constantly being sidetracked by cries of socialism and destruc-

tion of initiative. What kind of managing could be expected from Andrew Mellon, the venerated Secretary of the Treasury who spanned the career of all three Presidents? Personally honest, it would be impossible for the man whose family saw its wealth in securities increase by $300 million in a few years of one decade to avoid conflicts of interest. Mellon was seventy years old in 1925, old enough to remember the days when businessmen were held in disrepute by Roosevelt and Wilson and now basking under the new haloes they wore. His great passion was reduction of personal income taxes, even if that slightly postponed his ambition to do away with the national debt. His first efforts at tax reduction under Harding were so baldly slanted to benefit the millionaire class that he had to settle for half a loaf, a surtax rate cut from 50% to 40%. Under Coolidge's leadership, he picked up the task again, working it down to 20%, while the inheritance tax was lowered— soon to be repealed—and the gift tax was repealed. It was a propitious time for dying as well as making fortunes and the choice must have bothered several of his contemporaries. Meanwhile the Treasury Department dispensed $3.5 billion in tax refunds, several millions of which went to Mellon companies. Coolidge could find more time to contemplate the feet on his desk or startle the White House kitchen staff by taking personal inventory. A national budget of less than $3.5 billion in 1927 reflected a reduction in government activity at every level. The released tax money helped feed the runaway boom in the credit markets since it benefitted upper income people particularly.

Herbert Hoover, Secretary of Commerce for both Harding and Coolidge, was head and shoulders above them in intelligence and ability. Disgusted with Harding, he bided his time under Coolidge (who disliked his energetic ways and dubbed him "The Wonder Boy") until the job was his, but he also was subject to the business syndrome. He made the Department of Commerce an extension of the Chamber of Commerce but he presented a sincere concept of Quaker idealism and service to the leaders of the business world and urged that they subscribe to it. In an article entitled "Backing

Up Business" which he wrote while awaiting the 1928 nomination, Hoover listed the limited but helpful activities of his modest agency and prophetically noted: "It is not through inflation or speculation that we make progress for they are bound to be followed by ultimate depression and unemployment."[17] Yet he soon helplessly watched the economy cave in, unable to change his point of view significantly about the role of government. His experience with the Tennessee Valley Authority provides an illuminating example of how this cast of mind paralyzed the able, intelligent Hoover, equating him with the cypher Harding and the do-nothing Coolidge as lacking in vision. In the early twenties, Senator Norris of Nebraska had proposed that the hydroelectric dams at Muscle Shoals on the Tennessee River be taken over by the government which had built them as a war measure. Norris's dream was to develop the nation's great water resources to provide cheap power for millions of people in an entire region. Such proposals, with their suggestions of public power and participation in business, received frantic opposition from the utility companies and their well-organized lobbies. Coolidge actually was willing to sell Muscle Shoals to Henry Ford who offered to buy it for private development but Ford's plan was blocked in Congress by the Norris forces. Coolidge thereupon vetoed Norris's first Muscle Shoals bill in 1925.

In 1931 an improved Muscle Shoals bill was submitted to Hoover after passage again by Congress. Hoover was the first engineer to reach the White House and superbly equipped to appreciate the technological possibilities of the project, as well as the crying need for public works for a nation deep in the grip of depression. Here was the engineer of Veblen's dreams laying aside his slide rule in favor of the rugged individualism of William Graham Sumner. He was unable to separate the technological justification from the political implication, unable to separate the practical tactics for solving unemployment from the political principles of conservatism. "For the federal government deliberately to go out to build up and expand an occasion to the major purpose of a power and manufacturing business," Hoover's veto message said, "is to break down the initiative and the enterprise of the American people . . . It is a negation of the ideals upon which our civilization has been founded."[18] Such a pontifical judgment upon the structure of an entire civilization could hardly have been shown to be more mistaken by events. The TVA Act of 1933, imaginatively expanded beyond Norris's concept by Franklin D. Roosevelt himself, went so far as to embrace a vast plan for "the economic and social well-being of the people" of the entire Tennessee Valley. The TVA Authority was directed to emulate "the flexibility and initiative of private business enterprise" and so it did, bringing to an interstate region of five million people a rebirth and opportunities far beyond the potential enterprise of Henry Ford, whose automobiles no doubt found welcome new markets in the area. It was "one of the greatest peacetime achievements of the twentieth century," notes Henry Steele Commager, not only in its material results but in opening new possibilities in the realm of government.[19]

Yet each time has its period for heroes and for martyrs. Irving Stone, in his book *They Also Ran*, contends John W. Davis was so superior to Coolidge that he would have used all the legitimate agencies of the federal government to control the stock and money markets and thus would have "sharply reduced, if not largely eliminated, the credit zoom of 1925-1929 and its attendant material collapse."[20] This is a highly doubtful conclusion. Davis was a man of great ability but he campaigned in 1924 on a platform of tax reduction and private enterprise in the style of the times, losing four million votes to Robert M. La Follette, the Progressive party candidate, accordingly. By 1932, Davis was blindly charging Hoover with "following the road to socialism at a rate never before equalled in time of peace by any of his predecessors."[21] After the election Roosevelt eliminated him from consideration for his cabinet, embarrassed by such fogyness from a former Democratic Presidential candidate. There were few geniuses available who could have averted the self-propelling doom of the twenties, including the callow Roosevelt of 1924, then employed as president of the American Construction Council and recently a defeated Vice-Presidential candidate with James M. Cox against Harding and

Coolidge in 1920. La Follette possibly, but a nation of Babbitts would not have him.

VI

In October 1924, Lewis published three delightful political tracts in the *Nation* magazine entitled "Be Brisk with Babbitt." Flushed with the success of *Babbitt* on top of *Main Street*, Lewis had already moved in and out of a stately home in Hartford, Connecticut, had been received with acclaim and some disdain in the highest literary circles of London and had completed his manuscript for *Arrowsmith*. For this novel of the scientist-hero, he had characteristically engaged Dr. Paul de Kruif, the bacteriologist, to tour the West Indies and Panama with him for background and research material and then to accompany him to London and Paris to complete the draft. Home again for a brief four months in 1924, Lewis and his sophisticated and already exasperated wife, Grace Hegger, who was to gain some revenge after their divorce with her book *With Love from Gracie*, sailed again for Europe just before the *Nation* articles appeared. Lewis was already showing signs of the creative writer's frequent pattern—struggle, success, fear of loss of creative power, personal disintegration and decline. Endowed with a bad temper and excessively callous in his personal relations, Lewis was extremely sensitive to female domination as a threat to his personal freedom, including the right to become an alcoholic. Well on his way also to becoming a millionaire at this point, he demonstrated symptoms of the proverbial American man at the top. Within a year one of his editors was to observe him explode with rage when the clerk at the New York hotel where he was staying asked for his name once too many times. "Do you realize," he shouted, "that you are talking to a fifty-thousand-dollar-a-year man?"[22] Just as the most unbalanced business executive becomes a synchronized machine in his office, however, Lewis at all times was serene at his typewriter and tremendously productive over a long span of years.

Writing as a reporter sent to Zenith to interview some of its worthy citizens on their choice for President, he calls first on George F. Babbitt. Babbitt is attracted by the character of Coolidge: "I know he isn't as showy as Harding and Bill Bryan and Dawes and a lot of obviously brainy men like that, but my feeling is that he's a fellow who takes his time to make up his mind and to weigh all sides of the question. He's not a fellow that goes off half-cocked, or that yields to every passing wave of the ill-balanced popular winds of fashion." Besides, Babbitt has just returned from a trip to Europe and his point of view has been expanded. "Europe is picturesque and quaint and historical and all that, but it's a gone goose; it hasn't got any pep . . . We've got it all over Europe. They simply want to make all they can out of us. And so—a thing that so many Americans can't understand, without they've had the privilege of studying Europe first-hand—our game is to keep clear of Europe, and it's my firm conviction first, last and all the time, that the man who can best keep us clear of European entanglements is that most American and even Yankee of all our great statesmen —Calvin Coolidge!"[23]

Lewis's next interview is with Paul Riesling, Babbitt's sensitive friend in Zenith who would rather have been a violinist than a small businessman. Paul is recently out of prison, having been sent there for attempted wife-murder, and he accompanied Babbitt on the trip to Europe. "So you saw Georgie Babbitt. Good man. He has all the reasoning of a child of eight. He's the real majority-rule democrat—he repeats whatever he hears the majority of his friends in the Zenith Athletic Club and the Boosters Club saying. And at the same time he's one of the kindest, most loyal, most trustworthy friends a man could have . . ." Not surprisingly, Riesling, who saw Europe as though he and Babbitt were on different planets, is for La Follette. "I have a queer notion that in this election the American people is showing itself up . . . We're going to say that we're content to be known as tight, cautious, timorous tabbies; or as loose and confused and purposeless followers of a party which has no policy and which in a generation has had no great man except Woodrow Wilson perhaps; or as mature and fearless people who are no longer colonial shop-keepers."[24]

The final interview is the surprise. Charles McKelvey, millionaire president of the construction company which built the Zenith Union Station and the State Capitol, president of the Alumni Association of the State University and so suave and forceful that he always makes Babbitt feel envious and uncomfortable, is for La Follette. He had previously been against La Follette because La Follette didn't understand the value of businessmen like himself and because of his obsolete desire to break up monopolies and go back to the days of small, competitive, inefficient business. Still he had been talking with students lately at State U. and found all the bright ones were looking at La Follette as a crusader. In New York, he was exposed to a "pro-Soviet Communist," who couldn't stand the idea of reformers like La Follette and Ramsay MacDonald bolstering democracy and heading off the uprising, and so this Communist was stronger for Coolidge than the "Rotary Club and Bankers' Association put together." On the train back, he was harangued to vote for Coolidge by a Klansman who said if he didn't Catholics would be appointing a President in 1928. "Well it happens that an ancestor of mine, some darned old Scotchman that turned Catholic just out of pure cussedness had to flee to the Quakers in Nantucket to keep from being imprisoned by the holy Puritans of Massachusetts . . . I felt that La Follette, like William Allen White, represented my own people and that I, who'd been croaking about Immigration and the Furriners, had been so closely associated with Hunkies and Wops—in the interesting position of their employer—that I'd forgotten to be an American."[25] Here was Lewis in one of his best roles, tolerant, tough-minded, endowing his art with passion for a cause.

In giving complexity to McKelvey, Lewis was casting for the business hero he had long been planning for to replace the petty Babbitt. In Sam Dodsworth, he produced a character to be liked and admired. Those who remember the young Walter Huston, gray, rugged and square-jawed, tripping down the gangplank with

Fran as they begin their tour of Europe, saw an exemplary movie replica of Dodsworth. Aside from making Dodsworth a successful and reasonably enlightened auto manufacturer, which annoyed Mencken and other business critics as a sell-out of the cause, Lewis had little to say about the business spirit. *Dodsworth* is a novel about marriage and its main interest is Dodsworth's marriage problem and the self-awareness he develops from it, not the production problems of the Revelation Automobile Company, which he hesitantly merges with the giant U.A.C. as the story opens.

Sam Dodsworth at fifty simply should not have retired. He was not prepared to become an expatriate in Europe with his forceful Fran. Having been so thoroughly engaged in business, he apparently left himself too little time for developing his resources as a human being outside the world of business. On the other hand, Dodsworth is far from being a one-sided character. He is a Yale graduate, reads occasional books, enjoys Beethoven, fishing and all in all is a most efficient, attractive, reliable person. In addition, Lewis specifies what he was not. "He was not a Babbitt, not a Rotarian, not an Elk, not a deacon. He rarely shouted, never clapped people on the back . . ." In the eyes of his restless, spoiled, socially ambitious wife, this stalwart man was dull, provincial and insensitive. The prospects for their new condition of constant companionship were perilous indeed. Not that Sam Dodsworth isn't willing to try to become a good member of the leisure class:

> "By God, I'll enjoy life if it kills me—and it probably will!" he grumbled. "You've got to give me time. I've started this business of being 'free' about thirty-five years too late. I'm a good citizen. I've learned that Life is real and Life is earnest and the presidency of a corporation is its goal. What would I be doing with anything so degenerate as enjoying myself?"

There follows a tour of Europe with the sharp-eyed Lewis serving as a competent guide, considering his limited exposure as a traveller at that time. To his credit he does not portray Dodsworth as a

virtuous figure, an innocent abroad whose sterling American qualities contrast favorably with Old World deceits. If anyone is embarrassed by Dodsworth, it is Fran rather than the Europeans whose
society she crashes. They admire Sam as a latter-day version of
Henry James's *The American*. If he were anything else they would
have been disappointed, as it would be too much to contain the
best of two worlds. Europe in the 1920's still had a fatal charm
for Americans either rich or intellectual and the awkard Lewis was
overwhelmed by the casual arrogance of its upper classes. America
in relation to Europe was subject to as strong a yoke as the bond
between small town and sprawling city. Neither would persist as
a basis for American fiction.

In this setting, Lewis has the discrimination to show Dodsworth
as an increasingly bemused and unsure figure. One feels he has
gained an extra dimension of humility as he patiently stands by
while Fran leaves him in the hope of becoming an Austrian
Countess. In his own sober way, he learns that leisure must be
cultivated as a creative act, not to be compared with vacations,
that being a man is as important as being a businessman and more
difficult. He recognizes that his best friends Tub and Matey Pear-
son, the banker and his wife, though wonderful people are more
welcome sights in Zenith than in Paris.

He also becomes aware that at this point in his life Fran just
isn't worth it, although the author, his own marriage disintegrating
as *Dodsworth* was being written in 1927-1928, gives her little
chance, making her a combination nag, chatterbox and bird of
prey. In the end, Dodsworth leaves Fran, after she has humbly
come back to him, to marry Edith Cortright, a more sympathetic
woman, "born in Michigan, daughter of a banker who became
Secretary of the Treasury of the United States." She was hardly
an adventurous second chance for Dodsworth but at least possessed
a European serenity acquired in American embassies with her late
husband. Together they enthusiastically contemplate returning to
Zenith to manufacture "caravans," a new-fangled idea resembling
today's trailers and one that would not have been commercially
successful as described by the author. With *Dodsworth*, Lewis

became something of an old-fashioned novelist, finished with the quiet revolt in the village and unwilling to begin with the angry revolt in the cities. His future business chiefs would not even have the heroic uncertainty of Sam Dodsworth.

A pale successor to Dodsworth is Myron Weagle, the poetic hotelkeeper who is the hero of *Work of Art*, which appeared in 1934. It was a pure pot-boiler, rushed to completion in four months as if to make sure the money would still come in. Illustrating Lewis's innate suspicion of the artist, he contrasts Myron with his brother Ora, a literary type who becomes a hack writer. The real artist is revealed to be Myron, whose idea of a masterpiece is the perfect hotel. For once Lewis was out of touch with his times, for Americans could hardly be less interested in this story of enterprise while the last ten per cent of rooms that a hotel needs for profit were vacant from coast to coast. That is, unless they were interested in becoming hotelkeepers, for again the research was remarkable.

It seems inconceivable that Lewis could have written such a dreary novel while married to Dorothy Thompson, the famous journalist and war correspondent who became his wife in 1928. Under her influence, he did produce the provocative and often powerful *It Can't Happen Here* in 1935, shortly after she became the first American journalist to be expelled from Hitler's Germany. *It Can't Happen Here* portrays America taken over by native Fascists and with uncanny timing appeared just after Senator Huey F. Long, the rubbery-faced dictator who served as the model for Berzelius Windrip, was assassinated in the State House at Baton Rouge at the age of forty-two. Lewis was unable to cope with Dorothy Thompson and their marriage, terminated by divorce in 1942, was a stormy and well-documented war of words and letters with carbon copies. In *Dorothy and Red*, their friend Vincent Sheean records the comic pathos of the match. Lewis toyed with the idea of naming Hitler as co-respondent in a divorce action against his globe-trotting wife. He had nightmares of Dorothy reaching across his chest to answer midnight phone calls from Roosevelt and Churchill. He later ungallantly used her as a model for Winifred Homeward, the Talking Woman of *Gideon Planish*.

The Lewis's summer home was in Woodstock, Vermont and Budd Schulberg, a talented student at nearby Dartmouth College, invited the celebrated author of *It Can't Happen Here* to appear as a speaker. Lewis was on good behavior until he suspected that some of the radical students were baiting him for being too harsh on the Left. The story goes that he jumped to his feet and shouted, "You young sons of bitches can all go to hell!" and stalked from the platform.[26] His alienation from these bright spirits would be revealed in his final novel about the business hero, *The Prodigal Parents*.

The Prodigal Parents, published in 1938, is so embarrassingly slanted towards old-fashioned middle-class morality that it seems to be a parody of Lewis rather than his own work. The man who had once satirized the business culture now offered an effective bit of propaganda for the defense of the American businessman. Fred Cornplow, an even-tempered and only slightly restless automobile dealer, is the salt of the earth:

> He has at times been too noisy or too prosy; he has now and then thought more of money than of virtue and music; but he has been the eternal doer; equally depended upon—and equally hated—by the savage mob and by the insolent nobility . . . He is the eternal bourgeois, the bourjoyce, the burgher, the Middle Class, whom the Bolsheviks hate and imitate, whom the English love and deprecate, and who is most of the population worth considering in France and Germany and these United States.

Fred and Hazel Cornplow are not only exemplary and productive people but they are burdened with radical and irresponsible children, a son and daughter whom many might consider superior to Babbitt's innocuous children, at least as far as intellectual curiosity is concerned. A parallel might be drawn between the aging Sinclair Lewis and the cartoonist Al Capp. Capp too became famous for his rollicking satire of small town life, although Dogpatch is closer to

Tobacco Road than to Gopher Prairie. In his present decline, Capp cannot identify with the long-haired, anti-middle-class revolt that for better or worse is a real happening among American youth. As a result he is ignored on the campus while three million subscribers read the socially-conscious *Mad Magazine* and most everyone senses the superiority of Peanuts over Li'l Abner.

VII

Thus Sinclair Lewis's search for a business hero helps us understand the twenties, that unpredictable decade which crowned Lindbergh, a hero of the spirit, after all. The predecessor business heroes, the amoral giants such as Frank Norris's McTeague and Theodore Dreiser's Cowperwood, the prototype of the traction magnate Charles Yerkes in *The Titan* and *The Financier*, curiously were not repeated in the business-dominated twenties. In their Faustian pursuit of power and their magnetic hold over women, the old heroes now seem to be period pieces strictly related to the pre-World War I era, when the great millionaires were a kind of American superman. Babbitt and Dodsworth and even F. Scott Fitzgerald's shady Jay Gatsby were only country cousins to these buccaneers. The mythology of the independent businessman, cut to neighborly size, faithfully mirrored the values of the twenties. While Lewis's books were best sellers in fiction, the top place on the non-fiction list through most of 1925-1926 was held by Bruce Barton's *The Man Nobody Knows*. Written by the advertising man and Congressman whom Roosevelt later taunted in the refrain, "Martin, Barton and Fish" for his isolationism, the book is an appalling biography of Jesus in which Jesus is portrayed as a hard-driving executive, inspired sales manager and "The Founder of Modern Business."[27]

Lewis himself was unprepared for the twenties and might have become a proletarian writer had the great depression come after the War. He had left Yale for a short time in 1906 to become a handyman and disciple in Upton Sinclair's cooperative colony of socialists and artists known as Helicon Hall on the Palisades in New Jersey. In 1914 as a struggling young writer he wrote a lengthy analysis of the contemporary novel entitled "The Passing of Capitalism" for the *Bookman* magazine in which he laments the untimely passing of Frank Norris in 1902 at age thirty-two:

> Gone is Frank Norris; McTeague has staggered to his death; the tentacles of the Octopus are still; but today, in the year of Tagore and the siege of Liège, young men are still discovering *The Octopus*, and reading it and asking themselves the why and how of Society-in-General. And if enough young men do that we shall have something—a new capitalism, it may be an autocracy, it may be a complete anarchism but it will be a condition of society in which such men as they of the San Joaquin shall not reap thistles.[28]

While Lewis shifted towards the philosophy of acceptance, younger men like John Dos Passos rejected the old order with cries of outrage. For Dos Passos, the Sacco-Vanzetti case acted as a catalyst to shape his great epic *U.S.A.* The agonizing case of the two Italian anarchists charged with murder in 1920 and finally executed in 1927, after Justice Holmes himself turned down an appeal for a stay, was a *cause célèbre* that reverberated throughout the world. For millions it symbolized, probably unfairly, an alliance of the business class with the political establishment as a frightened plutocracy betraying at the least the American principle of scrupulous fairness, especially for minorities and dissenters. At the hands of a brilliant and impassioned craftsman such as Dos Passos, the harassed businessman received a new image, ages away from Babbitt and Dodsworth. "All right we are two nations," wrote Dos Passos, ominously faulting the oath of allegiance in *The Big Money*, the third part of the *U.S.A.* trilogy which describes the boom and the crash of the twenties.[29] His businessmen such as J. Ward Moorehouse and Charley Anderson are reprehensible operators, doomed figures of greed and corruption and one step away from class warfare although Dos Passos was essentially a

Veblenian individualist and not a Marxist. He is labelled a conservative today.

In summary, there is a consistent hostility to business to be found in our literature without searching for it too strenuously. Often it is satirical, ranging from Mark Twain's Connecticut Yankee in King Arthur's Court to Milo Minderbinder, the inspired hero of enterprise in Joseph Heller's *Catch-22*. Sometimes it is bitter as are the times. The question may well be asked: Why not? Ours is a business civilization. Our writers and artists, particularly those who choose to be involved with their consciences, would hardly win the respect even of businessmen if their work were all banality and flattery. The tension, even the hostility, is good for both sides. Where power resides, it is important that it be ridiculed from time to time and sometimes challenged, lest it accelerate its axiomatic tendency towards corruption.

Footnotes

CHAPTER 2

Sinclair Lewis:

The Search for a Business Hero

Mark Schorer has become Sinclair Lewis's major biographer with his impressive *Sinclair Lewis: An American Life*, published in 1961. In an article about writing the book, Schorer states: "I know more about the life of Sinclair Lewis, day by day, sometimes hour by hour, than he himself could possibly have known." He notes on his flyleaf that his children grew up while the book was being written. Surely any writer interested in Lewis must be grateful for his Boswellian 800-odd page book, although one wishes that Schorer might have known Lewis first hand. *With Love from Gracie* (New York, 1955) by Grace Hegger Lewis and *Dorothy and Red* (London, 1964) by Vincent Sheean strip more clothing from the agitated author, the latter drawing on the Dorothy Thompson papers in the Syracuse University Library.

A collection of all the best critical essays on Sinclair Lewis has been conveniently gathered into one volume, *Sinclair Lewis: A Collection of Critical Essays* (New Jersey, 1962), under the editorship of Mr. Schorer. Among analyses of Lewis related to the business spirit, some valuable recent additions are Chapter 7 of Thomas Reed West's *Flesh of Steel* (Vanderbilt, 1967) and "Businessmen in American Fiction" by Henry Nash Smith in *The Business Establishment* (New York, 1964), edited by Earl F. Cheit. Helpful in reviewing the 1920's, aside from the well-known sources, are Elizabeth Stevenson's *Babbitts & Bohemians* (New York, 1967) and the special issue on the twenties of *American Heritage* in August 1965.

---

[1] Mark Schorer, *Sinclair Lewis: An American Life* (New York, 1961), p. 298.

2 *Ibid.*, p. 302.

3 Henry L. Mencken, "Portrait of an American Citizen," in *Smart Set*, (October, 1922), reprinted in *Sinclair Lewis: A Collection of Critical Essays* (New Jersey, 1962), Mark Schorer, ed., p. 21.

4 William Manchester, *The Sage of Baltimore* (London, 1952), p. 135.

5 Rebecca West, "Babbitt," *The New Statesman*, (October 21, 1922), reprinted in Mark Schorer, ed., *op. cit.*

6 *Kiwanis Magazine*, X, November 1925, p. 473.

7 *Colliers*, LXXVI, November 21, 1925, p. 23.

8 *New York Times*, August 21, 1925, p. 15.

9 *Nation's Business*, XIII, June, 1925, p. 40.

10 *Ibid.*, December, 1925, p. 8; September, 1925, p. 34.

11 Simeon Strunsky, "About Books More or Less; The Truth About Georgie," *New York Times Book Review* (January 22, 1928), p. 4.

12 *Rotarian*, XXXIV, March, 1929, pp. 14-16.

13 *Ibid.*, XXX, June 1927, pp. 12-13.

14 Perry Miller, "The Incorruptible Sinclair Lewis," *Atlantic Monthly*, April 1951, p. 34.

15 Arthur M. Schlesinger, Jr., *The Crisis of the Old Order*, (Boston, 1957), p. 61.

16 William Allen White, *A Puritan in Babylon* (New York, 1938), p. 344.

17 Herbert Hoover, "Backing Up Business," *American Review of Reviews* (September, 1928), p. 278.

18 Henry Steele Commager, *The American Mind* (New Haven, 1950), pp. 343-344.

[19] *Ibid.*, p. 345.

[20] Irving Stone, *They Also Ran* (New York, 1943), p. 339.

[21] *New York Times*, October 30, 1932, Part II, pp. 1-2.

[22] Schorer, *op. cit.*, p. 434.

[23] Sinclair Lewis, "Be Brisk with Babbitt," *The Nation* (October 15, 1924), pp. 409-411.

[24] *Ibid.*, October 22, 1924, p. 437.

[25] *Ibid.*, pp. 437-439.

[26] Schorer, *op. cit.*, p. 612.

[27] Bruce Barton, *The Man Nobody Knows* (New York, 1925), Introduction.

[28] Sinclair Lewis, "The Passing of Capitalism," *The Bookman* (October 1914), p. 284.

[29] John Dos Passos, *U.S.A.* (Boston, 1960), three-volume Sentry edition, p. 413.

Chapter 3

MARRINER ECCLES:

Stormy Petrel of the Federal Reserve

Long before the hawks and doves wheeled over Washington, Marriner Eccles was there as the "stormy petrel." He stayed on from 1934 to 1951, outlasting every prominent New Dealer. Lately his voice has been heard once again, this time raised against the Administration on Viet Nam. Eloquent as ever, the salty banker's remarks were extended in the *Congressional Record* of January 23, 1967. A million copies were then circulated by the American Friends Society.

The Quakers were sounding the trumpet of the Mormon who had come from Salt Lake City in 1934 to become the sharpest and most intelligent businessman to serve in Franklin Roosevelt's war against the depression. In the light of his government experience, he is revealed as a most attractive and selfless businessman in the role of public servant, a latter-day Ben Franklin, self-trained and uncannily wise. He was also just original enough to stand the first Franklin's stricture on thrift on its head while the second Franklin was still talking about a balanced budget.

Businessmen who dream of glory in the corridors of power can profit by the rough and tumble encounters of Marriner Eccles in Washington. Through it all he survived with an abiding good humor, strongly fortified by a net worth of many millions of dollars, even in the thirties. The toughest blow was being demoted from Chairman of the Federal Reserve Board to plain Board Member by Harry Truman in 1948, providing the President with something of a warm-up for firing the equally formidable General MacArthur three years later. Eccles took his time about fading away, dominating the Board through his personality until 1951 when he resigned and returned to Utah to make more millions under the capitalist system he had helped save.

His first appearance before a Congressional Committee as a member of the Administration was all sweetness and light. In 1934, as a new assistant to Secretary of the Treasury Henry Morgenthau, he had characteristically promoted himself into taking the lead in drafting the Federal Housing Administration Act. In this capacity he appeared before the Senate Banking and Currency Committee, producing the following colloquy:

> *Senator Barkeley:* Are you a real mariner from Utah?
>
> *Mr. Eccles:* Yes, sir; I am from Utah. I do not know that I am a real "mariner." I am from Utah, however.
>
> *Senator Barkeley:* You are so close to the Great Salt Lake that I did not know but what you are a real mariner.
>
> *Mr. Eccles:* Well, if this drought continues, we might have to become pedestrians instead of mariners.[1]

While Congress almost danced with Eccles, the savings and loan and banking lobbies harassed the bill mercilessly, torn between their rivalry for each other and a generally conservative attitude towards government mixing into private enterprise, even for its own good. When the bill, with its masterfully ingenious principle of government insurance of private lending as a stimulus to private building, was passed in June 1934, it remained practically inactive until 1938, except for its Title I provision for home repair loans. In 1938, with the country reeling in a recession, lending terms under FHA were liberalized, an effective administrator took over and the banking and savings and loan system finally proceeded to take advantage of the immense benefits to private home-building conferred by the Act. Again carrying the ball for the Administration, Eccles had persuaded Roosevelt to appoint a committee of businessmen, including S. Sloan Colt, president of the Bankers Trust Company, Gerard Swope, president of General Electric Company and Robert E. Wood, president of Sears, Roebuck & Company to help draft the FHA amendments and thus bring the weight of their benign influence on Congress. As a fellow millionaire who had met large payrolls back in Salt Lake City, Eccles was an invaluable link between the New Deal and the chastened, resentful, powerful business world of the thirties.

II

Marriner Eccles is one of twenty-one children of David Eccles, a legendary Scottish lad from Glasgow who arrived in America in 1863 at age fourteen, a member of a poverty-stricken brood led by a blind father. This father had barely survived in Glasgow by turning out wooden kitchen utensils which David and the other children hawked in the streets. Their life and conditions were straight out of the misery of *Oliver Twist*. Adam Smith, Professor of Moral Philosophy at the University of Glasgow, had written *The Wealth of Nations* seventy-four years before David Eccles was born. This manifesto for *laissez-faire* was now being challenged by Marx and Engels who could well claim that the appalling slums of the industrial revolution were a case in point for the

Communist Manifesto. The saga of the Eccles family, from the blind grandfather of Glasgow through David the rugged individualist who conquered all obstacles and thence to Marriner the millionaire converted to social responsibility by the great depression, is the story of the great change in political economy of modern times.

As in a tale from Dickens, the grandfather harkened to a Mormon missionary and accepted the story of the Book of Mormon and the golden tablets that Joseph Smith had found in upstate New York in 1827. Any doubts brought up by his Scottish theology were offset by the opportunity to borrow from the Perpetual Immigration Fund of the Mormons and lead his family away from the Gentiles into the Promised Land of Utah. When he arrived there, completing the leg from Omaha by covered wagon, he found Salt Lake City equally worried about the Indians and the United States Army, which had sent a regiment to observe this peculiar people who were more suspect than ever as the Civil War progressed. The Mormons had already petitioned Congress for admission as a state in 1862 but were to knock on the door in vain until 1896, six years after the Church finally prohibited the practice of polygamy as a condition for statehood. Five years before this Church action, David Eccles married a second wife, Marriner's mother, who produced nine of the twenty-one children. Marriner, the eldest, was born in 1890.

By the time his second family was started, David Eccles had become a millionaire. With incredible fortitude, hard work and thrift, he had risen from woodchopper to owner of lumber mills in Oregon and holder of large interests in beet-sugar factories, coal mines, heavy construction, banking and utilities. Marriner Eccles has written:

> The very character of the inheritance he left summarized the economic possibilities of the nineteenth century. Though the entire cash capital of the Mormons in Utah in 1847 has been estimated at about $3,000, my father's own estate was appraised for state-inheritance tax pur-

poses at more than $7 million. By present-day values,
this would be equal to over $25 million. The state tax
was five per cent; there was no federal tax.[2]

Before his father died in 1912, Marriner completed the high-
school level of education at Brigham Young College in 1909 and
gaily set off for Europe to serve two years of missionary work
expected from the Mormon youth. Back to Glasgow he went and
the picture of the spirited young man clad in the high silk hat
and frock coat of the missionary haranguing the crowds on the
Glasgow green is colorful indeed. For all its insularity, the Mormon leadership has always been immensely practical and anxious
to compete with the world of trade in the best Calvinist tradition.
It clearly recognized the valuable education and business training
that would come from the exposure of its young missionaries.
Surely Marriner Eccles gained sophistication and debating ability
from the missionary episode.

With it he gained also an intellectual curiosity and open-minded-
ness that were to crystallize slowly but in time to be of great
service to his imperilled country. The story of his mental development in economic terms makes the dry economics textbook come
to life. His father, for example, took pride in the fact that he had
never had to look to the East for capital. In fact he had avoided
debt completely and preached this course as a guide for business.

> I, of course, nodded my head approvingly when I heard
> him say this. But later on I was to learn that if everyone
> kept out of debt, there would be no capitalist system;
> that the very essence of capitalism implies a debtor-
> creditor relationship; that to save successfully, someone
> has to borrow what is saved; that bankers, the arch sym-
> bols of capitalism, are the greatest borrowers in our
> society. Indeed, anyone else who had as many debts as
> bankers in relation to assets would go broke. Later on,
> I was to challenge in a direct way a further belief held
> by my father and his friends that there would always
> be a shortage of capital in the land and that saving was
> a good in itself.[3]

What seems commonplace to almost everyone today, that too much savings can mean over-investment or, more likely, under-consumption, was a strange heresy in those pre-Keynesian days. The corollary idea, that deficit spending by a government in time of depression is an absolute necessity for recovery, was not even a heresy, since no heretics had yet advanced it. It was not a matter of there being no depressions. America had been wracked by depressions or panics, as they were called, in 1865, 1873-1879, 1884, 1893 and 1907 to list the more severe ones in David Eccles's period. It was a matter, as far as government was concerned, of not feeling responsible for the type of action that would produce deficits in the national budget. Grover Cleveland, the first Democratic President following the Civil War, expressed the prevailing concepts when he vetoed a $10,000 appropriation by Congress for drought-stricken farmers in 1887. "Though the people support the Government," he said, "the Government should not support the people."

Actually, these depressions wrung themselves out without government aid, the overall economy responding to the open frontier, the railroads that crossed the country, the stimulation of new inventions and heavy industry and the availability of cheap labor. Although the corruption, labor exploitation and monopolies generated in the post-Civil War period now seem morally indefensible, there is another side to consider. How else were railroads to be pushed across the continent and giant enterprises to be created in time to serve a population that would increase from 39 million in 1870 to 76 million in 1900, as America opened its doors to desperate immigrants from Europe like the Eccles family? We now see that this richly endowed, uninhibited country had enough resources to squander them recklessly in land grants, homesteads and prizes for the fittest, and to that extent the exploits of the Carnegies, Rockefellers, Harrimans and other captains of industry are justified. Can we deny that they are any less necessary for their times than our own new class of corporate managers are necessary for today's managed capitalism? One of Americas most distinguished liberal theorists, Thurman Arnold, jolted his contemporaries in his *The Symbols of Government*, published in 1935, by assigning to folklore the notion that these early capitalists were all bad. He pointed out that great constructive achievements have quite often been accomplished by unscrupulous men and that these tycoons raised the level of productive capacity beyond the dreams of their fathers.[4] Even the authors of the *Communist Manifesto* were willing to grant the floodtide force of private enterprise seeking profit, stating the following in 1848:

> During its rule of scarce one hundred years (the bourgeoisie) has created more colossal productive forces than have all the preceding generations together. Subjection of nature's forces to man, machinery, steam navigation, railways, electric telegraph, clearing of whole continents for cultivation, canalization of rivers, whole populations conjured out of the ground—what earlier century had even a presentiment that such productive forces slumbered in the lap of social labor?

Both father and son would gladly have accepted this out-of-context tribute to capitalism from the system's most deadly critics. Even the later and purely American warnings of Theodore Roosevelt, Woodrow Wilson and Louis D. Brandeis about the dangers of economic instability lurking in the trend towards monopoly and bigness failed to disturb David Eccles, whose own demonstration of success within the system was beyond questioning. If one added to the Eccles world the underlying base of Mormon fundamentalism, even the outrages of previous depressions could be rationalized in Biblical terms, for example the lean years that followed the fat ones as in Pharaoh's day. Not only the Mormons but practically the entire academic world at the start of the twentieth century transferred such Biblical injunctions to economic theory with unbelievable smugness and certitude. Against this background, the young heir to the new family fortune could hardly be expected to mount a soapbox against the status quo, nor did he. "All this I too believed until the fortieth year of my life," states Marriner Eccles.[5]

Until his fortieth year, which occured in 1930, Eccles labored hard and successfully in the world of business. Under Utah law, two-sevenths of the inheritance went to the nine children of the second wife and the remainder to the first wife and her twelve children. As might be expected, there was bitterness among the inheritors. Marriner Eccles, as leader of the minority group, refused to join forces with his elder half-brothers and sisters and eventually, through a process of survival of the fittest, emerged as the richest and most powerful of the clan. In 1929, just before he received his vision of the new economics, he was president of the Eccles Investment Company, president of the First Security Corporation (a bank holding company with twenty-eight branch banks), president of the Eccles Hotel Company, president of the Sego Milk Products Company, president of the Stoddard Lumber Company, vice-president and treasurer of the Amalgamated Sugar Company and a director of the Utah Construction Company (soon to be under his presidency and one of the six companies involved in building Boulder Dam), to name his major interests. Almost forty years later he still presides over First Security, now holding over 100 branch banks with assets exceeding $900 million, and is Chairman of the Board of Utah Construction & Mining Co., a firm doing over $100 million a year of varied enterprise throughout the world.

III

Although the collapse of the nation's banking system came to a head in the weeks before Franklin Roosevelt's inauguration on March 4, 1933, resulting in the temporary closing of all banks by Roosevelt under a "bank holiday" order as the first act of his Administration, thousands of banks had already gone under in the last two years of Hoover's Presidency. Even in the twenties, the American banking system had been notoriously weak and uncontrolled. Excessively chartered and lacking deposit insurance or effective Federal Reserve operations, banks closed on an average of several hundred a year during times of prosperity. In the last half of 1931 alone, over one thousand banks closed as frightened depositors made a run for their money. It was at this time that Marriner Eccles established a rather exaggerated reputation for bringing all his banks through the depression without a closing. He did it with a mixture of luck and psychology, quickly taking over neighboring banks when their impending doom threatened his own or actually bluffing his depositors out of their hysteria by rolling in armored trucks from the Federal Reserve bearing currency or hoisting banners proclaiming "Your Money is Here. Come and Get It."

Eccles took scant pleasure out of these escapes which then put his banks in the position of having to force liquidation of loans and securities in order to remain solvent, adding to the distress and unemployment in the nation. He could not reconcile himself to the fact that a banking system or a political system which allowed such a futile and illogical procedure should be viewed as ordained wisdom. "As the pursuit of money had been the organizing principle of my life for almost twenty years," he reflected, "the pursuit of an idea of economic balance replaced it."[6]

Having lost faith in his business heroes in the citadels of the East, men like Ogden Mills and Andrew Mellon, the Treasury Secretaries in Hoover's Administration, or Albert Wiggin, Charles E. Mitchell and J. P. Morgan representing Wall Street, Eccles, a comparatively small-time banker, began to do some monumental thinking on his own. Rejecting the "wringing-out" theory of correction, he came to the conclusion that the economy could remain paralyzed if left to recover by statements of optimism and formulas of hard work and thrift. In an entirely common-sense way he deduced what the practically unknown Keynes was advancing through erudite theory, that a more or less permanent breakdown had occurred in the job-creating investment of savings on such a grand scale that only government, through monetary and spending programs, could end it. Before the Utah Bankers Convention in 1932 he stated:

I believe, contrary to the opinion of most people, that the depression in our country was primarily brought about by our capital accumulation getting out of balance in relation to our consumption ability. Our depression was not brought about as a result of our extravagance. It was not brought about as a result of high taxation. We did not consume as a nation more than we produced. We consumed far less than we produced. The difficulty is that we were not sufficiently extravagant as a nation.

The theory of hard work and thrift as a means of pulling us out of the depression is unsound economically. True, hard work means more production, but thrift and economy mean less consumption. Now reconcile those two forces, will you?

There is only one agency in my opinion that can turn the cycle upward and that is the government . . .[7]

This was strong language to use before a bankers' association and probably unique from a bank spokesman at the time. The speech did not touch on Eccles's ultimate thought, that the priming of the pump required not only low taxes on the part of government but actual spending of billions, regardless of budget deficits, to put the millions of unemployed on temporary government payrolls for performing public works. This would then create the effective purchasing power which would stimulate the stricken private sector to re-employ once again. Eventually the budget surpluses of prosperity would balance out the deficits and meanwhile the intolerable depression would be broken. The theory disregarded the prevalent idea that a spendthrift government would cause business to lose confidence and thus refuse to budge. Eccles had lost confidence in the ability of business to budge without government prodding it to life in the first place.

But government policy is made along the Potomac and not the Great Salt Lake. Though Eccles had not the slightest idea at the time his destiny would lead him to Washington, he took little comfort from the speeches of Hoover and Roosevelt as they campaigned for the Presidency. Hoover was running against a record of a stock market crash, industrial production cut by more than half, the closing of 5,000 banks and the unemployment of thirteen million workers, close to one third of the entire labor force. Finally in June 1932 he ineptly authorized the use of United States Army tanks under General MacArthur to rout a pathetic group of melancholy veterans calling themselves the Bonus Army from their shanty-town in the Capitol's Anacostia Flats. Hard working and diligent, he was doomed to defeat. He had performed some major feats such as creating in December 1931 the novel Reconstruction Finance Corporation. The RFC lent millions to insurance companies, banks and railroads in distress, causing Democratic sharpshooters to raise charges of favoritism and financial irresponsibility, even socialism. In the summer of 1932 his Administration created the Federal Home Loan Banks to provide relief and central banking for the savings and loan industry. The first reaction of Fiorello H. La Guardia, a fiery young Republican Congressman, to this aid for the banker class was to shout: "The bastards broke the people's back with their usury and now they want to unload on the government. No . . . let them die."[8] The same year the Federal Reserve Board poured money into the nation's banking system on a scale never before imagined but there were few loans for bankers to make. In spite of these admirable moves, made largely on behalf of creditors and investors, the economy remained stagnant as Hoover also concentrated on balancing the budget and shied away from massive government spending to create consumer purchasing power. Nevertheless his energetic steps made better campaign oratory than that of Roosevelt, who played it safe, knowing he was bound to win and being a member in good standing of the budget-balancing club himself at that point. The economic confusion of the times was illustrated by the 1932 conventions in which both parties actually devoted more time to discussing prohibition than curing unemployment. La Guardia in the House and La Follette in the Senate preached economy and budget balancing, showing no more economic insight than those they criticized.

Which candidate made the following speech?

> The credit of the family depends chiefly on whether that
> family is living within its income and that is equally
> true of the nation. If the nation is living within its
> income, its credit is good. If, in some crisis, it lives be-
> yond its income for a year or two, it can usually borrow
> temporarily at reasonable rates. But if, like a spendthrift,
> it throws discretion to the winds, and is willing to make
> no sacrifices at all in spending; if it extends its taxing to
> the limits of the people's power to pay and continues to
> pile up deficits, then it is on the road to bankruptcy . . .
>
> I regard reduction in federal spending as one of the
> most important issues in this campaign. In my opinion
> it is the most direct and effective contribution that gov-
> ernment can make to business.

It was Roosevelt in Pittsburgh on October 19, 1932, shortly
before the election. Although the speech now looks like a giant
misprint, fortunately the new President grew on the job and
cheerfully turned from one expedient to another as he led the
nation to recovery behind the force of his indomitable will. He was
hardly a guide for the education of Marriner Eccles, however, who
in retrospect seems to have possessed all the answers through some
sixth sense even then.

A snowstorm brought Eccles, previously a lifelong Republican,
into the bosom of the New Deal. The University of Utah had been
sponsoring some lecturers on economic problems, including Stuart
Chase in February 1933. For over forty years Stuart Chase has
been one of America's most provocative and useful thinkers. Something of a consumer's champion in the twenties, he had eagerly
joined the Roosevelt forces and his 1932 book on economic reform
entitled *A New Deal* gave them their name. When Chase was
stalled by the storm, Eccles's friends at the head table prevailed
upon him to advance his strange views once again as a substitute.
Chase caught the gist of the remarks and later when Eccles asked

him questions about men like Moley, Berle and Tugwell, Roosevelt's "brain-trusters," Chase challenged him with "Why not get yourself a larger audience?" and arranged for him to meet Tugwell that same month.

IV

Eccles had already caught a mild case of Potomac fever and was scheduled to appear along with some two hundred other leaders in business and economics before a "lame duck" session of the Senate Finance Committee investigating the cause and cure of the depression. This was a period when a puzzled country desperately cast about for answers. The week after Roosevelt's inauguration, it was reported that close to a half million letters arrived at the White House, thousands with plans for beating the depression. College students switched from the study of humanities to courses in economics. Controversial lecturers on politics and economics such as Stuart Chase, Lincoln Steffens and John Strachey, the British socialist, found large audiences throughout the country. "Social significance" was the measuring rod in the arts and the church as well as on the campus. It was a time of great speculation and receptivity to new ideas, an ironic by-product of living so close to the margin of existence. There was a friendly interest in Russia, for example, at that time too weak a country to transform the interest into fear. Henry Ford was hosting seventy Soviet engineers inside the Dearborn plant one day in 1932 while 3,000 unemployed workers demonstrated on the outside. Norman Thomas polled 885,-000 votes in 1932 as the Socialist candidate for the Presidency, his shining integrity and impeccable background attracting voters from all walks of life.

It was also a time of compassion and trust brought about by the common misfortune. Hitchhikers were picked up by motorists without fear and the parks were walkable at night. Yet violence lurked below the level of this decency. Frustrated and hungry people could be expected to follow strange leaders and they soon did, dangerous ones like Huey Long, Father Coughlin and Gerald L. K. Smith, or harmless ones like Dr. Townsend and Upton Sinclair. A great deal of the unrest was directed at the business and banking class, the natural scapegoats of any economic débacle. In conservative Iowa, farmers had mauled agents of mortgage companies and formed a militant association under the effective leadership of Milo Reno to sabotage food production. Roosevelt regarded Reno's Farmers' Holiday Association with grave concern from the day he took office and undertook his first efforts at currency inflation largely to pacify them with farm price increases. In Pennsylvania miners appropriated coal seams on company property and sold the ore for what they could get daily. The Governors of Minnesota and Nebraska were forced to declare a moratorium on foreclosures to avoid worse trouble. In the very month that Eccles went to Washington, protestors seized the county-city building in Seattle. The breadlines were a standard city scene. Bonnie and Clyde were robbing a dwindling supply of banks.

With grim humor, Eccles no doubt realized that bankers were among America's least favorite people, in the halls of Congress or elsewhere, as he arrived to testify. Hoover had already launched another Senate investigation in the Spring of 1932 directed against stock market speculators, painfully aware that the business community whose cause he had championed had badly let him down. This investigating committee gained impetus after the election when Ferdinand Pecora took over as counsel and began smashing reputations right and left. Eccles watched some of his old heroes, such as Charles E. Mitchell of the National City Bank and Albert Wiggin of the Chase Bank, lose their jobs as the result of dereliction revealed by Pecora. Public opinion was further exasperated by the disclosure of tax evasion, legal but excessively greedy, on the part of Mitchell, Wiggin and J. P. Morgan in addition to their stock rigging (commercial banks could issue securities at that time), insider transactions and grandiose salaries. Mitchell admitted to Pecora that he sold millions of dollars of securities at a loss to his wife to establish offsets to his taxable gains and then bought back the securities at the same price. It seems incredible that such "wash sales" should have been permitted by Hoover's tax collectors but so they were and Mitchell was arrested on tax charges shortly before Roosevelt's inauguration. Richard Whitney, President of the New York Stock Exchange, was a tougher witness. He coldly refused information to Pecora in 1933 with the explanation that, "The New York Stock Exchange is a perfect institution." In 1938 he was taken to Sing Sing for embezzling his own accounts including $1,125,000 in funds belonging to the Stock Exchange Gratuity Fund. The advent of the New Deal was something of an open season for shooting at bankers, producing some of the game humor which made the depression bearable. "Don't tell my mother what I'm really doing," a banker pleads to his friends, "she thinks I'm playing a piano in a sporting house."

Forty-seven of the two hundred experts, including the busy Charles E. Mitchell and Albert Wiggin, joined Eccles in testifying before the committee and another sixty sent written reports. Eccles recalls that these experts were almost unanimous in their chant for a balanced budget. Bernard Baruch, adviser to Presidents, was particularly emphatic:

> With the monotony and persistence of old Cato, we should make one single and invariable dictum and theme of every discourse: balance budgets. Stop spending money we haven't got. Sacrifice for frugality and revenue. Cut government spending—cut it as rations are cut in a siege. Tax—tax everybody for everything. But take hungry men off the world's pavements and let the people smile again.[9]

Eccles scoffed at these ideas and proceeded to outline a five-point program for the restoration of purchasing power as a start to end the depression. It involved an immediate grant of a half billion dollars to the states for relief to carry them through 1933; at least two and one-half billion dollars to be spent on self-liquidating public works regardless of deficits incurred by the government, or as an alternative, the restoration of the four billions of deposits lost by depositors in closed banks, along with a new plan for federal deposit insurance to avoid such losses in the future; an experimental allotment plan for farmers which would artificially restrict production and raise farm prices; an agency that would bail out farm mortgages through long-term financing; and settlement or cancellation of World War I loans owed by our allies, which had been subject to a moratorium since 1931, in order to stimulate American exports. In addition the Utah banker, to the horror of his fraternity, called for higher taxes for the upper brackets only, increased inheritance taxes, national child labor, minimum wage, unemployment insurance and old age pension laws; federal agencies to regulate securities, transportation and communication; and to top it all, a national economic planning board such as Baruch had presided over in World War I. Having made an indelible and unfavorable impression on a good many Senators, Eccles then caught the next train to New York to keep his appointment with Rexford Tugwell. The forty-two year old unknown Westerner would return within two years to face the Senators as the powerful head of the national banking system re-shaped to his specifications. *Fortune* in February 1935 commented on Eccles's testimony before the Senate Finance Committee:

> Anyone who will translate these suggestions into their present alphabetical symbols and compare the earlier general statements of economics with the economics of the present Administration will be forced to conclude that M. S. Eccles of Ogden, Utah, was not only a Mormon but a prophet.[10]

V

A full-blown compensatory economy scheme could not have sprung completely unaided from the mind of Eccles. There were other economic heretics on the scene who had deplored Hoover's emphasis on reinforcing creditor institutions so that relief would "trickle down" to the stricken populace rather than putting the unemployed directly on the government payroll to get the machinery started. For that matter, the list of welfare benefits that Eccles offered was as old as Bismarck, the "Iron Chancellor" who had stolen the socialists' thunder in the 1880's by handing out a good many of these benefits in Germany. States like Wisconsin, New York and California were well-advanced for the times in social legislation and the La Follettes of Wisconsin had come to Washington in the hope of bringing the "Wisconsin Idea" of the Progressives to the national government. In the midst of a great depression, however, welfare benefits were far less important than the underlying question of whether or not capitalism itself was capable of restoring normal employment.

Thus the seminal thinkers who searched in terms of a "middle way" or a "mixed economy" instead of clamoring for the strongly established, in theory at least, socialism of Veblen, Marx and many of the New Dealers deserve attention. Such men were not to be found where one might look today, for example, among the business leaders of the Committee for Economic Development or in the more enlightened schools of business administration, since there were few of either species then in circulation. Those twin pillars of business spokesmanship, the presidents of the National Association of Manufacturers and the United States Chamber of Commerce, were replete with platitudes and limited vision, an occupational hazard for holders of these offices throughout the twentieth century, to the great delight of the more biased historians. John Edgerton, in his presidential address to the NAM in October 1930, blamed the jobless themselves. "If they do not . . . practise the habit of thrift and conservation, or if they gamble away their savings in the stock market or elsewhere, is our economic system, or government, or industry to blame?"[11] Early in 1933, Henry Harriman, president of the United States Chamber of Commerce, officially advocated a cut of more than $1 billion in government spending by reducing federal activities to the level of the 1925 Administration.[12]

When Eccles testified before the Senate Finance Committee, two other businessmen associated themselves mildly with a deficit budget, J. David Stern, publisher of the *Philadelphia Record* and Ralph Flanders, a machine tool manufacturer who was later to become an outstanding Senator from Vermont. In his own testimony, Eccles acknowledged the influence of William Trufant Foster, an economist and writer who anticipated more sharply than any other public figure the anti-depression prescriptions to be advanced by John Maynard Keynes. Most interestingly, this former president of Reed College stated his position during the prosperity of the twenties. With Waddill Catchings, a former manufacturer who was then a partner in the high-flying investment trust promoting firm of Goldman, Sachs, Foster wrote *Business Without a Buyer* in 1927 and *The Road to Plenty* in 1928. Emphasizing the primacy of purchasing power for economic stability, the authors, as Keynes was also to do, discarded the famous classical theory of Jean Baptiste Say, which economics teachers taught as Say's Law. The law implied that total production created, in the form of wages and dividends, enough purchasing power to buy the goods produced. Some of the income was drained off in savings, to be sure, but these savings were the vital stuff of which new investments in job-creating machines and services were created, guaranteeing a new round of high employment. The interest rate acted as an automatic adjuster for this neat process, falling when savings were excessive, thus encouraging low-rate loans for needed production and discouraging redundant savings. When savings were inadequate, a rising interest rate withdrew purchasing power from the market and transferred it towards savings and investment. Similarly, when employment dropped, low wages would tempt business to rehire. Most businessmen and economists must have realized that the theories of a nineteenth century popularizer of Adam Smith were irrelevant in a world of mass production, cautious bankers, labor unions and administered prices wherein neither wages nor prices responded flexibly enough to supply and demand to sustain Say's Law. The myth persisted, however, and both Foster and Keynes found it necessary to demolish Say's toothless theory to provide the intellectual underpinnings of their new precepts. More important to men like Foster and Eccles in

their search for a current economic law was to recognize the importance of purchasing power. Thus the invention of the automobile
and more particularly Henry Ford's deliberate raising of wages
against the opposition of his fellow businessmen were seen as a
practical explanation of what caused a healthy economy and
a rising standard of living.

Still there was the problem of recurrent panics and depressions
and it was here that Foster and Catchings made their essential
contribution. The present system carried within it the possibility
of a stagnant economy, stabilized at a low level of employment
either through over-production or under-consumption. This could
arise from the efficient and profit-laden Ford plant, for example,
producing more cars than its well-paid workers and others could
buy. Or it might arise from consumers and corporations saving
too much for all the various reasons, or "propensities," as Keynes
would call them, including the psychological, attached to savings.
This would be particularly true in an economy of abundance rather
than the one of scarcity which had prevailed in the nineteenth century. Government spending, claimed Foster and Catchings, happened to be large enough to create the additional margin of
purchasing power needed to take goods off the market, which
helped explain the current but unpredictable prosperity. In retrospect, Foster and Catchings underestimated the excessive use of
foreign and domestic loans and speculative credit which so greatly
accelerated the happy times of the twenties and contributed to
their downfall. Still, their recognition of the dynamism of government spending, or fiscal policy, as we glibly use the phrase today,
to iron out the cycles in the nation's economy was a feat of the
first magnitude. With Yankee bluntness in contrast to the elegant
words Keynes would issue to the same effect, they summed up
their cure for the next depression: "When business begins to look
rotten, more public spending." In such times, an increase in the
national debt would be completely acceptable, since—and these
words of apparent double-talk were bound to disqualify Foster
and Catchings in respectable quarters—"It means scarcely more
than that the people of the United States collectively owe them-

selves more money." This condition, they added, was infinitely preferable to idle plants and idle workers. Franklin Roosevelt is reported to have written on his copy of *The Road to Plenty:* "Too good to be true. You can't get something for nothing."[13]

When the country staggered under the great depression, Foster alone pursued the theme with the conviction of a man who had predicted the causes of the depression and therefore was entitled to recommend a cure. The depression did not arise from a spend-thrift record, Foster stated, isolating the stock market binge from his analysis: "Far from having been profligate, the nation wasted its substance in riotous saving." For three years private enterprise had failed to turn the corner. Now it was necessary for government to restore purchasing power by public works, tax reduction, paying the soldiers' bonus, anything that would put spending dollars in the hands of consumers. He clinched his argument for the success of government intervention with an example generally tabooed in economic discussion because of its painful association with immorality. If the United States were to declare war tomorrow, declared Foster, Congress would immediately appropriate billions of dollars, men would rush to the factories and the farms and prosperity would return. Eliot Janeway, in *The Economics of Crisis,* coolly reminds us that wars have done just that in American history, although he finds the first exception about to appear in Viet Nam.[14] What is needed, men like Foster, Eccles and Janeway would agree, is a moral equivalent for war, namely a consciously directed economic system supplying a constantly rising standard of living for more and more people. Ironically, it took World War II to lift America out of its depression but the logic of the mixed or compensatory economy, making the best use of private enterprise, had already been established. In turn the alternative of a fully socialist economy had been rejected because, among other reasons, it was clear that the new system could work without repeating the old blunders.

The role of government greatly expanded through trial and error during the depression years and World War II. Its formal canonization occurred when Congress passed the Employment Act of 1946, which made it the duty of the federal government and its agencies, including the newly created Council of Economic Advisers, to use all practicable means "to promote maximum employment, production and purchasing power." More a statement of intent than a detailed law, this means primarily that Congress voted to use government spending and taxing, or fiscal, powers and government monetary powers, such as central banking policy, for the purpose of preventing major swings in the business cycle. Since then, of course, the mandate has been enlarged to include the alleviation of social discontent and the maintenance of an annual rate of economic growth sufficient to outstrip the claims of any rival major power. At any rate, for the solution that brought about the reasonably happy marriage between business and government with which these great endeavors were launched, the nation owes a vote of thanks to Foster and Eccles. Among others, they were influential in advocating the best way to end the depression to a reluctant Congress and a reluctant but open-minded President.

VI

Franklin D. Roosevelt's relations with the businessmen of America were the most complex of all our Presidents. If it is true, as Roosevelt's admirers say, that he was basically a conservative who saved capitalism from following the path to socialism, a vast majority of capitalists failed to appreciate his efforts. Like his cousin, Teddy, he did not hesitate to use demagogic criticism, such as 'the practises of the unscrupulous money changers" in his first inaugural address and to denounce the "economic royalists" at the start of his campaign for reelection in 1936. A detached aristocrat with inherited money, he did not particularly enjoy the company of energetic, powerful businessmen and his political base did not depend on their support.

In turn the emotion he inspired among hundreds of thousands of intelligent, educated and patriotic businessmen was often one of downright hatred. Some of it was a peevish snobbism directed against a man who was a "traitor to his own class." Others resented his scorn and public scoldings which affected their image in their communities and in their own families. Many had a vivid fear that he and his professors were going to confiscate their wealth through coddling of labor, wild inflation and discriminatory taxation. Still others were genuinely concerned that a mushrooming, bureaucratic government would lead the country along the road to serfdom. Under the circumstances, his strained relations with the business community are understandable. With his ebullient sense of humor and tendency to tease, FDR probably enjoyed the discomfiture of the rich.

The class of businessmen from which he felt most estranged were the bankers and financiers. He felt the landed squire's contempt for the continual revelations of misconduct and unethical transactions that were the aftermath of their most specialized activity, the stock market, and his 1932 campaign promise to take action against the holding companies, for example, was intensely felt. For their part, the bankers and financiers, in spite of their misfortunes, could not adjust to the new conditions wherein they were no longer consulted as equals of government, especially on economic matters such as the affairs of the Treasury Department and the Federal Reserve System.

What were Roosevelt's economics? They were as experimental and non-doctrinaire as his politics. "This country is big enough to experiment with several diverse systems and to follow several different lines," he remarked to Adolf Berle in expressing his preference for a mixed system. "Why must we put our economic policy in a single systemic jacket?"[15] His objections to the business interests were based not on their capacity to produce but on the feeling that they were not cooperating in helping all groups of the country to recover. He particularly felt that the banking and investment communities were passively resisting cooperation in order to discredit his Administration. As might be expected, he thoroughly rejected the hands-off-business policy of his predecessors. Yet he never accepted the technique of pump-priming and deficit financing with the conviction of an Eccles or a Keynes and it was not until the late thirties that he regarded it with any enthusiasm. Even then he was too timid and too late with his spending programs to restore the country to full employment before World War II.

Though Roosevelt and Harry Hopkins, his great relief administrator, will always be known as profligate spenders, they actually spent too little, assuming they could have pushed more massive programs through Congress. As a result, ten years after the crash, there were still seven million unemployed. Roosevelt never realized how effective increased peacetime spending could have been for the New Deal. He not only had the conflicting views of forceful advisers to consider in his perplexing job but among them deficit spenders were decidedly in the minority. Above all, his own temperament led him to take the middle course and to avoid total commitment to any one scheme.

Although the budget-balancing actions of his first months in office, such as vetoing the soldiers' bonus (which Congress passed over his veto) were quickly ended, his thrifty Dutch instincts in that direction were never abandoned. Typically he would listen with interest to expansionists like Eccles and the economist Leon Henderson and at the same time pay heed to Henry Morgenthau and Lewis Douglas, his Director of the Budget, who were horrified by deficit financing. When the total dollars are considered, the man who was reviled for his deficits was parsimonious, granting the crisis and assuming the efficacy of spending. Total deficits from 1930 through 1938 were $17 billion compared with $12.4 billion, the largest peacetime deficit in history, which arose during the 1959 fiscal year of the Eisenhower Administration.[16] The Eisenhower deficit, incidentally, came from a deliberate and successful program of government spending to overcome the 1958 recession. Of course the 1930 dollar was worth two 1959 dollars in purchasing power, but the comparison is a valid one. At the same time, from the viewpoint of history, Roosevelt's resiliency and daring to go as far as he did were remarkable in every way.

Even in the field of government lending, the New Deal's greatest

effort in the area of traditional business enterprise, Roosevelt in-
stinctively preferred guaranteeing private mortgages, as in the
FHA Act, rather than direct lending. His early advisers, particularly Tugwell and Berle, were men whose temperament and
training prepared them to contemplate major changes in institutions, such as state ownership of the banking system, rather than
the reform and tinkering which appealed to Roosevelt. In this
sense, the fact that no area of private enterprise was nationalized
during the New Deal can be taken as another sign of Roosevelt's
innate conservatism. Certainly he was in a position to nationalize
the banks after closing them to avoid chaos the day after his
inauguration. It is more than likely that the Congress which
stampeded within another week to approve the bank closing, the
temporary abandonment of the gold standard (through an em-
bargo on gold outflow) and the abrogation of the contract to
exchange dollars for gold would have acquiesced. Probably no
action would have given more pleasure to voters than such retaliation. A nation which had recently voted alcohol both out and in
was capable of expropriating banks as well.

One field of economic theory in which Roosevelt had a lively if
misguided interest was the matter of gold and its relation to
prices. Long before he accepted deficit financing, Roosevelt subscribed to devaluation of the dollar as a means of bringing relief
to the irate farmers who were a major concern of the New Deal as a
badly neglected casualty of the Hoover Administration. When the
Agricultural Adjustment Act was passed in the First Hundred
Days, the farm interests attached to it the Thomas Amendment
giving Roosevelt discretionary authority to cause price inflation
by altering the gold content of the dollar, among other expedients.
Lewis Douglas and other conservatives in the Administration ex-
horted the President not to indulge in any "soft money" experiments.
When a special monetary policy committee of Douglas, James P.
Warburg, a liberal representative of Wall Street, Dean Acheson,
Under Secretary of the Treasury, William Woodin, Roosevelt's
Republican Secretary of the Treasury and George Harrison, head

of the Federal Reserve Bank of New York, failed to come up with anything better than suggesting a quick return to the gold standard, Roosevelt turned in exasperation to Professor George Warren of Cornell. Warren's unorthodox and professionally suspect theory was for the government to buy gold at gradually increasing prices. This would increase farm commodity prices, in terms of dollars, as the gold value of the dollar fell, in other words, monetary rather than "supply and demand" inflation. This called for a fireside chat in October 1933 in which Roosevelt announced to his radio listeners that he was "authorizing the RFC to buy gold from time to time at prices to be determined by the Secretary of the Treasury and the President . . . thus continuing to move towards a managed currency." Though most of his listeners probably could not comprehend what it was all about any more than the next generation could follow the recurrent gold crises of the 1960's, they could identify the opposition from the outraged reaction of the banking community. It is difficult to conceive of great passions being aroused by monetary theory as they were in Bryan's day and again following the gold-buying program. While Wall Street and a committee of forty conventional economists launched an attack, Roosevelt found dubious allies in Elmer Thomas and Father Coughlin, who drew fifteen thousand people in November to the New York Hippodrome to hear their defense of inflation.

One of the most amusing and hopefully top secret stories of those days of crisis is narrated in the *Diaries* of Henry Morgenthau, who succeeded the ailing Woodin at that time as Acting Secretary of the Treasury. While Roosevelt ate his soft-boiled eggs at morning breakfast meetings with the serious Morgenthau and bluff Jesse Jones of the RFC, he would gaily set a price for buying gold at some arbitrary margin over the world price sufficient to curb speculators.[17] The gold-buying finally ended with the passing of the Gold Reserve Act on January 30, 1934, which established the price of gold at $35 per ounce and returned the U.S. to a semi-gold standard, embarrassed as a result of the purchases with an inflow of most of the world's gold, a new problem in itself.

The experiment failed to raise prices noticeably but it did help farm exports as foreign countries used their newly acquired dollars to buy American goods. The negative value consisted of forestalling the increased deflation which would have followed a return to the uncontrolled gold standard. Although this high-spirited maneuver was supposed to have appealed to the debt-ridden Western and Southern business interests as well as the farmers, Marriner Eccles, observing the scene from Utah, was unimpressed. He had already gone on record with the Senate Finance Committee the previous February to the effect that "devaluation would not by itself bring about any increases in prices. Prices could be raised only if the government created effective purchasing power by a spending-lending program based on deficit financing."[18]

Although Eccles would grant that Roosevelt's gold-buying, however faulty in theory, was at least a step towards placing monetary policy squarely in the hands of Washington rather than New York, which was soon to be his own special mission, other Roosevelt advisers regarded the action as unforgivable. Dean Acheson expressed such forceful reservations that Roosevelt demanded his resignation. Lewis Douglas resigned in 1934 and wrote to Roosevelt that his place in history and perhaps the fate of Western civilization depended on his balancing the budget. James Warburg, who had refused an office in the Treasury Department in 1932 but nevertheless had made a hopeful alliance with the Administration, broke with Roosevelt and became a severe and articulate critic. Al Smith, a recent convert to big business, took a crack at "baloney dollars." The few bridges to the business establishment that Roosevelt possessed were badly burned by his gold-buying adventures. It must have been with particular relief that he welcomed Eccles into his Administration shortly afterward.

VII

Eccles's brief interview with Tugwell (over lunch in a drugstore booth) resulted in a call to Washington six months later, in October 1933. Tugwell invited him to meet some key New Dealers and expound his views to them. Eccles went to the scene of action with barely concealed enthusiasm. Supremely confident of the rightness of his views, he had observed with dismay Roosevelt's original attempts at budget-balancing and the subsequent effort at price inflation through gold devaluation. Finally he had misgivings about the brass-band introduction of the National Industrial Recovery Act (NRA), which he thought would bring about monopolistic price increases instead of increased consumer purchasing power. He was churning with answers, he later reminisced, that would set the world aright if only men in high places would listen to him: "Any peep from Washington bounced back as a roar from my mountain side."[19] Meanwhile, he expressed himself in broadsides to his fellow Utahan, Secretary of War George Dern, who slipped them into Cabinet meetings or to Treasury Secretary Woodin without effect. Woodin was particularly unreceptive to the idea of bank deposit insurance. In addition, there were telegrams to Senators and public speeches.

Another prophet without honor in the councils of power was John Maynard Keynes, whose erudite and sophisticated economics were so startlingly paralleled by the non-academic and wholly practicable Eccles. Keynes's economics provide the final touch in examining Roosevelt's economics.

The Keynesian Revolution has often been identified with the New Deal Revolution. This identification in turn has been deemed to be a stretching of facts. Conscious Keynesianism is now perceived to be much more the property of succeeding Presidents than it ever was of Roosevelt. The $10 billion dollar tax cut of 1964 was a classically Keynesian policy, with an estimated cumulative flow, or "multiplier effect," of three times that amount added to the economy, according to President Johnson's economic advisers. President Kennedy, who initiated the 1964 tax decrease, exhibited his mastery of Keynesianism in his speech at Yale's Commencement in 1962. This was fitting inasmuch as the center of the Keynesian Revolution in America had been Harvard, led by interpreters and disciples of Keynes such as Professors Alvin Hansen and Seymour Harris.

Roosevelt was leaning heavily on Harvard in his first term but not on Keynes, in spite of the fact that Keynes was lecturing him on what to do as early as 1933 in an open letter to *The New York Times*. Unable to sway the political leaders in his own country to massive governmental economic operations, Keynes hopefully adopted the New Deal as the testing ground for his theories. In the past, the letter stated, only war was considered a legitimate reason for job-creating government expenditures. "You, Mr. President, having cast off such fetters, are free to engage in the interests of peace and prosperity the technique which has hitherto only been allowed to serve the purposes of war and destruction."[20]

Felix Frankfurter had met Keynes while lecturing at Oxford in 1933 and for the first time recognized the possibilities in deficit financing. Bearing an introduction from Frankfurter, Keynes arrived at the White House for tea in May of 1934. The meeting between two of the world's greatest revolutionists was less than happy. Roosevelt could hardly have appreciated Keynes's Olympian public advice and Keynes himself was generally an arrogant and impatient person. Frances Perkins, Roosevelt's Secretary of Labor, with feminine receptivity was awarded confidences by both participants. "I saw your friend Keynes. He left a whole rigamarole of figures. He must be a mathematician rather than a political economist," FDR told her. Keynes in turn said he had "supposed the President to be more literate, economically speaking."[21] Keynes was rarely discussed by Roosevelt thereafter.

Keynes then made the rounds of Washington under the guidance of Tugwell, astutely bought some depressed public utility stocks, sent another letter of instructions to Roosevelt via *The New York Times* and returned home. When Eccles similarly met the New Deal brain-trusters under Tugwell's sponsorship the following October, he found the influence of Keynes a minor one:

> With the exception of (Mordecai) Ezekiel and Tugwell I doubt whether any of the men in my room had ever heard of John Maynard Keynes, the English economist who has frequently been referred to as the economic

philosopher of the New Deal. At least none of them cited his writing to support his own case, and the concepts I formulated which have been called "Keynesian," were not abstracted from his books, which I had never read. My conceptions were based on naked-eye observation and experience in the inter-mountain region. Moreover, I have never read Keynes's writings except in small extracts up to this day.[22]

For that matter, few others have waded through the difficult, highly theoretical and mathematical *The General Theory of Employment, Interest and Money*, Keynes's basic book, which was not published until 1936. This is not unusual for the works of great minds. We are all likely to be Darwinians, Marxians, Freudians and Keynesians without having to go to the original sources. Such men, whose times are so ready for their ideas, inevitably become institutionalized by interpreters and public acceptance.

Amusingly one institution, the American businessman, was a force which the irrepressible Keynes wished to treat with a far gentler hand than the one offered by Roosevelt. By 1938, Roosevelt had largely written off his reconciliation attempts with business. He had gained its animosity with his 1935 tax bill which, with its increased corporate tax rates, estate taxes and similar features, was known as the "Soak the Rich" bill in the Hearst press. It was a tax bill which upper-income individuals and corporations would gladly exchange for succeeding tax bills, both during and after World War II, but at the time it was considered a personal vendetta on the part of Roosevelt. Marriner Eccles, by then a member of the Administration, disapproved of any increases in tax rates in the midst of depression, consistent with his clear-eyed view that raising taxes and worrying about inflation at such times was a kind of fiscal madness. The Administration had committed additional offenses against business with its "death sentence" for public utility holding companies Act in 1935 and its short-lived undistributed profits tax against corporations in 1936 (of which Eccles approved on the grounds of increased purchasing power). Finally there were the Senate's Temporary National Economic Committee (TNEC) investigations of monopoly, launched in 1938 under the crusading Leon Henderson and the still unappreciated Securities Act of 1933 and Securities Exchanges Act of 1934. All in all, 1938 was hardly a year for encouraging business to put its shoulder to the wheel, even for a President who regarded himself, with some justification, as a man who was saving capitalism for America. Keynes, sitting on the sidelines, comfortably immune from political pressures such as the current defection of enough Southern Democrats to enable the Republican-conservative Democratic coalition to slash Keynesian spending, decided to give Roosevelt a final bit of advice.

The advice has special merit not generally associated with Keynesian economics. It is simply that if a government is resolved to work through the agency of private capitalism, rather than substitute the state itself for the direction of overall investment, then it must recognize how delicate business confidence has proven to be ever since government invited itself in as the senior member of the firm. President Kennedy, who was not popular with business, and President Johnson, who has been popular with business on the grounds of confidence, might have shared Roosevelt's amusement upon reading Keynes's cynical letter of 1938, as revealed in Morgenthau's *Diaries*, published in 1959:

> Businessmen have a different set of delusions from politicians; and need, therefore, different handling. They are, however, much milder than politicians, at the same time allured and terrified by the glare of publicity, easily persuaded to be "patriots," perplexed, bemused, indeed, terrified, yet only too anxious to take a cheerful view, vain perhaps but very unsure of themselves, pathetically responsive to a kind word. You could do anything you liked with them if you would treat them (even the big ones) not as wolves and tigers, but as domestic animals by nature, even though they have been badly brought up and not trained as you would wish. It is a mistake to think that they are more *immoral* than politicians. If you

work them into the surly, obstinate, terrified mood, of
which domestic animals, wrongly handled, are so capable, the nation's burdens will not get carried to market;
and in the end public opinion will veer their way.[23]

One can imagine an alternate Roosevelt reaction to this letter
which seems more suitable for a Rex Harrison libretto than for
the pressing business at hand, including a frustrating unemployment problem domestically and the rise of Mussolini, Hitler and
Stalin internationally. Keynes, incidentally, not only became a
millionaire speculator in securities and foreign exchange but also
managed an investment trust and guided the finances of a life insurance company in the course of his varied career, which may
explain his claims as an authority on businessmen. In the end this
talented Englishman left his mark on America after all. The "revolution" in which he and Roosevelt collaborated, however coin-
cidentally, made government supremely responsible for achieving,
administering and maintaining prosperity. As Keynes once claimed
for his profession:

The ideas of economists and political philosophers, both
when they are right and when they are wrong, are more
powerful than is commonly understood. Indeed, the
world is ruled by little else.[24]

VIII

The development of a mixed economy, or middle way, at a time
when the old individualism was bankrupt and the new collectivism
demanded a ransom of freedom, is indebted to men like Marriner
Eccles as well as to Roosevelt and Keynes. In February 1934 he
became an assistant to Treasury Secretary Morgenthau and the
following September was offered the position of Governor of the
Federal Reserve Board, as the Chairmanship was then known,
by Roosevelt.

Eccles was quite aware of the fact that his status as a millionaire
banker and industrialist made his "gospel of logical radicalism"
acceptable to a broad spectrum of groups including the financial

conservatives in the Administration itself. There were only a few other "tame millionaires" associated with the Administration, notably Jesse Jones, Bernard Baruch, Joseph P. Kennedy and Averell Harriman.

The major difference between the one millionaire and the others was that Eccles, for all his lack of formal education, was capable of sustained theoretical analysis and comprehension of the new directions capitalism needed to take for survival. Jones was a Texas banker who took over the RFC for Roosevelt and with great gusto turned it into the nation's largest bank and investor. Untroubled by theory, he regarded the RFC as his private domain and as an engine for expanding the nation's economy. Altogether $50 billion passed through his capable hands. A myriad of subsidiaries as diverse as the Commodity Credit Corporation, the Electric Home and Farm Authority and the Export-Import Bank were assigned to this most successful recovery agency. Baruch enjoyed his role as a power behind the throne, placing protégés such as General Hugh Johnson in charge of the NRA and sustaining the legend of his own influence with Southern legislators. President Kennedy's father was a typically bold Roosevelt appointment as the first Chairman of the SEC in 1934. The forty-six year old businessman had participated as recently as 1933 in the type of stock market pool his Commission now was charged to prohibit. Roosevelt jauntily informed his Cabinet that Kennedy could do the job because he knew "the tricks of the trade." Kennedy acquitted himself in fine form, urged Wall Street to start floating new issues and resigned while ahead a year later to work on increasing the family fortune as the base for future operations. Averell Harriman's durable career in government penetrated to all corners of activity and at that time he was busy helping to run the NRA. An interesting comparison with Eccles was Lewis Douglas, Roosevelt's recently departed defender of the balanced budget. Similar to Eccles in so many ways as a Western small-state banker, Douglas was as completely dominated by orthodox ideas as Eccles was liberated from them. Douglas now graciously admits, Eccles reports, that he was 100% wrong in his opposition to deficit financing.[25]

In the light of this background, Eccles's Bank Act of 1935, a major contribution to the mixed economy, is a revealing example of how a typical piece of New Deal legislation became law.

Eccles accepted Roosevelt's offer on the condition that the Administration sponsor a new Act for the nation's banking system. Over the years, he pointed out, the Federal Reserve System had seen the Reserve Board in Washington reduced to impotence. The System had originally been designed to represent a blend of public and private interests but the private interests, dominating the regional Reserve Banks, had made the System serve their own purposes first. The Board in Washington, charged with representing and safeguarding the public interest, was powerless to do so under the present law and in the face of the opposition of the men who ran the Reserve banks, particularly the New York bank.

The bill was not intended by Eccles to be another popular barb at "Wall Street control." He sought legislation even more basic than the Securities legislation, which originated as a reform measure to protect the public, although it eventually became a stimulus to investment. From the very start, Eccles conceived of the banking bill as a method of making the nation's banks, especially the large city banks, the useful servants rather than the masters of the nation's financial system. It involved a basic philosophical attitude towards private or public control in relation to the prevention of future depressions.

A key feature in the bill was to be the establishment of the principle that open-market operations of the System be centered in Washington. When the Federal Reserve banks purchased or sold government securities in the open market, they directly influenced the reserves of member banks. Through the reserves they influenced the volume of deposits; through the deposits the loanable funds made available to the commercial banks; and through the commercial banks they influenced the minutest operation of the economy. When the Reserve System was established in 1913, the public debt, in the form of government securities, stood at $1 billion. In 1935 it was $27 billion and open-market operations had an effect not even contemplated in the original Act. As a result of custom and ineffectual regulations, the open-market activities now rested under the domination of the New York Federal Reserve Bank, through which private interests in the New York financial district exercised enormous influence over the national economy. Responsibility for the open-market operations had to be unified and vested in a clearly authorized body. Other reforms in relation to reserve ratios, eligible paper for rediscounting by member banks and the organizational structure of the Board itself were proposed by Eccles and his able drafting chief, Lauchlin Currie, one of the junior brain-trusters at the time. "If the monetary mechanism is to be used as an instrument for the promotion of business stability, conscious control and management are essential," stated Eccles in a summary of the proposed bill presented to Roosevelt.[26] It was a classic statement of a "middle way" between the driving force of private enterprise and the guiding force of government technique and responsibility in a vital era that had been revealed to be painfully inadequate. A press release was issued about the new appointee, emphasizing in effect that he had met payrolls and kept his banks open, as both Roosevelt and Eccles braced themselves for the storm from the unregenerate bankers.

It took five months before the Senate would confirm Eccles's appointment and it was obvious that the bill itself would be discredited if he were not confirmed. Meanwhile Roosevelt's Comptroller of the Currency, J. F. T. O'Connor and the head of the Federal Deposit Insurance Corporation, Leo Crowley, both directly involved in the banking system, opposed the bill, as did Jesse Jones. The frustrations of the plans of even so powerful a President as Roosevelt are illustrated in this split in his ranks. The Administration had let it be known that in November Congress would be asked to approve a $4 billion work-relief program. The Federal Reserve System would be the channel through which the banking system would have to absorb the securities and provide the credit for financing the program. Under the prevailing Reserve structure a group of individuals in the Reserve banks dedicated to budget-balancing had the latent power to block the program by dragging their feet on the whole operation if the new Banking Act were not passed. An Advisory Council of the Federal Reserve Board had just issued a statement demanding a balanced budget without clearing it with the Board itself, much to Eccles's indignation.

The inevitable parade of distinguished economists, led by Professor Walter E. Spahr of New York University, on behalf of sixty-six well known professors in various universities, testified before the House Banking and Currency Committee against the bill, just as their forebears had done in 1913.

The House, under the leadership of Congressman Goldsborough of Maryland, an extremely well-informed legislator, passed the bill with ease but the Senate was to be a different story. Carter Glass, Senator from Virginia, was an elder statesman who possessed immense power over banking legislation as a result of his career as Secretary of the Treasury under Woodrow Wilson and creator of the Federal Reserve System against the opposition of the entrenched bankers of pre-World War I. Roosevelt committed the error of not clearing the appointment of Eccles with the proud old man beforehand and the fledgling appointee was caught in a political trap. Glass devoted himself first to preventing Eccles's confirmation, failing to swing the Senate Banking and Currency Committee by a single vote. He then cast the sole vote against Eccles in the full Senate.

Having failed to kill the bill by blocking Eccles's appointment, Glass next turned to the bill itself, calling sixty witnesses who provided a solid core of great names in finance in opposition. The gist of the argument was that the whole System was working well enough and would now become subject to the political domination of the President. Yet under cross-examination of Senator Couzens of Michigan, even so articulate an opponent as James Warburg, a member of the family of the banker Paul M. Warburg, who as much as Glass was the father of the Federal Reserve System, was forced to admit that private control presently existed. Quoting Woodrow Wilson, Eccles reminded the Senators in his own testimony that, "The control of the system of banking and of issue which our new laws are to set up must be public not private; must be vested in the Government itself, so that the banks may be the instruments, not the masters of business and of individual enterprise and initiative."[27]

By the terms of the Banking Act of 1933, which established the FDIC and separated banking and the securities business, any bank officer who did not pay back loans to his own bank by July 1, 1935 would lose his job. Craftily tying in some extensions to this deadline in his new bill, Eccles kept most of the bankers' opposition in line. Meanwhile, with some prodding from Roosevelt, Chairman Steagall of the House Committee held firm against strong Senate pressure and the bill was passed on August 23. The Joint Committee that ironed out the details awarded many compromises to Glass, fed to them by Eccles, and Glass boasted to the press: "We did not leave enough of the Eccles bill with which to light a cigaret." Eccles was delighted with his victory and proudly displays a photograph of Glass, himself and Congressman Steagall in front of a bronze plaque to "Carter Glass, Defender of the Federal Reserve System," in the foyer of the Federal Reserve Building. The small, lean, sharp-visaged and dark-eyed Eccles stands in profile behind the older adversary, whose profile and physique in turn bear a startling resemblance to that of the younger man. The self-trained Keynesian reveals himself to be a self-trained Freudian, noting in his autobiography: "We seem to be father and son, which may account for our troubles . . ."[28]

IX

The on-going conflict between American business and government rose to a maudlin pitch with the phenomenon of the American Liberty League as a factor in the 1936 election. By this time the New Deal itself had changed direction from its initial efforts towards a semi-planned economy, most notably expressed in the energetic partnership between business and government in the NRA. The "Second New Deal" emphasized a restoration of competition within a centrally defined social framework as an economic system. Politically, its support would come from a coalition of non-business groups as a check against business dominance.

This new tack on behalf of less centralization received little commendation from the business community, which did not distinguish between government intervention of the NRA type and the more subtle efforts of the "Second New Deal." In this sense, business was correct as the Administration basically was forced into its new phase by Supreme Court decisions and typically developed it by trial and error.

Astute observers such as Justice Brandeis and Keynes, otherwise great supporters of the Administration, rejoiced as much as the most conservative businessmen in the extinction of the NRA when it was declared unconstitutional on May 27, 1935. Brandeis voted emphatically with the majority as an expression of his deep-seated antagonism towards bigness and centralization. Keynes equally feared excessive power of the state and was supremely confident, as was Eccles, in the ability of "pump-priming" techniques and regulation to restore prosperity under the leadership of traditional, unplanned business enterprise. Roosevelt fumed over the "horse and buggy" thinking of the "nine old men" on the Supreme Court. Still unsure of his economic theory, he imperturbably turned to the spending and reform measures that Eccles, Leon Henderson, Thomas Corcoran and Ben Cohen would advocate as "compensatory" economists. On the political front, he had the sureness of a master and turned deliberately to the new coalition.

The business community saw the series of anti-New Deal Court decisions as a call to action against a spendthrift, unfriendly Administration. The United States Chamber of Commerce, which had given Roosevelt and the NRA a rising ovation at its convention in 1933, declared the honeymoon over at its 1935 convention, voting opposition to the social-security bill, the extension of NRA beyond its approaching two-year termination date, the Eccles banking bill and all labor legislation. "Businessmen are tired," declared President Silas Strawn, "of hearing promises to do constructive things which turn out to be only attempts to Sovietize America."[29] Roosevelt's ragged band of business supporters outside the government, notably Thomas J. Watson of International Business Machines, Myron Taylor of U.S. Steel, Gerard Swope and Robert E. Wood, disassociated themselves from such extremism but the exasperated Roosevelt reluctantly accepted the estrangement. Ironically, he could find champions among sophisticated large corporation executives but had practically no support from the small or medium business class throughout the country. Meanwhile business and employment conditions were showing substantial improvement in 1936, a further invitation to the business community to take a defiant stand.

The call to arms to businessmen to halt the New Deal came strangely enough from conservatives in the Democratic party. The American Liberty League was formed in 1934 under the leadership of Jouett Shouse and John J. Raskob, the Democratic chieftains who led the Presidential campaign for Alfred E. Smith in 1928. This alliance, reinforced by a large group of the du Pont family, traced back to the Association Against the Prohibition Amendment. With prohibition conquered, Shouse now organized the American Liberty League ". . . to defend and uphold the Constitution" among other worthy objectives. Roosevelt heartily endorsed the objectives when his old friend Shouse called at the White House to announce the new organization.[30]

With John W. Davis, the defeated Presidential candidate against Calvin Coolidge, and Al Smith in the fold, the non-partisan front of the League was soon abandoned. By 1935 the League was tremendously active and spent twice as much money as the Republican party itself. Although it claimed 120,000 members, over half of its funds came from a few dozen bankers, industrialists and businessmen. In 1936, one-fourth of its funds came from the du Pont family alone.

The League was effectively organized and produced over one hundred skillfully written propaganda pamphlets against the New Deal between 1934 and 1936, distributing over five million copies and receiving tremendous reprints in the generally anti-Administration press. There were 10,000 college student members in 346 university chapters throughout the country, all unexposed to Keynesian economics at the time.

Speaking from the loftiest of motives, the League accepted the classical doctrine that depressions were natural and would work themselves out through automatic processes. Not only had the New Dealers failed to bring recovery, but there was the suspicion they actually prevented recovery in order to perpetuate power and transform the country into a dictatorship. A favorite of Shouse's own economic preaching was the identification of thrift in government with the virtue of thrift in the individual, of the federal budget with the household budget, a position which Eccles was to challenge so articulately. "You Owe Thirty-One Billion Dollars" was a favorite speech of Shouse in 1936.

The League reached its high point, both in publicity and bad judgment, on January 25, 1936. Two thousand guests gathered at the Mayflower Hotel in Washington, representing, according to the *New York Times*, "a large portion of the capitalistic wealth of the country." The speaker of the evening was Al Smith, incongruously resplendent in white tie and tails, who launched into a shallow comparison of the New Deal and "communistic Russia." His old vice-presidential running mate, Senator Joseph T. Robinson of Arkansas, was tapped by the Administration to deliver the reply to the man who was more familiar in a brown derby on the sidewalks of New York. Robinson's scorn reflected the mood of the nation: "The voice is Jacob's voice but the hands are the hands of Esau." Jim Farley joyfully branded the League as an adjunct of the Republican Party and the horrified Republican leaders were unable to disown their unwanted allies. Alf Landon, a moderate and able opponent, recognized the League as the "kiss of death" and went down before Roosevelt's most smashing victory.

Eccles did not take part in the 1936 election, it being considered inappropriate in view of his new fourteen year appointment as Chairman of the Board of the Federal Reserve System. It may have been with amusement that he saw so many of his fellow businessmen, including ex-Treasury men Dean Acheson and James Warburg, embrace the Liberty League and its faulty economics. Yet there were other adversaries on which to exercise his skill in defending Administration policies. Roosevelt asked Congress in April 1938

to resume large-scale spending, being convinced that his retrench-
ment moves in 1937 had been premature and had caused a serious
recession. Senator Byrd of Virginia thereupon broadcast an attack
on Roosevelt's "nine years of fiscal insanity" and paid his respects to
Eccles "for the crackpot legislative ideas of those holding important
office." It did not help that Treasury Secretary Morgenthau in a
public speech had called for a balanced budget the previous
November.

With Roosevelt's approval, Eccles engaged in a public debate on
the radio and in the press with the junior Senator from Virginia.
His arguments are a reminder of how difficult it was to promote
his theories at the time.

> Early in your speech you extolled . . . "those time-old
> virtues of thrift, frugality, self-reliance and industry."
> Somewhat later, however, you expressed alarm at the in-
> crease in debt in the past five years. I am at a loss to
> understand how you reconcile these two ideas. Certainly
> if it is good for people to save, i.e., practise the virtues
> of thrift and frugality, it must also be good that someone
> should borrow money and put it to productive uses.
> Private enterprise has in the years since the depression
> began been in no position to employ profitably anywhere
> near the total of the country's savings, because there was
> not sufficient buying power in the hands of the public to
> purchase the output of existing facilities of production.
>
> Debts and obligations of various kinds are but the other
> side of investment, and if we ever tried to liquidate the
> whole amount of them, or even any substantial fraction,
> we would precipitate a crisis so severe that general
> economic paralysis would result. When there is a con-
> traction of total debt, private and public, we have de-
> flation. We have never had prosperous conditions without
> an accompanying expansion of debt, either private or
> public, or both.

*   *   *

The Senator has warned you that the total debt of all
public bodies in the United States now amounts to $430
per every man, woman and child, that it is a mortgage
on you and your property, and that your children and
grandchildren will have to pay off this mortgage. But he
failed to tell you who owns the mortgage. You, of course,
know that it is owned by all the people and amounts to
an average of exactly $430 owed to every man, woman
and child. In other words, all of the people are borrowing
through their public bodies from all of the people.

The whole problem of internal debt, public and private,
must be considered in relation to the total real wealth
of the nation.[31]

Dry reading perhaps. Yet the knowledge that debt is not some
monstrous villain but instead is a servant capable of achieving
heroic deeds such as ending a depression belongs high on the list
of discoveries. Whereas Senator Byrd was never able to agree with
Eccles, the latter found himself entirely in agreement with Senator
Byrd's economizing when the post World War II round of inflation became the order of the day. Similarly, Eccles opposed Treasury Secretary Snyder's easy-money policies as consistently as he
opposed Morgenthau's budget-balancing tendencies.

X

Eccles was to have his share of defeats as well as triumphs in
the thirteen years he would spend as Chairman of the Federal
Reserve Board until 1948 and the three years as dominant member
until his retirement in 1951. A favorite of the press and the magazine journalists, he was described by Raymond Clapper in 1935
as "the all-powerful head of our banking system . . . the strangest
character in that strange wonderland of Washington. His revolutionary ideas bring shudders to his fellow capitalists."[32] Yet his
first attempt at banking reform after the election of 1936 met with

defeat. He wanted a unified banking system as a more effective instrument for dealing with the nation's monetary and credit needs. This would involve requiring the state banks to join the Federal Reserve System instead of enjoying an option not to do so even though becoming members of the FDIC. In addition, unification would eliminate the overlapping regulatory authorities of the FDIC, Comptroller of the Currency and Federal Reserve Board. This would result, for example, in uniform relaxation of bank examinations when an easier credit policy was desired in periods of recession. The banking community has always resisted the logic of a unified system with its own logic of "divide and conquer" and lack of enthusiasm for federal encroachment. For eight years, Eccles badgered Roosevelt to give his full support to such a bill. The President, somewhat leery of the competitive disadvantages he sensed might result for the smaller banks in the state banking system, outdistanced his able banking chief until attention was diverted by World War II. As usual, the Eccles proposals evoked a feud with Morgenthau who was not about to give up control of the Comptroller of Currency's office.

Still another trying experience occurred as a result of the sharp raising of reserve requirements of member banks of the Federal Reserve System, first by 50% in August 1936 and again by a total of 33-1/3% in March and May of 1937. Increasing reserves to this extent is done for the purpose of stemming inflationary forces but there was hardly a threat of inflation at that time of continued massive unemployment. Pressure from the banking community and its academic economists, based on the potential "threat of inflation" arising from the excessive inflow of gold from foreign countries, mounted until the generally unflappable Eccles, devoted to easy money during depressions, reluctantly raised the reserves. Since the recession of 1937-1938 soon cast its shadow, largely caused by Roosevelt's premature reduction of government spending and the $2 billion withdrawn from the purchasing stream as the result of the social security system's first tax collection year, Eccles was sorely tried to explain his actions. He insisted in a public statement that he was still an advocate of easy money, but the explanation was somewhat unconvincing and the prior approval of the business community unappreciated. Meanwhile, Morgenthau had rushed to Roosevelt in March, complaining that the Eccles action had driven the government bond prices down, which would mean an increase in the cost of financing the government. The Board in turn agreed to stabilize these prices by open-market purchases of government securities. This was a prelude to the famous "accord" lasting until 1951 between the Treasury and Federal Reserve Board wherein the latter compromised its prized independence on behalf of the Treasury's understandable desire to finance close to $200 billion of war expenditures at low interest rates. Similarly the *contretemps* over the raising of reserves foreshadowed the great problem Chairman William McChesney Martin would face throughout the fifties and sixties. It is the delicate matter of timing the application of Federal Reserve Board brakes to that most welcome but elusive "other side" of the compensatory economy, the period of boom and inflation.

XI

No one so vital as Marriner Eccles should be bid adieu on the dry ground of timing of reserve changes and the pegging of bond prices. Fittingly his showdown with Harry Truman came from his mighty clash with Amadeo P. Giannini, the colossus of California who made the Bank of America the world's largest bank.

The colorful A. P., obsessed with the desire to build a nationwide banking system, fought with regulatory officials at every level as he ingeniously bought and acquired banks in the Western states. In 1928 his Bancitaly corporation added 51% control of the prestigious Bank of America of New York to some previous New York bank holdings, comprising the most adventurous step so far towards fulfilling his national ambitions. The Federal Reserve Board demanded that Bancitaly divest itself of the Bank of America of New York stock shortly after the purchase and A. P. acquiesced for the moment. The next step was to form a new bank holding company,

Transamerica Corporation, which took over the stock of both the New York and Western banks under one massive corporation with $1.3 billion in assets. The Federal Reserve Board complained that this tactic circumvented the Bancitaly agreement to divest itself of the New York bank stock which Transamerica had acquired once again. The move horrified his Wall Street contact, J. P. Morgan & Co., who promptly severed relations with Giannini. The void was thereupon filled by A. P.'s impulsive selection of Blair & Co., which he merged with Transamerica, naming Blair's president, Elisha Walker, as chairman of Transamerica in 1930. Vice-chairman was none other than Jean Monnet, Walker's associate at Blair & Co., who would return to France two years later and become its great political economist and administrator. A. P. installed his son Mario as president and went off to Europe to nurse his failing health.

Monnet's return to France was expedited by his expulsion from Transamerica along with Walker after one of the grandest proxy fights in the history of American business. Sadly the Gianninis realized their mistake when Walker attempted to meet the demands of the depression by stopping dividends and preparing to liquidate Transamerica holdings at sacrificial prices. A. P. bombarded Transamerica with telegrams of dissent only to find the Transamerica board, including his most trusted lieutenants, solidly against him. "THERE'S NO COMPROMISING WITH RIGHT OR PRINCIPLE REGARDLESS OF CONSEQUENCES. NO SIR, NEVER MY BOY," he telegraphed the doggedly loyal Mario, who had been so humiliated by Walker he had resigned his presidency.[33] Summoning unexpected resources of health, A. P. left the baths of Germany, secretly arrived in America under an alias and launched the proxy fight. The old magic of the Giannini name flashed like Napoleon's on his return from Elba as A. P. and his insurgents stormed the country, raising the cry: "Save the bank from Wall Street racketeers!" On February 15, 1932, the proxies were counted. Giannini won by 7,000,000 shares.

This was the type of man who would warm the heart of a Roosevelt or an Eccles and vice versa. After bailing out the Bank of

America in California (the New York banks had already been sold by Walker to National City Bank) with $40 million from President Hoover's RFC, A. P. denied Hoover's personal request for his support in the coming election. He went to Washington for the inauguration of Roosevelt, whose will was as mighty as his own, and returned to California to await the signal to open the Bank of America on March 13, 1933, the scheduled end of the bank holiday for banks in the larger cities. His old opponent, John U. Calkins, governor of the Federal Reserve Bank in San Francisco, had other plans, recommending against reopening the Bank of America because of its financial condition. It took the combined strength of Senator McAdoo, William Randolph Hearst and Jesse Jones to force Secretary of the Treasury Woodin to override Calkins.

Soon A. P. was a favorite of the Administration and one of the few bankers publicly supporting it. When Eccles was facing a hard fight with the Banking Act of 1935, he received strong Giannini support, even though a hoped for extension of branch banking to a regional basis was dropped from the final bill. Transamerica had already received a windfall from Carter Glass's Banking Act of 1933 which allowed national banks to open branches on a parity with state banks for the first time. A. P.'s staunch support in 1935 was reflected in this statement to the press: "Personally, I would rather that this power be exercised by a public body in the public interest than by the New York banking fraternity."[34] In a press release from Bank of America he noted: "The Federal Reserve Board is a political body only in the sense that its members are nominated by the President and confirmed by the Senate. So are the members of the Supreme Court." "GREATLY APPRECIATE YOUR STATEMENT," Eccles wired A. P. "IT WAS BOTH A PLEASURE AND A PRIVILEGE," beamed A. P. to Eccles.[35]

Transamerica and the Administration were soon to be at each other's throats, however, first under the fire of Morgenthau and his Comptroller of the Currency, next by the SEC and finally by Eccles and the Federal Reserve Board. The Comptroller's office, as the result of its bank examinations, charged on September 13,

1938 that Bank of America's assets, particularly its real estate loans, were unsatisfactory and forbade payment of dividends until the situation was remedied. Dividends were immediately paid by the bank and the wrangling went on until December when a "sweeping victory" was won by the bank, in the words of the bank's biographers, Marquis and Bessie James.[36] The victory terms included the bank's agreeing to add $30 million of new capital, again obligingly supplied by the RFC, which had become an investor in bank stocks as well as a lender under Jesse Jones. Meanwhile the SEC entered the fray as the New Deal showed a principled disregard for one of its original supporters. The SEC hearings started in 1939 and fizzled out in 1947, failing to prove the charges of false and misleading information in a Transamerica securities registration and the payment of dividends in excess of true earnings. The SEC probe was encouraged by Morgenthau who supplied the Commission with his examiners' figures. In its early stages it was not regarded with enthusiasm by Eccles who expressed doubts about the wisdom of the action, much to Morgenthau's chagrin.[37]

By 1943 Eccles had taken the lead in trying to contain Transamerica's mushrooming growth. When John N. Snyder succeeded Morgenthau in 1946, the Comptroller's office began to approve Transamerica branches again after a temporary freeze. Eccles had already requested Attorney General Tom Clark to prosecute Transamerica as a monopoly under the Sherman Antitrust Act but Clark deemed this approach would not be successful. A bank holding company bill aimed at Transamerica was then promoted by Eccles but it failed to get support in 1947. Finally, the Federal Reserve Board unanimously decided to conduct its own investigation of Transamerica in relation to a possible violation of the Clayton Act, which did not require proof of monopoly but only "being in a position to exert monopolistic power." Again a request for prosecution had failed even to elicit a response from the Attorney General's office.

Shortly thereafter President Truman demoted Eccles from his position as Chairman of the Board (his Chairmanship was about to expire) but asked him to stay on as a Board member. There was no doubt in Eccles's mind about the political pressure bearing down on Truman from California in a critical election year. Swallowing his pride, Eccles stayed on, disqualifying himself as a member of the proceedings. In the midst of the hearings in June 1950, the Comptroller of the Currency suddenly granted permission to Bank of America to acquire and branch twenty-eight Transamerica-owned banks. After doing so, Bank of America was forced by a court injunction, under threat of contempt, to transfer them back to Transamerica within thirty days. Under such strained conditions, the hearings finally came to an end in June 1951, having consumed 13,000 pages of testimony. Rudolph Evans, the presiding Board member, summarized the findings against Transamerica and its 667 banking offices in five Western states: "Its acquisitions," said Evans, ". . . have concentrated more economic power in one small group of men—perhaps only one man—than probably has ever happened before in the business life of our country . . . Not even the great railroad, steel, oil, tobacco or aluminum cases disclosed the existence of greater power in one organization directly affecting the economic life of so great a geographical area . . ."[38]

As in a Greek tragedy, death, departure and irony made their appearances. A. P. died on June 3, 1949, at age seventy-nine, having seen Bank of America, with $5 billion in assets, pass New York's Chase National Bank to become number one in size in 1945. His great bank had transformed California into a major, flourishing state and his influence on banking had been fundamental. Mario survived his powerful father by only three years, wasting his frail physique on the unimportant outcome of the case, too ill at the end to be told of the decision. Eccles immediately resigned. "Now the time has arrived," he stated, "when I can . . . return to my home."[39]

The irony of the case is that while Transamerica was awaiting a ruling on its appeal, it calmly completed the divestiture of the Bank of America stock which it had commenced fifteen years earlier, having been satisfied with minority control. At the time of the hearing decisions, it had only 7% of Bank of America stock left. Within two months after Mario's death at age fifty-seven on August 19, 1952, the remaining shares were sold. Mario was the last of the interlocking directors between Bank of America and Transamerica. The Federal Reserve Board had ruled that Transamerica was to divest itself of everything but the Bank of America. Instead Transamerica had accomplished the opposite. In July 1953 the United States Court of Appeals set aside the Federal Reserve Board ruling, declaring it had failed to prove the monopoly charges against Transamerica after all. Transamerica in turn decided to give up its other banks in the face of new bank holding company legislation. Occidental Life Insurance Company, which the hapless Elisha Walker picked up as a stray in 1930, is now the ninth largest life insurance company in the nation and the chief adornment of the new multi-billion dollar Transamerica empire.

Footnotes

CHAPTER 3

Marriner Eccles:

Stormy Petrel of the Federal Reserve

Marriner Eccles has written his own superb record of public service and intellectual pilgrimage, *Beckoning Frontiers* (New York, 1951), published as a valedictory upon his departure from Washington in 1951. The other side of his epic struggle with A. P. Giannini and Transamerica is well told in *Biography of A Bank* (New York, 1954), by Marquis James and Bessie R. James, which inevitably becomes a biography of the great A. P.

No one ventures into the history of the New Deal without gratefully acknowledging Arthur M. Schlesinger, Jr.'s monumental trilogy *The Age of Roosevelt* (Boston, 1957-1960), which combines history, philosophy, economics and the author's sure touch for the dramatic. James McGregor Burns's *Roosevelt: The Lion and the Fox* (New York, 1956), and William E. Leuchtenburg's *Franklin D. Roosevelt and the New Deal* (New York, 1963) are among the most valuable new analyses of FDR. Everyone in the New Deal, of course, seems to have written his memoirs or published his diaries, testifying to the literary and intellectual bent of the New Dealers *en masse.*

Caroline Bird's *The Invisible Scar* (New York, 1966) and Robert Bendiner's *Just Around the Corner* (New York, 1967) are helpful additions to understanding the Great Depression. Robert Lekachman's *The Age of Keynes* (New York, 1966) finally brings us a first-rate American biography of Keynes. *The Revolt of the Conservatives* (Boston, 1962) by George Wolfskill tells the fascinating story of the business world's opposition to the New Deal at its peak moment.

148   *Business at Bay: Critics and Heretics of American Business*

¹ Marriner S. Eccles, *Beckoning Frontiers* (New York, 1951), p. 156.

² *Ibid.*, p. 36.

³ *Ibid.*, p. 20.

⁴ Thurman W. Arnold, *The Symbols of Government* (New Haven, 1935), p. 125.

⁵ Eccles, *op. cit.*, p. 37.

⁶ *Ibid.*, p. 71.

⁷ *Ibid.*, pp. 83-84.

⁸ Arthur Mann, *La Guardia, A Fighter Against His Times* (Philadelphia, 1959), p. 306.

⁹ Eccles, *op. cit.*, p. 100.

¹⁰ *Fortune*, February 1935, p. 65.

¹¹ William E. Leuchtenburg, *Franklin D. Roosevelt and the New Deal* (New York, 1963), p. 21.

¹² *Ibid.*, p. 37.

¹³ Arthur M. Schlesinger, Jr., *The Crisis of the Old Order* (Boston, 1957), p. 136.

¹⁴ Eliot Janeway, *The Economics of Crisis* (New York, 1968), pp. 2-3; pp. 264 ff.

¹⁵ Adolf A. Berle, Jr., *Power Without Property* (New York, 1959), p. 16.

¹⁶ Robert Lekachman, *The Age of Keynes* (New York, 1966), p. 115. (The budget concept employed is the national income and product account method.)

[17] John M. Blum, *From the Morgenthau Diaries* (Boston, 1959), p. 69.

[18] Eccles, *op. cit.*, p. 124.

[19] *Ibid.*, p. 123.

[20] Arthur M. Schlesinger, Jr., *The Politics of Upheaval* (Boston, 1960), p. 651.

[21] Frances Perkins, *The Roosevelt I Knew* (New York, 1964), pp. 225-226.

[22] Eccles, *op. cit.*, pp. 132-133.

[23] John M. Blum, *op. cit.*, pp. 403-404.

[24] J. M. Keynes, *The General Theory of Employment, Interest and Money* (New York, 1936), p. 383.

[25] Marriner S. Eccles to the author, June 22, 1967.

[26] Eccles, *op. cit.*, p. 173.

[27] *Ibid.*, p. 213.

[28] *Ibid.*, p. 248.

[29] Arthur M. Schlesinger, Jr., *op. cit.*, pp. 271-272.

[30] George Wolfskill, *The Revolt of the Conservatives* (Boston, 1962), pp. 28 ff.

[31] Eccles, *op. cit.*, pp. 315-319.

[32] Raymond Clapper, "Banker or Bureaucrat?" *Review of Reviews* (July, 1935), pp. 22-25.

[33] Marquis James and Bessie R. James, *Biography of A Bank* (New York, 1954), p. 321.

[34] *New York Times*, April 28, 1935, Part III, p. 1.

[35] Marquis James and Bessie R. James, *op. cit.*, p. 389.

[36] *Ibid.*, p. 454.

[37] Chester T. Lane (counsel for SEC) in the Oral History Collection of Columbia University, 1951, pp. 493-496.

[38] *Time*, June 25, 1951, pp. 58-59.

[39] *American Banker*, June 22, 1951, p. 1.

Chapter 4

T. K. QUINN:
A Heretic in the House

Theodore K. Quinn was an underprivileged youth who quickly climbed the ladder at General Electric Company and then kicked the ladder away. "I quit monster big business," was the delayed but heretical announcement of this former youngest vice president of G. E.

Corporation executives are rarely heroic figures of self-sacrifice. They suffer fears and tensions as much as other people but their separations, especially near the top, are rarely voluntary. Nor are they often forced. Vice presidents are seldom given the sack. As in the Foreign Service of the State Department, it is more convenient to promote them or assign them to new duties out of harm's way. Too many people are involved in their previous promotions and there is always the tendency to close ranks over such tragic prospects.

Having quit G. E. in 1936, Quinn lived just long enough to see

151

three G. E. executives sentenced to jail in February 1961 as punishment for their part in the great electrical industry price-fixing conspiracy. One of them was William S. Ginn, at 45 earning $130,000 a year as head of the Turbine Division. Ginn was a vice president at 41, the current counterpart of Quinn and, like Quinn, was being groomed as a possible president of the nation's fourth largest enterprise in sales. No doubt the philosophical and mellow Quinn viewed the predicament of the younger man with self-projection if not pity. Still, in a *New Republic* article in March 1961, Quinn commented cynically that Chairman Ralph Cordiner had stopped short of firing Ginn though several lesser convicted executives had been discharged or demoted.[1] Ginn had won his reprieve when Cordiner royally decreed a "three year statute of limitations" (antitrust laws go back for five years) for company offenses, which just happened to cover Ginn. When Ginn returned from his thirty-day sentence, however, Cordiner icily dismissed him. Quinn was thus proved wrong and another exception was made to the generalization about the security of vice presidents.

The "incredible electrical conspiracy," as *Fortune* called it, was the most shocking exposure of big business shortcomings in modern times. The investigation was launched with unexpected vigor by the Justice Department of President Eisenhower and continued under Attorney General Robert F. Kennedy. The antitrust attorneys developed incontrovertible evidence—a good deal of it "state's evidence" supplied by frightened or vengeful executives—that some $7 billion worth of heavy electrical equipment had been sold over a period of seven years at secretly rigged prices to such customers as the Tennessee Valley Authority and private utilities throughout the country. G. E. carried off the honors, although twenty-nine other companies including Westinghouse were found guilty, along with a total of forty-nine top-drawer executives. The drama of the case, of course, rested in the almost unprecedented jail sentences given to the seven good organization men who claimed they were simply carrying out orders from above. Exotic codes, such as "phases of the moon," determined whose turn it was to win a sealed bid for giant transformers or turbines.

Federal Judge J. Cullen Ganey made it clear that he thought not all the guilty parties were in court. He found it incredible that the heads of G. E. and Westinghouse did not know what was going on in relation to such a large percentage of their sales and would gladly have sentenced them if he had the evidence. The corporate fines were $1,787,000, the merest fraction of these sales, but the purchasers of the price-fixed commodities were entitled to treble damages. As a result, G. E. alone paid out close to $200 million in claims to its outraged customers, whose executives had no choice but to collect, even if somewhat puzzled and apprehensive at the excessive morality bringing about their windfalls.

What happened to the cast? Cordiner and Robert Paxton, G. E. president, discreetly accelerated their own retirements. Most of the fired executives found other jobs including a major presidency for Ginn. The union leaders who had piously asked for Cordiner's resignation and sent games of "Monopoly" to the seven inmates returned to their normal activity of seeking wage increases. G. E. recovered from the trauma rather spectacularly. Its annual sales increased over 60% in the next seven years and its stock went up 50%, percentages indicating a continued respect for profitable pricing. The Justice Department in 1961 tried to get G. E. to sign a consent decree that it would not now *cut* prices to levels that would eliminate smaller competitors. G. E. archly refused and antitrust in relation to price conspiracy subsided with the advent of Democratic Administrations. The new order saw President Kennedy kindly admonish the stricken business community to "lift this shadow from its shoulder." A year later in April 1962, he was furiously engaged in threatening retaliation against U. S. Steel for ineptly raising the price of steel—a further instance of the dilemmas of pricing in a "mixed economy." In short, of all the perplexing areas of public policy, none are more elusive than the questions of the monopoly power of big business, its attendant price rigidities and the concept of "free enterprise." Was Judge Ganey really in tune with the times when he stated: "What is at stake here is the survival of the kind of economy under which America has grown to greatness, the free enterprise system."?

Some of the unreality of the situation is illustrated in a humorous *New York Times* ad run unwittingly by the Barclay Hotel (where competitors had surreptitiously met to discuss turbine prices) on February 2, 1960:

> Antitrust corporation secrets are best discussed in the privacy of an executive suite at the Barclay. It is convenient, attractive and financially practical.

II

Since our story is about men, some great and some not so great, whose lives reflect the actions and passions of twentieth century American business, a brief summary of T. K. Quinn's career and philosophy is in order. He was an articulate man and a prejudiced man, which helps establish a basis for useful discussion. His name is unknown beyond a small circle but this distinction is shared with the new élite of unknown personages who now head the billion dollar corporations he deplores. He is probably the only senior officer of big business who ever left the fold and then attacked ideologically the giant hand that fed him. Since his point of view is neither Marxian nor sour grapes, but in the American tradition of anti-bigness, he makes a credible witness. Over the years he was frequently called upon to testify before monopoly subcommittees of both the House and the Senate. In addition, he left a modest testament in his books and articles.

The background for his dissent from the Establishment is easily traced to his father. In his autobiography, *Giant Business: A Threat to Democracy*, T. K. Quinn tells about his engaging sire who was short on cash but long on ideas. A descendant of non-Catholic Irishmen from Limerick, Timothy Quinn was a Chicago labor crusader who expired on the platform at age eighty after a stirring oration to the Chicago Federation of Labor in 1932. The boy Ted had intimations of the father's greatness when at age eight they went for a swim in Lake Michigan and he saw for the first time knife gashes and bullet scars on his father's arms and legs, souvenirs of the wars between capital and labor. The father was a lion-hearted optimist, however, who gaily turned the boy's mind towards the great poets and the great contemporaries. In the Quinn household these latter were Eugene Debs, the labor martyr, Governor Altgeld, the tragically heroic figure of their own state of Illinois, William Jennings Bryan and Robert G. Ingersoll. Ingersoll the freethinker and agnostic, the man who bowed to no man, was the patron saint of the otherwise devout household. His influence was magnified by his close friendship with T. K.'s grandfather and namesake, Dr. Theodore Kinget Quinn, who appropriately was jailed for advocating birth control. Ingersoll's *The Liberty of Man, Woman and Child* rested near the family Bible and was the more worn of the two. T. K.'s favorite Ingersoll quotation may explain his subsequent fall from the grace of big business: "Take those chains from the human soul. Break those fetters. If I have no right to think, why have I a brain?"

The children of the "lower class" neighborhoods of pre-World War I Chicago had an uncomplicated vision of their world. It was too much with them for rejection, too harshly real for any dreams other than the American Dream of success and status. The key to upward mobility for T. K. and all his German, Irish, Scandinavian and Jewish classmates was education. College was out of the question but how many collegians might secretly envy the intoxication of T. K.'s first important book purchase at age eighteen when he already was holding down a factory job! The investment was in Dr. Eliot's *Five Foot Shelf of Harvard Classics*. Every Saturday the collector would meet him upon his return from work to collect the fifty cent instalments. Finally the instalments were completed and eventually the books were read. From then on, Quinn took pleasure in being known as a philosopher as well as a businessman. Harvard, mother of heretics as well as Presidents, had exerted its insidious influence.

T. K. had decided on law. Since there was no night law school in Chicago, he went to Cleveland where he landed a job at the

Cleveland Miniature Lamp Works at seven dollars a week and enrolled at the Cleveland Night Law School. Three years later he passed the Ohio bar examination with flying colors. He had done too well at the lamp works, however, and decided he liked it enough at the head office, National Lamp Works, to make a career of corporate managership.

In 1911, the United States Government, acting under the relatively new Sherman Antitrust Act, took one of the first of its long line of actions against the incorrigible General Electric Company. It forced General Electric to disclose to the public its secret control of the National Lamp Works which in turn controlled a dozen other bulb manufacturers including the Cleveland works. Gradually the comradeship and feeling of autonomy that T. K. and his fellow executives enjoyed at the National Lamp Works gave way to the forces of integration in the G. E. empire; but T. K. had already been marked as a comer and was on his way to the parent company itself. Amusingly, he tells of his important contribution towards getting around the law that prohibited control of the resale price of lamps. Instead of selling lamps to distributors and dealers, at Quinn's suggestion G. E. "consigned" them. The distributors and dealers thus became agents of G. E. rather than retailers and their prices could be maintained with impunity. Such ingenuity, which served its purpose of bolstering G. E.'s profits for several years, attracted him to the attention of Gerard Swope and Owen D. Young, the great leaders of G. E.'s post-World War I burst of growth.

Years later, when he was on the other side of the fence, Quinn was particularly eloquent about the "lamp bulb stranglehold" maintained by General Electric and Westinghouse, who still control about 80% of the market.[2] The public would find it difficult to get excited about these charges. Bulbs seem reasonably cheap. Few manufacturers would want to challenge the leadership of G. E. and Westinghouse in this field, even with the original patents now expired. And the 20% outside their control represents a vast number of bulbs. We will have to look for more compelling evidence against the giant corporations than the bulb monopoly.

III

From lamps, as bulbs were then known, T. K. jumped to appliances. In 1927, Swope made him head of G. E.'s new refrigerator department at the precocious age of thirty-four. He became a vice-president in 1930 in charge of all home appliances. Now the missionary element in T. K.'s personality came to life, released for the time being in the great American art of salesmanship.

The prosperous twenties were a good time for introducing a new product and within three years G. E. refrigerators rose from scratch to sales of $50 million a year. Quinn points out that as usual G. E. did not invent this product, which already was dominated by General Motors's Frigidaire and by Kelvinator. In fact, states Quinn, arguing against the popular assumption that big research creates new products, G. E. laboratories have produced no new consumer products that he knows of other than the household garbage grinder.

In the case of G. E.'s refrigerator, the Tom Edison of its famous mechanical feature was a lonely French monk, the Abbé Audiffren, who, working in seclusion, had somehow come across the idea of the hermetically sealed compressor now used in practically all refrigerators. G. E. developed the idea for kitchen use and came out with a box at the top of which was the well-remembered crown of condenser coils. This superstructure was not only repulsive aesthetically but was also a dust-catcher. Here the promotional talents of Quinn rose to the occasion. He named it the "Monitor" top, summoning up the heroic values of the revolving turret of the Civil War ironclad Navy vessel, and launched it as a virtue in a million dollar wave of advertising.

Price competition was the last thing either General Motors or General Electric wanted then or now and General Motors did not respond by cutting prices to meet the threat of G. E. refrigerators. Quinn was engaged in the type of competition that is a plain but often embarrassing fact for most of contemporary America's competitive enterprise. It is the competition of style, service, advertising, brand name or alternate choice rather than price. Quinn modestly acknowledges that most important of all for G. E.'s success were its immense capital resources and staying power. To this he added advertising, a national distributing organization and his new General Electric Credit Corporation, which offered that priceless ingredient, instalment credit. Of course, by 1931, a great oversight—the necessity for sustained employment—had paralyzed the land. G. E. limped along, managing to show profits largely because of its position in bulbs.

Operating as a top-ranking G. E. vice president in New York, the introspective Quinn felt vague yearnings of disbelief. He did not like the idea that his present and future lay in the hands of one man, Gerard Swope, although he claims that Swope dangled the succession in front of his eyes. The same Swope, however, reprimanded him for postponing a Sales Committee meeting to attend his father's funeral, the ultimate in petty testing for company devotion.

Offsetting his success on the job were other negative factors. His constant travels throughout the country were robbing him of his home life. G. E. was continually involved in antitrust proceedings. There was resentment against what he regarded as G. E.'s reactionary labor policy. Writing in 1948, T. K. reveals the ghost of his stiff-necked father urging him on:

> Eventually in the summer of 1935, I determined to resign. Being a symbol of so-called "success" was never going to satisfy me. My father had been a liberty-loving Irishman and a life-long fighter for the underdog. There I was on the wrong side of the fence. I disliked the centering of power in any one man or small group. The decision might be in my favor but that was beside the point. It was an autocratic decision in any event. I do not suppose that General Electric was much worse or much better than any other giant, impersonal corporation, but there was no satisfaction in that . . . I only knew that I wanted to get "unwound" and get into something —anything—else.[3]

This is drama in a minor key, to be sure, and the syndrome is too universal to evoke pity. Ironically, it is somewhat insincere to boot. T. K. did not go into the labor movement or on any other errand of mercy. Instead he walked straight into the plush world of Madison Avenue advertising, bearing with him the good wishes of all his colleagues and some fat General Electric appliance advertising contracts.

Like all of us, Quinn reads better through the blur of time or in the pages of approved biographies. There is no doubt that he was fed up with big business when he left but the withdrawal came in easy stages. This inconsistency gives him the flaw that one looks for in the better type of heretics.

Besides serving as president of Maxon, Inc., from 1936 to 1943, T. K. had the indiscretion to write his first book in 1943 called *Liberty, Employment and No More Wars.* A good deal of the book is in praise of big business:

> Let us oppose unfair taxes, persecution and unwarranted government restrictions that tend to destroy uselessly our great economic industrial and commercial organizations. Moreover, let us oppose the vain, costly, artificial attempts to preserve inefficiency, incompetence and pitifully small business in this new collective era.
>
> *   *   *
>
> Our large corporations have worked out, better than government, practical ways and means of getting men to work together in a common cause. Indeed they have done such a good job of it that human adjustments and equilibrium of desires and loyalties beyond anything attained by government have been achieved by private industry.[4]

General Electric grasped rather feebly at this book to answer Quinn whenever he appeared as a witness against big business or General Electric. The plain fact of the matter is Quinn changed his mind but not officially until 1948 when he wrote a small book called *I Quit Monster Business.* One would suppose a man has the right to change his mind, just as business has the right to change its product, without being pilloried for the old model. The implication is that Quinn is intellectually dishonest and thus a discredited authority. This argument is unworthy of a $5 billion corporation which must meet the critics both in Congress and elsewhere on a loftier plane to insure its own credibility. After all, nothing succeeds like success and the giants can well afford to treat the giant-killers kindly. Big business often is at the mercy of its human assets, however, who tend to try to frame a Ralph Nader, as General Motors did in 1966, or to impugn the intellect of a thinking ex-vice president. Thus General Electric's public relations division even today issues a standard broadside inelegantly entitled "WHICH BOOK BY T. K. QUINN D'YA READ?", setting forth side-by-side contradictory statements by the Quinn of 1943 and the Quinn of 1953, when asked for more cogent information about their alumnus.

T. K.'s first starring role as an apostate executive came in 1949 when he appeared before Representative Emanuel P. Celler's House Subcommittee on the Study of Monopoly Power. Congressman Celler is a distinguished public servant who has sought to keep the limelight on monopoly trends without unreasonably restricting the cornucopia of mass production which he recognizes as an established benefit of big business. Celler in the House and Estes Kefauver in the Senate were a formidable team in the forties and fifties against unhealthy monopolies and conspiracies. Unable to find popular support of the groundswell type that ushered in the antitrust laws at the turn of the century, when big business tweaked the nose of government itself, they have at least reminded today's tamer business to stay in line. Together they added the Celler-Kefauver amendment to the Clayton Act which covers the former loophole of monopolistic acquisitions of assets rather than corporate stock. Kefauver was particularly effective in the drug industry, whose conspiracies were matched by its testing outrages such as that of the drug thalidomide. The cornucopia of the pharmacoepia was less benevolent than it seemed.

Before examining T. K. Quinn as a witness against big business, a further chapter in his career is relevant. Never really at home in

advertising, although Maxon's billings doubled while he was with
the firm, he responded in 1943 to the call of his former associate,
Defense Mobilizer Charles E. Wilson, president of G. E., to join
the war effort in Washington on the War Production Board. For
one dollar a year, Quinn's assignment was to be Director-General
of the War Production Drive, a special campaign organized to
create joint management and labor committees in the war plants
in order to increase production.

Quinn was a great success in this position, increasing the plant
committees to 5,000 by the time he left a few years later. Although
the committees were purely advisory, they were viewed with some
suspicion by both employers and unions who wished to keep their
distance from each other even during the emergency. From his
foxhole in Washington, Quinn publicly reproached Henry Ford,
president of Ford Motor Company and Alfred P. Sloan, chairman
of General Motors, for "paying only superficial attention" to establishing his committees while loafing and slow-downs were rampant
in Detroit.[5] This attack on America's arsenal was immediately
rebutted. General Motors's Charles E. Wilson telephoned General
Electric's Charles E. Wilson who issued a statement that T. K.
had made a mistake. In 1949, the second Wilson said T. K. was
mistaken again, this time before the Celler Subcommittee. "He is a
very able gentleman," said Wilson to Congressman Celler. "May I,
since he made those statements in *I Quit Monster Business*, just
give you for the benefit of the record some of the statements in this
(other) book that are completely contrary . . .?"[6]

When Quinn left WPB, however, it was with the warm com-
mendations of his boss Donald W. Nelson. He now planned to go
into business for himself and organized a cooperative group of
home-appliance distributors who would market a line of appliances
produced by about thirty smaller manufacturers. The distributors
included some ex-G. E. luminaries such as Rex Cole in New York
City. With Quinn as president of the managing company, a nationwide promotion of the brand name "Monitor" started with a double-
page, four color ad in the *Saturday Evening Post* in November,
1945. *Fortune* magazine publicized the venture, dubbing Quinn

"The Philosophical Promoter" and praising his recent book in defense of big business. Quinn the economist, *Fortune* noted approvingly, "assails existing antitrust legislation as 'mental windmills of outmoded competition,' thoughtlessly designed 'to prevent our economy from evolving naturally.'"[7]

Monitor was a failure and one wonders if Quinn's break with big business was related to this failure as much as anything else. The idea was good but it rarely has worked in the American marketplace, unlike outright franchising of independents which has worked. Only in the case of some small grocery retailers or in the farming business has an association of smaller units organized for cooperative merchandising and advertising been successful. In Monitor's case, according to Quinn, the steel shortage of 1948 dealt the death blow, even though 1947 sales to distributors exceeded $10 million. The steel shortage, connected with the pre-Korean cold war, did not hurt the big manufacturers. They did not get all the steel they wanted but they all were allocated enough to beat previous sales records. Meanwhile, Monitor's manufacturers were forced to buy in the gray market at excessive prices. Most of them gave up or merged or became fabricators for the giants who could provide them with steel. Quinn's roll call of Monitor manufacturers who disappeared or merged is a requiem for smaller business versus the giants: John W. Young Company of Fall River, Massachusetts for washers, Electromatic of Detroit for ranges, Crosley of Cincinnati for washers, Savage Arms of Utica for home freezers, Quaker Heater of Chicago for heaters, Globe-American of Kokomo, Indiana for gas ranges. While forces other than the steel shortage may have been more responsible for Monitor's demise, the resentment against the giants by Quinn was traumatic.

IV

In 1962, Quinn's final book, *Unconscious Public Enemies*, was published posthumously. Some of the chapters had appeared as articles in *The New Republic* and *Nation* magazines, publications with an anti-big business bias, to which he brought rare credentials. Using this book as his valedictory and bearing in mind his unique personal history, his crusade can be summarized. Hopefully we can then relate these thoughts to a reasonably balanced appraisal of bigness, antitrust and some of the options facing American business.

Quinn had the dramatist's flair for overstating his case. Big business is termed the "public enemy," as though it deserves billing with subversives and the F. B. I.'s ten most wanted men. The difference is that business does not even know it is an enemy of the people.

The dimensions of the American corporate structure are always amazing and quickly forgotten. Since Berle and Means wrote their epochal analysis demonstrating the progressively increasing concentration of corporate assets and control in 1932, the facts have been treated like the weather, interesting but not much to be done about it. Quinn ticks off the well-known score. There are about seventy billionaire industrial corporations in the country, many with hundreds of thousands of employees. (General Motors now employs 750,000 persons, one out of every one hundred of our work force.) More than half of American workers are employed by less than one per cent of the corporations and the one per cent represents over half of the total corporate wealth. More to the point, since corporations flourish at the stroke of a pen, making this ratio meaningless, the top 500 corporations control over two-thirds of all corporate assets. These facts no longer boggle the imagination since we are used to size in all aspects of contemporary life. Interestingly, a relatively new study (Professor Adelman's of M. I. T.) has been receiving widespread attention. The rate of growth of big business assets in relation to total business assets has long since failed to reach the saturation point predicted in the thirties.[8] Apparently it has tapered off at 45 per cent, moving "at the pace of a glacial drift," as Berle now acknowledges, rather than an avalanche.[9] Still, size and heavy concentration among the few is the dominant feature of our business landscape.

Granted the dimensions, Quinn proceeds to more subjective

routes. He finds the leadership of big business deficient in morality because it is a self-perpetuating hierarchy accountable only to the inner control group, consisting mainly of the trustees of banks, funds and other institutions which vote controlling blocks of stock. In addition, he notes that the top men are all too likely to represent nepotism and luck rather than ability in obtaining their exalted jobs and expense accounts. This comment about how to succeed can be dismissed summarily but the comment about personal morality is heavy-handed. Veblen's small-town merchants are capable of as much cupidity as corporation presidents. If businessmen as a class err, it is because the rules are not tight enough. If they are too powerful, that is another matter but a critic of business cannot mount a sound case on the other person's morality.

Quinn recognizes that cutthroat competition is out of the question but he charges that the administered (follow the leader) price system maintains prices and profits at excessive levels. If prices are going to be controlled, he wants the final decision to be public rather than private. He therefore would subscribe to a permanent Wages and Hours Board, a proposal that would lose him the labor vote in addition to the already lost business vote. This would be fitting as certainly strong unions contribute to price rigidity wherever there is administered pricing.

T. K. takes exception to the claim that there are four million independent businesses in the country, stating this includes hundreds of thousands of hot-dog and coffee stands. Two hundred thousand gas station operators, for example, are under the iron control of the giant oil companies and tens of thousands of other entrepreneurs exist at the sufferance of big business purchasing agents from day to day. Striking hard at General Motors, the biggest of them all, he cites the peonage of automobile dealers who are forced to sign one-way contracts with manufacturers and to take on cars they cannot sell. It is not easy to feel sorry for the auto dealers, most of whom are the big men in their towns and cities, dedicated to high living, hunting trips and boosterism. It is true their contracts were one-way. Perhaps they owe as much to Quinn as anyone else that a federal law was passed in 1956 outlawing such contracts after the dealers and Quinn protested to the House anti-monopoly subcommittee. Since then the auto companies have set up dealers' grievance councils, which work effectively and remind us that the giants can be curbed in many ways.

Quinn is quite right that the vast number of suppliers and sub-contractors for big business live at its mercy. In the present era of uneasy corporate power, however, something similar to the bomb's balance of terror does exist among the giants. General Motors and Ford may compete energetically with each other but the last thing in the world they want is the disappearance of Chrysler. It was bad enough to have lost Packard, Kaiser-Frazer and Studebaker. They realize that public opinion just would not stand for the ultimate use of their market power either among themselves or their satellites.

In his writing and testimony, Quinn repeatedly lapses into the "lost values" school of big business criticism. Here we have the most enticing and the most hopeless argument against big business. It is a native American strain which has vaulted from the Populism of the nineties to the New Freedom of Woodrow Wilson and the "curse of bigness" of his mentor, Louis D. Brandeis. Then on to the second New Deal and the TNEC investigations of 1938 and finally into the hands of the National Federation of Independent Business and certain Fourth of July orators. It turns back sentimentally to what young Walter Lippmann, differing from Brandeis, called a "nation of villagers," ruggedly independent, free and enterprising.

Brandeis, of course, was a sophisticated millionaire corporation lawyer who, like Quinn, turned against his former clients, undoubtedly with better reason. He was repelled by the first crude wave of mergers that saw the emergence of U. S. Steel, Standard Oil and similar trusts. The business oligarchy of his day was still a threat to government itself and only a few years back had shamefully dominated the Senate. Moreover, Brandeis had a lively fear of the spreading power of the uncontrolled financial interests as revealed in the Pujo Committee investigations. Since then the big corporations have at least become reasonably independent of Wall Street, meeting most of their investment requirements from huge amounts of cash in their retained earnings. Wall Street in turn has been domesticated by the government and by its own institutional reforms. The misgivings about a business-banker alliance have been replaced by other problems, notably that of a business-military alliance. At any rate, Quinn's revival of the Brandeisian concept that bigness is an evil in itself is archaic.

Because it is archaic, it fails to enlist the support of liberals who have long made their accommodation with giant business and are more concerned with controlling its power than dismembering it. Thus Quinn was saddened to note the defection of David Lilienthal, the TVA and Atomic Energy Commission administrator. A former New Dealer and disciple of Brandeis, Lilienthal wrote *Big Business: A New Era* in 1953, praising big business for its economic wonders; for its actually having stimulated competition and benefitted small business; and because "in Bigness we have the material foundation of a society which can further the highest values of men."[10] The irony of the two men rushing past each other to exchange positions was lost on T. K. "I suspect," Quinn wrote, "Mr. Lilienthal knows that we cannot welcome monster-big, collectivistic business without also welcoming a socialistic solution of our political problems. Karl Marx understood this . . ."[11]

The fear that General Motors and the other billionaire corporations are subverting America towards socialism is the final strand in Quinn's philosophy. It is one that establishes him in a class by himself as far as business critics are concerned.

> Monopoly and oligarchy are not compatible with democracy. This nation cannot long endure only partially free under conditions of concentrated economic power . . . The alternative is the abandonment of capitalism in favor of some other system for use rather than profit. Capitalism is presently weakening itself by its excesses.[12]

Most contemporary critics of big business, including T. K.'s fellow authors on *The New Republic*, start out with a cheerful bias in favor of socializing the giants if necessary. Quinn, on the other hand, is an unregenerate conservative in this respect, and a consistent one as well. Like Barry Goldwater, Quinn evokes American pieties of the frontier and deplores the decline of the old values and lost individualism. It is a safe assumption that Goldwater did not get Quinn's vote, however, as Quinn is unable to make the distinction between the evils of big government and the virtues of big business which comes so easily to the Goldwater faction.

For that matter, the legions of small businessmen—there are still about four million non-farm, self-employed in the country—were for the most part in the Goldwater camp. John Bunzel, in *The American Small Businessman*, has given us a probe in depth of the attitudes and philosophy of these entrepreneurs and their trade associations. It is true that they possess the fundamental virtues of thrift, industry and independence which have enriched the American character. They have not been neglected by a friendly government, as evidenced by the permanent House and Senate Small Business Committees and frequent resolutions on their behalf. There is a question of whether they can live up to their ideals, however, especially their expected devotion to competitive principles. They are, no doubt, happy to see antitrust actions against big business, but they also vigorously support price maintenance laws such as the Robinson-Patman Act of 1936 and anti-chain store legislation. Often they are not the enlightened examples of democratic leadership one would hope for, but instead anti-union, anti-civil rights, pro-crank supporters of right wing activities. In the final analysis, they too are for big business, so long as it does not directly impinge on their own success.

Thus Quinn is a lonely prophet warning us of the perils of bigness. He does not shrink from laying out a program consistent with his analysis. He would permit medium-sized corporations but would divide up General Motors and all the other giants into several survivors just large enough to obtain the efficiency of large scale production. (On efficiency, incidentally, Quinn speaks from experience that giantism is almost a guarantee of inefficiency carried along by other strengths. In all fairness, he should be granted this point. American big business, with its proliferation of white collar specialists, does contain an amazing amount of feather-bedding at the desk level. Typically, a corporation in profit trouble, such as Chrysler a few years ago, can eliminate a third of its administrative people and suffer through until time to rehire. Many people concerned about the effects of automation and employing an increasing population would see this as a virtue rather than defect of the system.) The giant corporations would have public directors appointed by the President to accelerate their decentralization and to limit their growth afterwards. There would be no thought of nationalizing industry. The giants would be forced into their new roles of regulated public utilities rather than private enterprises through prohibitive taxation on excessive size or sales. The threat of collectivism would be met and the quality of our life would improve.

T. K. Quinn could sincerely claim a goal of economic democracy and pluralism quite in harmony with the American goal of political democracy and diversity. The supreme fact of modern technology in the twentieth century, however, makes the active pursuit of such a goal a fantasy. Throughout the industrialized world increasing bigness in economic organization is inevitable, regardless of the sheltering political form. It seems to be as congenial to the progress of Russia as it is to America. Bigness has not only taken over business but perhaps much more seriously all aspects of our cultural life. Still it does not follow that billionaire corporations and democratic government are incompatible. It does follow that the responsible use of business power is a major concern. This will be considered in the following chapter.

V

But first back to Judge Ganey's court. There were no trials because the defendants and their corporations thought it best to plead either guilty or *nolo contendere*, a plea by the defendant that he is not guilty but will not contest the charge. Somehow the grand jury indictments never captured the public imagination as did other current scandals in the business world. The shock of the rigged TV quiz shows in 1959 hit Americans in the pit of the stomach—Shoeless Joe Jackson all over again—but rigged prices on heavy electrical equipment was another matter. The subsequent scandals of Bobby Baker, political influence peddler, and Billie Sol Estes, swindler of finance companies, were in the established tradition of greed, high living and ultimate punishment. In fact, had it not been for Senator Kefauver's determination to hold Senate Antitrust and Monopoly Committee hearings on the electrical case a few months after the jail sentences were completed and the witnesses could appear before him, a good deal of the record would never have been made public at all. The G. E. executives, fired to the last man, were more talkative than the Westinghouse executives, whose company took no action against them.

Having pleaded guilty or *nolo*, the defendants were at the mercy of the court. Judge Ganey listened to the recitals of the impeccably good citizenship of the veteran, near-the-top executives arrayed before him. No one expected jail sentences but there was a threatening uncertainty in the air. Since 1890, corporations had been in and out of antitrust trouble, depending on the changing attitudes of Presidential Administrations and the energies and budgets of their enforcement agencies. There was little shame attached to price-fixing violations, or, for that matter, to charges of monopoly. The fines were paid, or consent decrees not to repeat offenses entered into, whereupon government and corporation lawyers retired until the next skirmish. Jail sentences, if any, were usually suspended in cases of price conspiracy, the corporations rather than the individuals being viewed as the offenders. In 1959, however, an ominous note was struck in a case involving five medium-sized garden tool manufacturers in the midwest. For the first time in antitrust history, a defendant pleading *nolo* was sentenced to a ninety-day jail sentence by a Federal Judge in Ohio, although the federal prosecutor had recommended only a fine. One of the vice presidents, who claimed he had been promised leniency for pleading *nolo*, left the courtroom to drive to the U. S. Marshal's office to be taken to prison, pulled off the road and shot himself.[13] The shock of this precedent brought about some of the key confessions which enabled the Justice Department to break the case before Judge Ganey.

The outgoing Administration appointees in the Justice Department had recommended to Judge Ganey jail sentences for thirty of the individual defendants. The new Attorney General, Robert F. Kennedy, stated that he had reviewed the recommendations for sentences and strongly recommended that they be imposed.

Judge Ganey then sentenced the hapless seven to jail. He stated that the defendants had:

> . . . flagrantly mocked the image of that economic system of free enterprise which we profess to the country and destroyed the model which we offer today as a free world alternative to state control and eventual dictatorship.

Having defined our economic system so surely in terms of price competition and divided the world so neatly into free and dictatorial, Judge Ganey turned to popular social commentary:

> . . . in the great number of these defendants' cases, they were torn between conscience and an approved corporate policy, with the rewarding objectives of promotion, comfortable security and large salaries—in short the organization or the company man, the conformist, who goes along with his superiors and finds balm for his conscience in additional comforts and the security of his place in the corporate set-up.

The irony of the situation lies in the fact that these superiors, organization men themselves only a few years back, like Judge Ganey preached free enterprise and competitive pricing when they knew it did not exist in most of big business and has not for years. In fact, it had not existed during the entire business lifetime of the jailed defendants. Each of the defendants testified he had been taught the ropes of price-fixing, conspiratorially or otherwise, by his superiors all the way up the ladder.

The crudities of the secret meetings and the stupidity of being caught were the real offenses. There was even a lesson to learn from what happened when members of the price-fixing club broke the rules under pressure from time to time. Westinghouse became the hero of Wall Street in the late 1960's, its growth rate being the best of the top 500 industrial companies. Its dark days began with tremendous overproduction of heavy electrical equipment in the 1950's. It was forced into a deadly price war with G. E. and others which had similarly miscalculated. Discounts ran as much as 50 per cent, the years of the "white sales," as the distraught division executives later recalled them. These overzealous executives, for the good of the company and their jobs, thereupon eased the crunch by entering into another round of conspiracy leading to the débacle of 1961. Westinghouse's resurgence began in 1963 when a new president made cost consciousness a "way of life" at Westinghouse and abolished over 4,000 white collar jobs. Now a favorite investment of foundations, pensions funds and universities, Westinghouse presumably does not indulge in price-fixing conspiracies, but its prices strangely are close to competition and high enough to produce record earnings. As Galbraith points out in *The New Industrial State*, our giant corporations need stability, both in pricing and demand, to meet the disciplines of their long-term planning and rising labor costs. If they do not get these benefits our economic health is jeopardized. Galbraith, once a champion of antitrust as a countervailing force giving equilibrium to American capitalism, has second thoughts on the subject of size and has always recognized the propriety of administered prices. He simply acknowledges that such pricing is characteristic of our industrial state. Moreover, it works reasonably well and efficiently.[14] The modern corporation is too sensible to indulge in ruinous price-cutting and too intent on increasing sales—the real competitive goal—to price itself out of the market.

How would Galbraith sit on Judge Ganey's bench? He would find both Judge and Attorney General defective in their economics and presumptuous in their sanctification of the conventional wisdom of the so-called competitive, free enterprise system. He would reluctantly have to rule against the defendants—they were obviously guilty of breaking the law as well as guilty of ineptitude— but he might comment that the law, as Charles Dickens put it, "is an ass." At least the law, which was originally intended to prevent market power from raising and lowering prices to achieve monopoly in an era of scarcity, must now be regarded as an archaic law.

Even T. K. Quinn refused to gloat over the misfortunes of the executives whose life he would not lead. Cutthroat competition, he noted, could reduce prices below cost and finally force factories to close. The conspirators simply had the bad luck to be in custom-built lines, requiring, so it seemed, meetings to administer prices.[15] What annoys him particularly is the hypocrisy of the free-enterprising spokesmen for the giants, most of whom issued absolute disclaimers for their subordinates' activities:

> The industrialists who are determined to be free to set their own profits and prices so bitterly resent the implications of any kind of governmental control that they favor the alternate antitrust laws and price competition. What they really want is market stabilization, every last one of them, with prices, wages and profits fixed by themselves to serve their own purposes and this simply cannot continue to be permitted, not if we put the public interest first and the good of all against private greed.[16]

Well done, Galbraith would comment, but he would lose Quinn on the score of comprehensive government economic planning, which Galbraith foresees as the condition which should precede relaxation of the antitrust laws.

Meanwhile, the devotees of antitrust in the Administration and Congress seek to formulate policy in the public interest. They are aware of the paradox in a situation that does not dismember the giants but tries to prevent the emergence of new giants who might compete on stronger terms with the older giants. They proceed on the theory of lesser evils. Meanwhile, they face the problem of the unprecedented merger fever forced by technology and estate taxes.

Thorstein Veblen by Edward B. Child. About the time he was at the
University of Chicago, 1892-1907. The painting is in Sterling Hall
at Yale University.

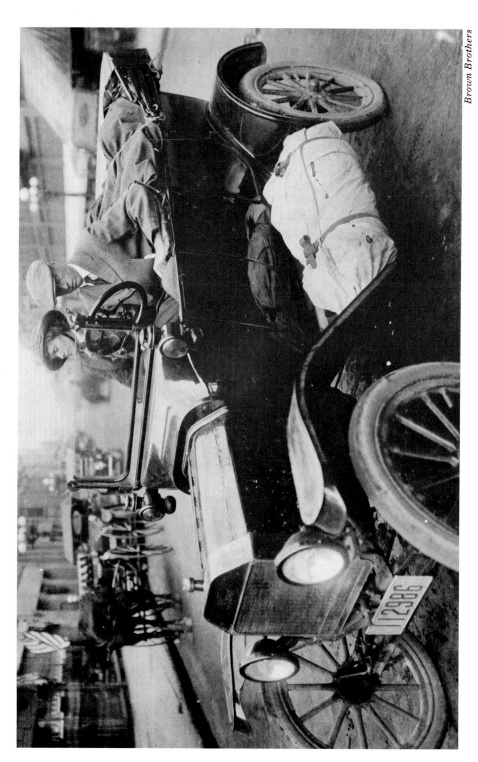

Sinclair Lewis. With his first wife, Grace Hegger Lewis, 1916. They travelled from Sauk Centre, Minnesota to Carmel, California in their

Marriner Eccles. About 1938. He stands between Carter Glass and Congressman Henry Steagall. Note the father-son resemblance between the adversaries.

T. K. Quinn. As author and business critic, 1953.

Cyrus Eaton. Hosting a lunch for Soviet Premier Khrushchev at New York's Hotel Biltmore, September 26, 1960.

Adolf Berle. With President John F. Kennedy, July 7, 1961.

Ken Wittenberg

Michael Harrington, 1968.

Los Angeles Times

Herbert Marcuse. At San Diego campus of University of California,
August 1968.

A new problem is the unexpected emergence of the conglomerates which so far have escaped the probing of antitrust.

Conspiracy actions are still being initiated but jail sentences no longer seem necessary. A good deal of government success lies in mergers and conspiracies which never hatch for fear of the consequences. *Fortune*, reasonable spokesman for big business, has called for a complete liberalization of the policy towards bigness and restraint of competition. This would have to start with a new set of antitrust laws as the Supreme Court, indicates Max Ways, *Fortune* editor, is out of its depth in these matters.[17] On the other hand, *Fortune* surprisingly supports action such as that taken against the electrical industry conspirators. It was a case of individual moral lapse, states *Fortune*,[18] leaving to critics like Galbraith and Berle the underlying question of reality versus outmoded principles.

Footnotes

CHAPTER 4

T. K. Quinn:

A Heretic in the House

T. K. Quinn wrote and published the four books mentioned in this chapter in the period from 1943 to 1962. He also contributed articles to *The New Republic* and *The Nation*, the latter of which saluted him as "T. K. Quinn, an old friend and a valiant fighter against that concentration of corporate power which represents one of the greatest threats to American democracy," when he died in 1961.

For the story of the great electrical price conspiracy, John Herling, a newspaperman, has written a most competent, balanced and painstakingly thorough account, *The Great Price Conspiracy* (Washington, 1962). *Fortune's* Richard Austin Smith told all in a lively article, "The Incredible Electrical Conspiracy" (April and May 1961), leading T. K. Quinn to marvel at the way *Fortune* had become more objective through the years.

This excellent coverage, supplemented by the transcripts of the Kefauver hearings, provided major portions for books by Walter Goodman, *All Honorable Men* (New York, 1963) and Fred J. Cook, *The Corrupted Land* (New York, 1966). Here we have passionate reporters, thinly veiling their distaste for corporation ethics and organization men, laying it on business in high-spirited, muckraking style.

A valuable summary of the dilemmas of antitrust may be found in Richard Hofstadter's "What Happened to the Antitrust Movement?" in Earl F. Cheit, *The Business Establishment* (New York, 1964). The case for and against antitrust is fairly set forth in *Fortune Readings* in *The Regulated Businessman* (New York, 1966).

John H. Bunzel's *The American Small Businessman* (New York, 1955) is a fascinating analysis of the beliefs and creeds of this venerated group in the American body economic. Like many university professors, Bunzel finds meanness and parochialism in this vestigial group. In turn, the professors feel an uneasy kinship with enlightened corporate executives, perha, s because both universities and business have succumbed to bigness.

[1] T. K. Quinn, "General Electric," *The New Republic* (March 20, 1961), pp. 10-11.

[2] T. K. Quinn, "The Lamp Bulb Stranglehold," *The New Republic* (February 27, 1961), pp. 9-10.

[3] T. K. Quinn, *Giant Business: Threat to Democracy* (New York, 1953), p. 159.

[4] T. K. Quinn, *Liberty, Employment and No More Wars* (New York, 1943), p. 83, p. 116.

[5] *New York Times*, December 23, 1943, p. 12.

[6] Testimony before the special subcommittee of the Judiciary Committee of the House of Representatives on November 30, 1949, p. 46.

[7] *Fortune*, October, 1945, pp. 279-280.

[8] M. A. Adelman, "The Measurement of Industrial Concentration," *Review of Economics and Statistics* (November, 1951), pp. 269-296.

[9] Adolf A. Berle, *The 20th Century Capitalist Revolution* (New York, 1954), pp. 25-26.

[10] David E. Lilienthal, *Big Business: A New Era* (New York, 1953), p. 190.

[11] T. K. Quinn, "Too Big," *The Nation* (March 7, 1953), p. 210.

[12] T. K. Quinn, *Unconscious Public Enemies* (New York, 1962), p. 109.

[13] John Herling, *The Great Price Conspiracy* (Washington, 1962), p. 11.

[14] J. K. Galbraith, *The New Industrial State* (Boston, 1967), p. 185.

[15] Quinn, *op. cit.*, p. 166.

[16] *Ibid.*, p. 167.

[17] Max Ways, "Antitrust in an Era of Radical Change," *Fortune* (March, 1967 — Supplement), p. 152.

[18] Richard Austin Smith, "The Incredible Electrical Conspiracy," *Fortune* (May, 1961), p. 224.

Chapter 5

CYRUS EATON:
Khrushchev's Favorite Capitalist

PART I

The most famous businessman in this century's mid-passage is Cyrus Eaton in his mid-eighties. Whenever American businessmen are charged with being colorless, other-directed conformists, they can point with mingled pride and horror to this giant variant in the nest of capitalism.

He spans this century like the pages of history itself, emerging as one of the most durable capitalists of all time. Starting logically enough as the office boy of John D. Rockefeller shortly before the Panic of 1907, he proceeded to make $100 million on his own in the vicious, dog-eat-dog, stock-jobbing style of the roaring twenties, only to be reduced to shattering financial and personal oblivion in the crash of the thirties. His comeback was in the form of a reincarnation, this time as a New Dealing, government-borrowing, labor-loving, Wall Street-hating wheeler-dealer who made his $100 million and more all over again.

Thus Eaton is one of the few American businessmen to be both a titan in the sense that Theodore Dreiser meant it for the robber barons at the beginning of the century and a tycoon as *Time* and *Fortune* popularized the word for contemporary businessmen whose affairs stagger the imagination. Now in his final years, he courts posterity in still another role, that of the crusader for peace, the bridge between American capitalism and its middle-aged bogeyman, the Russia of Khrushchev and Kosygin.

Behind the legend there is the man himself, as enigmatic as the Russia which has taken him to its heart, exhibited him on its TV to millions of viewers, sent Deputy Premier Mikoyan to Cleveland in 1959 with a gift of a troika sleigh and three white horses and finally awarded him the Lenin Peace Prize in 1960. His statement upon receiving the prize, which none of his fellow capitalists would touch with a ten-foot pole, is typical of the infuriating logic with which he confounds his critics:

> Such recognition of a capitalist provides new evidence of what I am sure is the sincere interest of the Soviet people and their government in peace for all mankind. I am firmly convinced that men of conflicting beliefs can reach a meeting of the minds if they are determined to do so.
>
> In working for peace I take lasting satisfaction in following the proud tradition of two of America's greatest industrial leaders, Andrew Carnegie and Henry Ford.[1]

Only a man with a sly sense of humor would remind his fellow Americans that if they attack him they are attacking two of America's most venerated business heroes. At the same time, only a man of Eaton's benign capitalist arrogance would assume that the capacity for making millions necessarily endows a man with the capacity for statesmanship. Yet such qualities are part of the charm and fascination of Cyrus Eaton. They have won him not only the praise of a host of European intellectual and political leaders but also of Franklin D. Roosevelt, Harry S. Truman and for a brief period Dwight D. Eisenhower.

Eaton is such an original phenomenon on the American business scene that he defies comparison. In appearance he is tall, slender, silvery-haired and courtly. So was Bernard Baruch, for example, but Baruch was all hard facts and common sense, whereas Eaton has in him a touch of the poet. In fact Eaton quotes poetry frequently in a most unbusinesslike way, revealing a romanticism which probably further draws him to Russia, the only country where poetry has box-office appeal. For a contrasting figure, there is Howard Hughes, certainly as famous in America as Eaton and many times richer. But Hughes the aging playboy, wearing tennis sneakers and operating mysteriously from his headquarters in Las Vegas, is as far removed from the non-smoking, non-drinking Eaton as Cash McCall is from Daddy Warbucks.

A more likely suggestion is to view Eaton as a character straight out of the plays of George Bernard Shaw. He represents the eccentric, erudite millionaire more familiar in the English tradition than the American. In his restrained good humor and his preposterous ability to stand accepted ideas on their ears and make them credible, Eaton is none other than Shaw's Sir Andrew Undershaft, the cynical merchant of munitions who drives his daughter Major Barbara to tears as he gently dispels all her myths about the morality of millionaires. Eaton of course would prefer to be known as the merchant of peace as he attempts to open the eyes of his fellow capitalists to the immorality of their attitudes toward the Russians and atomic armament. In this pursuit, he is both flattered and honored to have the friendship and support of Lord Bertrand Russell, the aged British philosopher who resembles Eaton in being greater than fiction.

Eaton's favorite photograph is a magnificent study by the famed Yousuf Karsh. Adorning the April 1966 cover of *Finance* magazine ("All the News of the Hire of the Dollar"), he looks for all the world like a Renaissance cardinal as he stands in his scarlet-red hunting jacket. In his hands he carries his riding crop like a scepter and also as a symbol of almost sixty years of happy residence on his eight hundred-acre Acadia Farms in Northfield, Ohio. In the background are his books which characterize the frustrated intellectual, another American achiever in a spotty line from Teddy Roosevelt to John F. Kennedy who prefers the after-hours company of anyone but businessmen. Rounding off the photograph's composition is a globe of the world, turned appropriately to afford a view of the Russian subcontinent.

Karsh omitted one element that must be considered in the total man. Always unpredictable, Eaton married Anne Kinder Eaton in 1957 when she was thirty-five and he seventy-four. A poised, articulate Vassar graduate, the previously divorced Anne has been confined to a wheel chair since a polio attack in 1946. She has been his intrepid companion ever since their marriage, sharing completely his views on poetry and the Russians and creating news in her own right as she led the vast peace demonstration before the United Nations building on the cold and rainy day of April 15, 1967. Her solid American background and social position further confuse the detractors of these unlikely Russian sympathizers. On a Mike Douglas show on April 19, 1962, her answer to the inevitable "Are you a Communist?" question was classic in its feminine logic: "Oh don't be silly," she gasped, "No, I am not a Communist. I am a dyed-in-the-wool capitalist." Thus Cyrus Eaton, joining the ranks of elderly men that include Count Pucci, Pablo Casals, Edward Steichen, Supreme Court Justice Douglas and Karsh himself, each of whom has married a woman half his age, counts his blessings.

II

He was born in Pugwash, Nova Scotia in 1883, the son of the village storekeeper. In his teens he came to Cleveland to visit his uncle Charley Eaton, minister of the Euclid Avenue Baptist Church where the great John D. taught Sunday school on his day of rest from the ruthless elimination of competition in the great era of free enterprise. He had already made up his mind to be a minister and he adored his Uncle Charley who was only sixteen years his senior. He actually became a lay Baptist preacher during his college years but the exposure to Rockefeller was more than his ideals could stand.

Rockefeller seems to have had a way with ministers, uncovering in them rather impressive gifts in the world of affairs. Only a few years ago, in 1902, Rockefeller had found his fortune increasing beyond control and had sought advice from another Baptist preacher, the forty-year old Frederick T. Gates. Gates's performance in business under Rockefeller's guidance exceeded his performance in the pulpit and soon he was selected to establish and administer the first of Rockefeller's great charitable foundations, the General Education Board. In addition Rockefeller had helped lure young William Rainey Harper from the ministry at Yale in 1891 to become the first president of Rockefeller's new University of Chicago. Harper made extensive trips to the land of the tsars and his son Samuel Harper headed the Department of Russian Affairs at the University of Chicago for many years until his death in 1942. From the Harpers, with whom he maintained close friendships, Eaton developed an early interest in the vast, turbulent country but his own first trip to Russia was not made until 1958.

Charley Eaton, living next door to his wealthy parishioner and always ready for a game of golf with him, succumbed in due time. With Rockefeller's backing, he moved on to New York's Madison Avenue Baptist Church in 1909 and before he knew it he was out of the ministry. His career included service on the War Shipping Board in World War I, editor of *Leslie's Weekly*, executive for the General Electric Lamp Division and finally Congressman from New Jersey. As Representative Eaton he served for almost thirty years as a distinguished and useful Congressman. He was the ranking Republican on the House Foreign Affairs Committee and one of the signers of the United Nations Charter at its founding in 1945. When Harry S. Truman ordered combat troops into Korea on June 30, 1950, the loudest cheers in the Congress were for the Republican Congressman's remarks: "We've got a rattlesnake by the tail," he said, "and the sooner we pound its damn head in the better." Representative Eaton died in 1953, just before his nephew started making news on the subject of Russia, but there never was any question about his own fears in that direction. "The Russian dictatorship has proved beyond question that its purpose is to destroy every capitalistic system of free enterprise in the world," warned Rockefeller's former minister in 1947.

After graduating from McMaster University in Ontario, Eaton became a trouble-shooter for Rockefeller's East Ohio Gas Company. In 1907, he was sent by a group of investors to secure a franchise for an electric power plant in Manitoba, Canada. His backers, frightened by the Panic of 1907, withdrew. Always cool in adversity, the young entrepreneur obtained the funds on his own in Canada, where the Panic was not so severe, built the plant, sold it in 1909 for a handsome profit and was on his way. From that point on, Eaton developed control of gas and electric companies in hundreds of cities throughout the midwest and southwest and from Canada to Brooklyn.

This was the age of the great utility holding company boom. Since Eaton's life reflects the business history of our times, a glance at that manic period which resulted in a catastrophic depression is in order.

In 1912 Eaton put together his first great utility holding company, Continental Gas & Electric Co. By the mid-twenties, he commanded the much larger United Light and Power Co. His utility empire was now the third largest, exceeded only by that of Samuel Insull and by Sydney Z. Mitchell's Electric Bond & Share. United involved assets of close to $2 billion. (The purchasing price of the dollar of 1929 was about twice that of today's dollar.)

It was an age of mergers in which the utility combinations were the outstanding examples of a new type of merger. Heretofore the typical merger was a case of a giant corporation such as U.S. Steel or Standard Oil swallowing up smaller companies in the same or related fields. The object was to eliminate competition, gain the advantages of size and dominate an industry regionally or nationally, with all the benefits flowing from such power.

The utility mergers of the twenties were partially a response to the cupidity and greed of investment bankers and promoters who were after the profits offered by an insatiable mass of investors clamoring for a place to invest their funds. They were also a result of the inevitable period of consolidation which follows every new industry. Electric power multiplied nineteen times between 1902 and 1929 and every town seemed to have its own electric light and power company under local ownership. Yet between 1919 and 1927 over 3,700 utility companies vanished as they were bought out by the big holding company groups. The rationale of these mergers was that central management and efficiency would result in increased sales, lower rates to consumers and higher profits for shareholders. Rather than eliminate competition, the object was to standardize operations, management and technology as was being done for the burgeoning chain stores. The prospect made sense and encouraged speculation in stocks since utilities filled a basic need and were protected by franchises. As a result utilities were sold and resold to the highest bidder until by 1932 thirteen holding companies controlled 75% of the nation's electric power.

The holding company then as now is simply one corporation which owns subsidiary corporations below it. As on an organization chart, there is a top box which gathers in the money and then buys the stock of an existing operating company whose umbilical cord reaches upward to the top box and downward to new operating companies or holding companies which it in turn has acquired. Men like Eaton, Insull and Mitchell are credited with developing the fine art of "leverage" that allowed the top box to control several levels of subsidiaries, which would then resemble a pyramid of boxes, with a minimum capital investment. This is what is meant by pyramiding control.

The art of leverage consisted of two elements. First, the upper box could control by holding only a majority or even an effective minority of the stock of the subsidiary below. This would suffice to control policy including the important payment of dividends, management fees and other *largesse* to the holding company. Secondly, there was the use of borrowed funds and preferred stocks as part of the holding company's initial investment. The resulting reduction in the amount of common stock needed to carry the enterprise obviously increased the profit per common share and enabled common stock-owning promoters to build empires on a trivial investment of cash.

Now a final bit of financial architecture was added to accommodate a generation of investors bellowing to be shorn, the investment trust. Cyrus Eaton's Continental Shares, Inc., established in 1926, was a classic though relatively modest example of this then perfectly legal and practically unregulated device. The investment trust pyramided in the same manner as the holding company. In fact companies such as Continental were both holding company and investment trust. The basic difference was that the investment trust did not seek to control operating companies in any one field. Instead it proposed to invest in a variety of securities. The price of its shares, however, did not reflect the market value of its purchased securities as one would expect today. This vital information often wasn't disclosed either to the buyers or the stock exchanges. Instead it reflected plain supply and demand based on the glamor and aggressiveness of the sponsor as much as anything else, with the result that prices wildly exceeded the already inflated value of the underlying securities. In turn the sponsor could be an investment banking or brokerage firm, such as the House of Morgan, Goldman Sachs or Eaton's own Otis & Co., enabling the sponsor to market and trade in its own securities as well as conveniently manufacture new inventory when needed! The investment trusts became the rage of Wall Street and were being launched at the rate of one a day in 1929. In that year they issued an estimated three billions worth of securities, practically all of which went for speculative rather than capital-creating purposes to the extent that they were used to purchase existing securities. It was a period, as J. K. Galbraith notes wrily in *The Great Crash*, of "fiscal incest." It is not possible to defend the old order and one can only reluctantly admire Eaton's singular return from the ashes.

III

Following Eaton as an archetype of his times, although hardly a conscience-stricken one at this point, his epic struggle with Samuel Insull is worthy of notice. Insull's headquarters were in Chicago, where he pyramided a national array of corporations, mainly in the field of utilities, into the realm of unreality. After his bubble burst, an experienced corporation lawyer, Owen D. Young of General Electric, completing a lengthy study of Insull's vast paper structure, rendered the final judgment: "It is impossible . . . for any man, however able, really to grasp the real situation . . . it was so set up that you could not possibly get an accounting system which would not mislead even the officers themselves."

In his palmy days, Insull was admired by all good Americans as a financial genius. The former private secretary and most trusted adviser of Thomas A. Edison, Insull lived on an estate in Libertyville, wore country-squire knickerbockers that reminded one of his English background and genially led Chicago in the financing and support of its plush Opera House. By 1930 the gross assets of his group amounted to almost $2.5 billion. Insull companies accounted for one-eighth of the country's electric power.

It was this formidable number one man that Cyrus Eaton chose to raid. The vehicle would be his Continental Shares Co., which was to achieve a peak capital and surplus of $156 million through retained profits and money poured in from Otis & Co. sales before the deluge. In the best leverage tradition, the resources also included tremendous bank loans secured by Continental shares, of which Chase National Bank of New York alone contributed $27 million.[2]

Continental began to buy secretly into Insull's most prized utilities, Commonwealth Edison Company, Peoples Light, Gas & Coke and Public Service Company of Northern Illinois. It didn't matter that the maneuver was constantly driving prices up beyond all reason as the mighty game was being played with other people's money. Insull recognized the threat to his empire and retaliated by pouring in money to buy up his own stocks and drive the price beyond Eaton's ability to pay. For this tactic an obliging public had subscribed massively to Insull's new investment trusts, Insull Utility Investment, Inc. and Corporation Securities Company. It was too late, however, for Eaton had amassed a stake in the three utilities that Insull could not tolerate. One would think the market crash of October 1929 would have ended the matter then and there but strangely enough the battle continued until 1930.

Finally a truce was declared in June 1930 when the two monarchs met to discuss the terms of the ransom. Minutes of the Corporation Securities Company note that Insull and Eaton haggled over whether Insull would have to pay a total of $350 or $400 per share for the 160,000 shares Eaton had assembled in these sources of light and power in the midwest. The shares went at $350, which was $6,000,000 above the market price, paid unwittingly by Insull's investors to protect his personal position. Continental proudly reported a profit of about $15 million over its cost of the shares. In order to pay out the $56 million involved, Insull had to overextend his debt to the banks. This is generally reported as having accelerated Insull's crash in March 1932 with Eaton being awarded the role of giant-killer. Eaton's modest disclaimer that he really was a friend of Insull and "thought Insull knew what he was doing" is hardly necessary. The fact is that both Eaton's and Insull's empires were doomed to crash even without their feudal in-fighting.

The record of Insull's fall from grace reads like a stern morality tale for errant capitalists. As his empire crumbled, he liquidated whatever he could from his own personal fortune and contributed it to Corporation Securities Company. He cashed in a half-million dollar life insurance policy, sold his four-thousand acre estate and turned in practically all the personal property of himself and his wife in a futile effort to stem the tide as well as to avoid personal bankruptcy. When the receivers took over in April 1932 Insull mourned: "I wish my time on earth had already come." By now the estimated losses for Insull's investors were $750 million, not to mention his own $100 million.

For two years Insull and his family had lived in a state of siege, protected from furious stockholders by no less than thirty-six bodyguards on a round-the-clock schedule. After a bullet whistled through his limousine and lodged in his chauffeur's shoulder, the old man used only an armor-plated Cadillac with plate glass windows an inch thick to go to his office. Finally he set up an $18,000 pension for himself and sailed quietly to France with Mrs. Insull in June 1932. It was the election year during which one of the candidates, Franklin D. Roosevelt, promised to place drastic curbs on corporation finance, with particular attention paid to holding companies.

Meanwhile a Cook County Grand Jury took up some of the tasks which would later become the province of the yet-to-be-born Securities & Exchange Commission. Soon the usual list of irregularities was produced, including "crossloaning" of collateral among related companies, questionable brokers' fees, padding of payrolls, a secret list of sixteen hundred insiders entitled to guaranteed profits and using the mails to defraud. Suddenly it was discovered that the scapegoat had fled to Europe and a nation of repentant speculators indulged in a great chase to bring him back. The resourceful fugitive had fled France for the asylum of Greece, with which the United States had no extradition treaty. His "pension" having been cancelled, he was living on the handouts of friends and was a rather popular personage in Athens. The Greeks stoutly defended their curious prize but finally capitulated and ordered him to leave by March 15, 1934. He escaped from the Greek authorities on a tramp steamer which he had chartered for his own use and became front page news as he wearily knocked on the doors of exotic ports for refuge. A vigilant Congress hastily passed an emergency law giving the United States the power to arrest Insull in any country in which it had extraterritorial rights.

Finally the drab steamer put into Istanbul for provisions. The confrontation with the American government was too much for Turkey regardless of its sympathies for the penurious little wanderer who had escaped the dragnet thus far. Under heavy guard, Insull was returned to America.

In April 1934, he entered Cook County Jail, half-supported by his guards, still wearing the Homburg and pince-nez of the executive, his large white mustache drooping on a pallid face. The lesson was plain for all to see — even the mighty Insull must pay the price for the great binge.

Strangely enough Insull was acquitted on all counts, probably because he had muddled up the books so much that no ordinary juror could feel free from reasonable doubts. In July 1938, age seventy-nine, he dropped dead on the streets of Paris, leaving $1,000 in cash and $14 million in debts.

IV

"A holding company," said Will Rogers, "is a thing where you hand an accomplice the goods while the policeman searches you." Operating companies below the top of the pyramid were at least subject to some state regulations of their stock and bond issues as well as their rates to consumers. Holding companies, however, as Professor Felix Frankfurter pointed out, were practically immune from regulations. As a result the worst of them made exorbitant demands on their operating companies, selling them excessive services, profiting from the supply of materials, even receiving loans "upstream" from subsidiaries in order to finance their raids and promotions on the stock exchanges. Far from reducing the ultimate rates to consumers, the excessive capitalization and loading of charges at the top tended to increase rates, as Thorstein Veblen had gloomily predicted. As with all abuses, the excesses finally brought about a reform — the so-called "death sentence" of the utility holding company — which constitutes an interesting chapter in the nation's economic history.

It was not until 1935 that Roosevelt felt prepared to pursue his anti-holding company legislation. The resulting turmoil over the Wheeler-Rayburn bill produced a great clash between the forces of government and the forces of business. The result was a compromise bill in which the death sentence was slightly commuted when the bill became law on August 26, 1935. Another result was the emergence of Wendell L. Willkie, president of the Commonwealth & Southern holding company, as a national spokesman for the business interests who would challenge Roosevelt for the Presidency in 1940.

The private power industry has always been one of America's most highly organized industries in terms of trade associations and effective lobbying. The reason is easy to see. It is always a candidate for public ownership and as such has to be prepared to man the barricades at a moment's notice. In spite of the congenial occupants in the White House during the twenties, it never let its guard down. Sam Insull had his own front, the Illinois Committee on Public Utility Information and on the national scene there was the National Electric Light Association. The NELA conducted a relentless attack against the perils of public ownership, mounting its campaign in the schools, universities, churches and legislatures at a reasonable cost on the consumer's light bill. It had reason to be concerned. There were liberals in Congress such as Senator George W. Norris of Nebraska. This crusty old man had dared to oppose the declaration of war in 1917 and had recently co-authored the Norris-La Guardia Act outlawing "yellow dog" labor contracts. He spoke of the "power trust" as "the greatest monopolistic corporation that has ever been organized for private greed." In the summer of 1935 Norris could happily contemplate the new Tennessee Valley Authority which had already begun operation in 1933 and he could dream about rural electrification programs and other heresies of public power on the drawing boards of the New Deal.

Against this background a giant offensive was mounted to defeat the holding company bill, not only by the power industry but also by allies such as the United States Chamber of Commerce and officials of the American Bar Association. In retrospect the bill seems almost conservative. It had nothing to do with public ownership and certainly none of the dire predictions such as the "paralysis of the nation" and "nationalization of the industry" came to pass. The bill was presented by the Administration as an effort to return the power industry to more independent private ownership and Roosevelt could artfully claim he was fighting "the private socialism of concentrated economic power."

Lobbying is a necessary device in the American form of government, enabling pressure groups to coordinate and present their case. Most businessmen would agree with this stand but the newspaper reports of 660 power lobbyists descending on Congress in 1935 would seem to be too much of a good thing. Over 800,000 messages poured in on Congress in June alone. A young freshman Senator, Harry S. Truman, reported that he burned 30,000 letters and telegrams which had reached his desk and he must have wondered at the groundswell of opposition, especially from shareholders whom one would suspect had been burned enough by holding company investments. Another young Senator, Hugo Black, conducted a Senate Subcommittee investigation which revealed that a great percentage of these messages from the proverbial "widows and orphans" had been sent by Western Union over city directory names provided and paid for by the utility lobbyists.

In its final form the bill directed the SEC to permit a holding company to control more than one integrated public utility system only if the additional system could not economically stand alone. This and other reforms in the bill were as good as death for the old order. Wendell Willkie fought the bill to the end and resisted compliance until the Supreme Court cut off all hope. Yet Willkie at no time defended the actions of the speculative holding companies such as Eaton's, which he felt should be strictly controlled by state regulations, and his own company was shown to be a model of the proper use of a multiple holding company. His evangelism for his cause was well-received by the country and turned out to be an unexpected preview of 1940.

V

While all these historic events were taking place, Cyrus Eaton was benched on the sidelines at the lowest point of his career. Like Insull he had suffered a $100 million personal loss but his crash had come approximately a year earlier in April 1931. Continental shares which had once been quoted on the New York Stock Exchange at $300 had dropped to $3 and 18,000 bitter stockholders were never to forget his name. The inevitable suits were filed against him for millions of dollars. The record of these suits indicates that Eaton obtained personal loans in the millions from Continental and entered into other transactions that would never be tolerated in a public company today.[3] Eaton rarely if ever has lost a lawsuit — he seems to win them all — and none of these were successful. The banks that had called Continental's loans in 1931 insisted that he resign and the corporation was turned over to his friend and neighbor George T. Bishop and four Cleveland banks. Within two years Continental was liquidated. The new utility regulations accelerated the disposition of the remaining assets.

Unlike Insull, Eaton apparently was not harassed personally and being only forty-seven at the time he was in better condition to stand the shock. "The others all died under the strain of panic or never recovered from it," he calmly observed years later.[4] It helped matters that he was not broke as so often reported but ended up with at least a million dollars after Continental was liquidated. Still in 1934, when this father of seven children was divorced by his wife of twenty-six years of marriage, the divorce papers referred to his net worth as being less than $105,000. He still owned and maintained his large residences and farmlands in Northfield and Deep Cove, Nova Scotia. He also owned a majority of a greatly subdued Otis & Co., where he went to work every day, nursing his fierce pride and ambition for the comeback.

Always an amateur philosopher, Cyrus Eaton had time now to reflect like a fallen emperor on the fantastic changes in his fortunes. The utility and investment banking fields had been only a part of his operations in the booming twenties. He had also moved in on the rubber industry and the steel industry. The rubber industry was still suffering from the effects of the 1921 depression, when the price of crude rubber had collapsed severely. The competition among these companies, some with their headquarters in nearby Akron, was intense and the profits were low. Through Continental, Eaton bought up virtual control of Goodyear and he also had a growing position in Firestone and Goodrich. As a business doctor of sorts, he promoted a series of friendly meetings of the rival executives in the library of his home where he pointed out to them the disadvantages of competing pricewise too vigorously. There was a resulting stabilization of prices and profits for the time being. In spite of such good counsel, which seems to have bordered on flagrant price-fixing collusion, the rubber families of Akron must have sighed with relief when Continental and Eaton went under in 1931.

His steel venture was on a much grander scale. Steel is America's basic industry, the very sinew of its being, and only a few men may be listed among the great steelmasters. There were several smaller steel companies in the midwest and Cyrus Eaton dreamed of combining them into a huge integrated company that would challenge the supremacy of the eastern colossus, U.S. Steel. Aside from whatever benefits would come from "integrating" and "rationalizing" midwest steel — to use substitute words for plain "merging" — there would also be good underwriting opportunities for Otis & Co.

The story of how Eaton made his start in steel has frequently appeared in America's business journals and popular magazines. Through the years, as with so many other business stories, it has gained a life of its own and considerable dramatic appeal. The scene is the ailing Trumbull Steel Co. of Warren, Ohio, fallen on bad times in spite of the good year 1925. Young Cyrus Eaton, age forty-two, soft-spoken and unknown to the receivers of Trumbull, proposes a solution for the company's troubles. Noting their skepticism about his credentials, he utters the now famous lines: "Gentlemen, if you have any doubt about my ability to underwrite it, just call the Cleveland Trust Co. and ask if my check for $20,000,000 will be honored."

VI

The deal was made and Eaton soon became known as the "little giant" of the steel industry as he cast about for additional mergers. The Cleveland Trust Co., incidentally, is still concerned forty-two years later about calls from Cyrus Eaton. For years it has been trying to out-maneuver him in a long-standing dispute about the proper method of voting some thirty-four per cent of the bank's common stock which happens to be administered by the bank's own trust department. Traditionally the bank has voted the stock at its annual meeting on behalf of its own slate of directors. Eaton has contended that the bank like any other Ohio corporation legally may not vote what is to all intents and purposes its own stock. The bank claims it is exempt from this Ohio law because the Ohio Banking Act permits such voting.

Eaton is an ex-director and substantial stockholder of the bank. The bank is quite aware that if the thirty-four percent is neutralized, Eaton may be on his way to naming himself and others to the board and assuming control of Cleveland's largest bank.

At its annual meeting on March 23, 1966, the bank voted the stock again and knowing that Eaton intended to file suit to declare the vote invalid, surprised him by filing court action for a declaratory judgment seeking approval of the voting of the stock.

On June 9, 1967 the Ohio Court of Common Pleas ruled for Eaton. The episode illustrates the tenacity and ingenuity of the wily old financier who never seems to lose legal cases. It illustrates also his continuous gravitation towards new political centers of power over the years. His attorney in the case was State Representative Carl B. Stokes, who a few months later was elected Cleveland's first Negro Mayor, having received substantial financial support from Eaton in his victory over Seth Taft, with whose family Eaton has long carried on a feud.

VII

Having captured Trumbull, Eaton moved ahead quickly and soon gained control of United Alloy Steel of Canton, Central Steel of Massillon and Donner Steel of Buffalo. With the help of Continental Shares, Inc. an investment of $10 million in Republic Iron & Steel gained his group enough power to package them all together as Republic Steel, the nation's third largest steel combine, in December 1929. At the same time, Otis & Co. successfully marketed an issue of $60 million of Republic preferred stock, coming in just under the wire.

All the publicity and honors that go with such financial derring-do were now showered on the former divinity student from Pugwash. He became a trustee of the University of Chicago and made a trip to England where he rented an estate and entertained royally, unburdened by thoughts on Russia, which the U.S. did not officially recognize at that time. He was invited to serve on boards and commissions as he happily assumed that a permanent New Era of business prosperity, engineered by businessmen such as himself, had come to this favored country.

For chairman of Republic Steel, Eaton proudly hand-picked Tom Girdler of Jones & Laughlin, which poses an interesting moral dilemma Eaton was saved from facing when he lost his Republic holdings a few years later.

Girdler prospered at Republic Steel and became known in time as the industry's toughest rugged individualist and labor-baiter. His feelings about Eaton are recorded in his book *Boot Straps*, published in 1945: "Cyrus Eaton had fashioned his ideas into a remarkable plan . . . Eaton was smart as any man I ever met; and he was rich."[5]

But could Eaton share similar warmth for Girdler — that is, the Eaton of the second $100 million? Long after U.S. Steel had capitulated to the CIO's drive for union representation, Tom Girdler refused to follow suit. He gathered the "Little Steel" companies behind his leadership and issued a defiant challenge. "I won't have a contract, verbal or written, with an irresponsible, racketeering, violent, communistic body like the CIO and until they pass a law making me do it, I am not going to do it," he announced, calmly ignoring the Wagner Labor Relations Act and the National Labor Relations Board. On Memorial Day 1937, outside Republic Steel's South Chicago plant, Chicago police and company deputies broke up a crowd of demonstrators — men, women and children in a holiday mood. Four were killed, six fatally injured and ninety wounded, some thirty of them by gunfire and many shot in the back, according to the Senate Subcommittee records of the hearing on Republic

Steel. Girdler of course was not personally responsible. Yet from the viewpoint of history he occupies a very low rank for industrial responsibility.

By 1947 Cyrus Eaton published the following in an article in the *University of Chicago Law Review* entitled "A Capitalist Looks at Labor":

> To avoid extinction, if for no loftier motives, we who are capitalists will have to make immediate and radical changes in our attitude toward labor and our methods of dealing with labor. We will have to begin by muzzling such organizations as the National Association of Manufacturers and by recognizing, and sincerely regretting, that there is a bad feeling on both sides. For every corporation officer who characterizes a union official as a crook there is a labor leader willing to label an industrialist a bandit.
>
> Our next step ought to be a full and ungrudging acceptance of labor as human beings and as our partners who do the work. American management has exhibited the greatest genius in mass production and mass selling that the world has ever seen, but no automobile manufacturer ever thought of making denunciation of motorists the keynote of a sales campaign. On the other hand, many are the scathing statements that have been issued from the skyscrapers of Detroit against the United Automobile Workers.
>
> *   *   *
>
> The classical example of managerial folly is found in one especially vain and strutting corporation head who some years ago announced that he would retire from business before he would let his plants be organized. He wasted twenty million dollars of his stockholders' money in a futile fight against a strike for union recognition. Having spearheaded the attack on labor, he expected his fellow industrialists to reward his company with more

business, but found that they placed their orders with
other concerns whose more dependable labor relations
assured better delivery.

*   *   *

Such extreme cases are the exception, but they do
capitalism untold harm. The men at the top may think
they are omniscient, and that their system is omnipotent
in that, of itself, it can confer on humanity all of the
material blessings. But both capitalism and the men in
it have all the weaknesses and limitations that have racked
every system, economic, political, and religious, devised
by man during his millions of years of martyrdom. What
counts in any system is the intelligence, self-control, conscience, and energy of the individual.[6]

It is amusing to note that a year before he published this article,
the man who had once hired and admired Tom Girdler hired one
Harold J. Ruttenberg, a former economist for the United Steelworkers of America, to be vice-president of Portsmouth Steel, a
new Eaton venture organized in partnership with the Kaiser-Frazer
automobile company. Ruttenberg was actually in charge of Portsmouth for a while and reports are that he was an excellent salesman,
although one wonders how he was received by his clannish fellow
executives in the industry. The unreal dimensions of Eaton's business career are symbolized in this turn of the wheel — involving a
long life, an opportunistic, flexible mind and the ability to make a
fortune twice over in successive eras.

VIII

Although Eaton's empire today consists of approximately $2
billion of assets[7] in a variety of fields, he is best known as the Chairman of the Board of the Chesapeake & Ohio Railroad. When he
writes letters to newspapers he is likely to sign his name as chairman
of the railroad's board. In 1960 he wrote such a letter to the *Herald*

Tribune chiding New Yorkers for their rude reception to Khrushchev. The editors of William F. Buckley's *National Review* sharply questioned the propriety of the identification let alone the contents of the letter.[8]

This raises an interesting question which officers of public companies have to face from time to time. At what point are they forbidden to use the majesty of their company's name as far as controversial personal causes are concerned? On the one hand they are exhorted by social critics and their own sons in the business schools to stand up and be counted. On the other hand, they must face up to their insecurity as minority-owning management, exposed to plotting fellow officers, corporate spies, journalists and a government poised to review their tax returns, expense accounts and government contracts. It is no time for heroism on the corporation front, aside from the personal heroism required for certain college recruiting. It is not therefore unusual to find the following *caveat* on newspaper petitions and fund-raising letters: "Company Names Are Used for Identification Only." Even this requires relative courage.

Cyrus Eaton stands above such groundling considerations. The only things he has perhaps ever feared are stockholders and their proxies. The "Chessy" has thrived under his control, having taken over the Baltimore & Ohio and being well on the way to taking over the Norfolk & Western. The stockholders, apparently as content as the sleeping kitten that symbolized C & O advertising for so many years, are more interested in their profits than their prophet.

It was not always so pleasant in the luxurious C & O suite on the thirty-sixth floor of Cleveland's Union Terminal Tower building. However resounding Cyrus Eaton's crash was in 1931, the collapse of his predecessors and fellow Clevelanders, the Van Sweringen brothers, was bigger and louder.

As an example of improper railroad investment banking, the Van Sweringen episode ranks high in business history. In 1929 the brothers were already legendary figures. Ambitious Americans thrilled to the story of their rags-to-riches climb from newsboys to great real estate developers to railroad kings. After making a fortune in developing Shaker Heights, a Cleveland suburb, they acquired their first medium-sized railroad in order to provide rapid transit for its residents. Now with the backing of the House of Morgan they established a railroad empire of great complexity. Using their Morgan-financed Alleghany Corporation as a holding company, they captured the coal-carrying Chesapeake & Ohio, the Missouri-Pacific, the Erie and other trunklines in the east until finally they controlled a sprawling network of 23,000 miles of track across the country, as much as in all of England at that time. With their coal mines, terminals and commercial properties thrown in, they overshadowed Eaton as he made his mark in the business circles of Cleveland and the midwest.

As personages, however, the brothers were unattractive. Business reporters who interviewed them generally found them commonplace, distinguished only by their single-minded acquisitiveness. The older brother, M. J., was a confirmed bachelor who did not let his younger brother, the pudgy, round-faced O. P., marry until he was old and sick. They lived together on a seven hundred-acre farm estate in Shaker Heights called Daisy Hill, a rambling collection of barns and wings remotely resembling a Swiss chalet. In an effort to cheer up their drab lives they completed a huge ballroom in 1930 but it was too late for dancing. Below the ballroom of all places was a giant swimming pool with walls of colored tiles and exotic columns no doubt inspired by William Randolph Hearst's similar monstrosity at San Simeon in California. A magnification of the strange Collier brothers, the rich recluses who finally had to be pried out of their overflowing New York apartment, these brothers acquired railroads like squirrels gather nuts. The mighty Alleghany corporation controlled six railroads and other properties in 1929 valued at close to three billion dollars. Both men had completed only grammar school and the name "Alleghany" itself, still listed on the New York Stock Exchange, was finally discovered to be a mis-spelling on their part which apparently none of their hirelings dared challenge.

Alleghany crumbled in the thirties when the Morgan interests could no longer keep on carrying it. Its leverage included $250 million of debenture notes and preferred stocks which were in default. On top of that, the brothers had personally borrowed almost $50 million, largely on Alleghany stock, from brokers who in turn had borrowed from Morgan banks, which was the main reason why they were kept alive after 1929. It was almost as if they were too involved in debt to be allowed to expire and they were still permitted to draw a combined salary of $150,000 a year long after the worst was known. In addition President Hoover's new Reconstruction Finance Corporation selected their Missouri-Pacific Railroad for a $23 million loan in 1932 that provoked outraged charges of financial favoritism in Congress.

In 1934 the bankrupt Van Sweringen holdings including the control stock of the Alleghany Corporation were auctioned off to the only bidder, the elderly George A. Ball, whose fortune rested on glass jars made in Muncie, Indiana. He was generally considered to be a front man for the Van Sweringen brothers who stayed on the payroll and were thought to have an option to buy the stock all over again. Within two years, both Van Sweringens died and Alleghany was on the block again.

At just about this time an amusing and quixotic challenge was thrown at Wall Street by Professor Charles A. Beard, one of America's great economic historians, and Matthew Josephson, a first-rate journalist who had just dedicated his sensational new book *The Robber Barons* to Beard in 1934. Both men had sought their share of the free ride of the twenties and were licking their wounds from losses in Van Sweringen and other securities. Regarding their endeavor as something of a mission, they constituted themselves and a few friends as the Missouri-Pacific Railroad Independent Bondholders' Committee and decided to challenge the latter-day barons in the protective arena of the New Deal. An accommodating Senator Burton K. Wheeler immediately gave them star witness billing in the Senate Committee railroad hearings he was about to open. Felix Frankfurter and other legal luminaries gave them free counsel. A friendly press gleefully reported the assault on Morgan and his cohorts by these intellectuals suddenly given the opportunity to test their theories. Their object was to prevent the reorganization of the Missouri-Pacific at the hands of the same bankers and management that had made such a mess in the first place. Beard was an eloquent witness, charging that the Van Sweringens had "milked" the Missouri-Pacific in a frantic effort to bolster the sagging Alleghany shares in the market and demanding protection for himself and other bondholders.[9] For amateurs they did considerable good and the Wheeler Committee and appropriate government agencies were inspired to produce needed reforms. On the other hand, Wall Street could hardly be replaced. It survived the attack and participated in the reorganizations.

The new atmosphere of reform and giant-killing now produced another performer on the Alleghany scene, Robert R. Young, who would soon become an important factor in the career of Cyrus Eaton.

IX

Young was referred to as a "new breed" of tycoon and as the "daring young man from Texas" (or "from Wall Street," depending on which magazine you read). At any rate he had a good press and a great sense of the use of publicity and public relations as weapons in the continual battles of his lively career. Small, thin, with prematurely white hair, he was still in his thirties when he bought control of Alleghany from the seventy-year old Ball who now had no further use for it. Called almost immediately to testify before Senator Wheeler, Young readily admitted he had bought control of the pyramid for only $254,000 of his own money as a down payment. Within five years, it was worth approximately seven million dollars.

Youthful wizards of finance appear in cycles on the American business horizon and for twenty years Young's star was in the ascendant. The son of a country banker, he went to the University of Virginia, worked in the accounting departments of Dupont and General Motors and ended up as an assistant to John J. Raskob. In the late twenties he went out on his own as a stockbroker, made a stake by anticipating the crash and now with the backing of the Woolworth heir Allen Kirby controlled Alleghany. Since his career thereafter was comet-like, ending with suicide in 1958, his character comes into sharp focus. He was racked with ambition, suffered from hypertension and failed to achieve any lasting reputation other than for his aggressive and flamboyant drive for power. Although he was known as a financier from Texas, he preferred the company of the wealthy and titled people at Newport, Rhode Island where he had a forty-room house overlooking the harbor. At Newport he made a certain splash with the lavish entertainment he provided for his close friends the Duke and Duchess of Windsor. It is not difficult for his detractors to visualize this driven man as a pathetic figure, yearning for acceptance and power in a world beyond his reach.

When Senator Wheeler questioned Young about his plans for improving Alleghany, Young came right to the point and declared he was going "to take the gravy out of Wall Street" by placing his railroad financing on a competitive basis. This heresy produced seismic shocks on an already battered Wall Street, which for years had always regarded railroad financing as a matter of negotiation between railroad management and certain time-honored investment bankers such as Morgan Stanley and Kuhn, Loeb and Co. These august firms had often put the lines together, were represented on their boards of directors and knew just where to place the securities at a reasonable price. The price was too high, Young argued, resulting in increased costs to consumers and reduced profits for shareholders. Perhaps more than the price, Young feared Wall Street interference with his plans.

The story goes that soon Young received an invitation to lunch from Thomas W. Lamont, the minister's son who had become chairman of the Morgan banking firm. Young discreetly leaked to the press in due time that he had been instructed to render to Morgan that which was theirs or face the consequences. To be known as the "only man who defied Morgan and lived to tell it" now became part of Young's mythology.

No one could have been more charmed by Young's declaration than Cyrus Eaton, whose Otis & Co., having sold its brokerage business and being estranged from the eastern forces that had accelerated Continental's demise, was starving for investment banking business. Eaton had already declared in favor of sealed bids for both railroad and utility securities and now he would have a formidable ally. Joining in the crusade was Halsey, Stuart & Co. of Chicago, which owes its present eminence to this turn of events. In 1938, Young's Chesapeake & Ohio, which he controlled sufficiently through Alleghany to exercise policy, brought out a $30 million bond issue, which Eaton and Harry Stuart snatched away from the traditional bankers by cutting the cost of selling it to the public by $2 million. By 1946 Otis & Co. was one of the top ten underwriting firms in the country and the base of operations for Eaton's new fortune.

In making his comeback, Eaton, formerly a Republican who had participated in a few medicine-ball cabinet sessions with President Hoover, quickly joined the forces that were chastising investment bankers in general and Wall Street bankers in particular. He had already advocated support of Roosevelt in 1932 but his own influence must have been negligible at the time. Now in his drive for open bidding, he had the support of the reform elements in Washington. Otis & Co. and Halsey, Stuart wanted to be in utility financing as well as railroad financing and their number one target was Eaton's old competitor Wendell Willkie, who was still president of Commonwealth and Southern. As might be expected, Willkie, whom political opponents were later to label "the barefoot boy from Wall Street," rebuffed them strenuously and refused to accept their low bid, asserting he preferred to do business with Morgan Stanley. Eaton then went to the SEC which eventually ruled in 1941 that competitive bidding would be mandatory for public utility issues.

Somewhat earlier Eaton had been turned down personally by Senator Taft on his request to bid on the financing for Cincinnati's new Union Terminal, for which Taft was serving as finance committee chairman. Again Eaton proceeded to Washington, this time to the RFC. He convinced RFC Chairman Jesse Jones that since railroads owing money to the RFC were going to pay for using the terminal, it should be built with the lowest cost of financing. Jones accepted this strained logic and eventually the Interstate

Commerce Commission also ruled that all railroad issues had to be exposed to open bidding. In retrospect these decisions represented one of the most momentous changes in Wall Street history.

Although allowed to participate, Otis & Co. did not turn out to be the low bidder on the Cincinnati terminal financing. Meanwhile Taft's sharp rejection of Eaton's original request earned him Eaton's implacable opposition thereafter. "We've already made a deal with people we trust," said Taft, "and I resent your coming here." In 1952, the Cincinnati *Enquirer* was up for sale and the Taft family's *Times Star* was poised to buy it. The *Enquirer*'s employees were anxious to buy the paper themselves but were unable to obtain the required $7,600,000 financing. The loan came quickly enough from an Eaton subsidiary, for a reported $250,000 fee. Eventually the employees found they couldn't run the paper and Scripps-Howard took over.

In painting a portrait of Eaton, this thirst for revenge must be noted. Just as Eaton rarely loses lawsuits, so do people who oppose him rarely become Presidents, although in the latter case we are dealing with the long arm of coincidence. At any rate he strongly opposed his fellow Clevelander and former Secretary of War Newton D. Baker in favor of Roosevelt at the Democratic convention in 1932. Baker had only recently savagely depicted Eaton as a "ruthless industrial Napoleon" exploiting like Insull "the life savings of the little people." This characterization was made in the course of a bitter and successful struggle on the part of Eaton and the Republic Steel forces to prevent the merger in 1931 of Baker's client, Bethlehem Steel, with Youngstown Sheet & Tube, also coveted by Republic. Similarly, when Willkie opposed Roosevelt in 1940, Eaton published a noteworthy paper in favor of the third term. The Taft family has always been able to count on Eaton for handsome financial contributions to any Taft opponent.

In 1942 Young was established strongly enough in C & O holdings to become chairman and a year later Eaton joined him on the board. Young became increasingly restless and now was consumed with ambition to take over the New York Central itself, the line of the Vanderbilts, whose sluggish assets he felt needed his strong

leadership. Eaton had been acquiring C & O stock on his own and
when Young resigned in 1954 Eaton made an additional investment of $14 million and became the C & O's largest stockholder and
new chairman. With the cash from Eaton's purchase and the backing of reinforcements from Texas, Clint Murchison and Sid Rich-
ardson, Young, Kirby and the Alleghany Corporation finally captured the Central in 1954. The victory came after a rousing proxy
fight that cost the Central stockholders at least $1 million, accord-
ing to the custom that allows recovery by the winner of much of
these costs after the incumbent loser has already spent a fortune
of the railroad's money defending itself.

Matthew Josephson knew Young as well as any journalist, having
written a *Saturday Evening Post* series on him in 1945, attended
a C & O board meeting as Young's special guest and spent a week-
end at his home in Newport. Granting the desirability of open bidding, Josephson's current verdict is that Young was an opportunist,
embracing the posture of the New Dealer in relation to Wall Street
only to advance his ends. Young was as anxious to manipulate the
holding company device as the old crowd before him and when
opposed by the government agencies that had befriended him would
rail against the bureaucracy.[10]

What about Cyrus Eaton in the same context? As always the
contradictions that enter the business executive's life — the "strains"
that are supposed to gnaw at his vitals according to seriously professional studies like *The American Business Creed* by Sutton,
Harris, Kaysen and Tobin—must be considered. Surely Eaton and
Young were sharply different personalities, Eaton as suave as Young
was blatant. Away from business, Eaton has cultivated an intellectual, concerned image with which he wishes to be identified;
Pugwash and Acadia Farms are as far from Newport as Khrushchev is from the Duke of Windsor. Yet Eaton and Young were
quite compatible for many years in their common pursuit of money.
Only with money could Eaton have purchased his particular brand
of independence.

As for New Deal ideology, Eaton has alternated between free-
enterpriser and New Dealer as the situation arises. Concerning the

usual distinction that would make a man of business accept the
New Deal — the recognition that big government bears the ultimate responsibility for policing the economy and maintaining full
employment — Eaton generally speaks in a strangely old-fashioned
vein. In his 1947 *Chicago Law Journal* article, which he has had
reprinted for current consumption, the man who made several rush
visits to Washington stated the following:

> . . . there can be nothing but criticism for the capitalists
> who have lately taken to running to Washington like cry-
> babies for help from politicians and the bureaucrats in
> suppressing labor. The whole story of governmental in-
> terference in business is foreign to free enterprise . . .
> One of our peculiar national traits is a pathetic eager-
> ness to believe that passage of a national law will solve
> any problem we have . . . Let it be recalled that the elabo-
> rate law that was passed to strengthen the transportation
> industry resulted in the establishment of the Interstate
> Commerce Commission, the biggest bureaucracy of them
> all, which has brought every known woe to the
> railroads.[11]

In 1961 he was quoted as delivering the following impeccable
conservative summation:

> I live happily and I hope productively by the doctrine
> that intelligent and enlightened private ownership and
> operation provide the ideal system of economics for my
> country, and that the greatest possible separation of poli-
> tics from economics is desirable.[12]

In his long career Eaton has had so many scraps with government
agencies — ICC, Internal Revenue, SEC and FBI to name a few —
that he could hardly be expected to love the bureaucracy. It is part
of the fascination of the man that he is not easily typed. Like most
controversial figures, he probably hopes that opportunism and
idealism are not wholly irreconcilable.

X

One of the most profitable trips Eaton made to Washington was in connection with Steep Rock Iron Mines in northwestern Ontario, which contain reserves of high-grade iron ore used in steel production estimated at one billion tons. Probably few visits to the nation's Capitol have been worth so much per mile travelled as this one. It helped Eaton create a fortune from still another source, the government lending agency in time of national emergency, spawner of such giants as the Henry Kaiser empire among others.

For years prospectors had noted evidences of floating iron ore in the four mile by fifteen mile "W" shaped Steep Rock Lake. One of them, Julian Cross, set up rigs on the ice one cold winter, drilled down through 150 feet of water at three points in the lake and struck rich ore. The only problem was that the lake contained 120 billion gallons of water. A company was formed under Major General D. M. Hogarth, Quartermaster General of the Canadian Army in World War I, who presented the venture for financing to several firms on Wall Street. Confronted with a cold "no" for his idea of draining the lake by an underground tunnel, Hogarth thought of Cyrus Eaton.

It was 1943 and the nation's steel mills were running full-blast, creating concern about ore reserves. Struck with visions of John D. Rockefeller's great *coup* in obtaining the Mesabi range years ago, Eaton took an option on the deal, reportedly for only $20,000 cash, and was on his way to Washington.

Apparently Roosevelt, who had an uncanny ability in times of great pressure to sort his mail correctly — for example, the letter from Einstein explaining the desirability of encouraging work in the field of atomic fission — looked approvingly at this preposterous idea for winning the war and gave Eaton his blessing. Next Eaton's labor leader friend, Phillip Murray of the CIO, introduced him to Harold Ruttenberg, whom Eaton later hired. Ruttenberg was the steel union's representative on the War Production Board and a good man to help with priorities on drills and pumps. Jesse Jones and the RFC came through with a $5 million loan. Eaton then called on the Canadian government in Ottawa and got $20 million of financing for railroad spurs, loading equipment, power lines and docks. Wishing to include everyone, he also obtained $5 million from the province of Ontario and capped the package with a modest $2,250,000 issue of debentures by Otis & Co. There were some last minute protests from the Russians, who complained that they badly needed the machinery and equipment, but Eaton insisted on America first.

Altogether about $40 million had been invested when the time came to drain the lake on July 22, 1943. There had been veteran engineers who had predicted that the vast project wouldn't work. It involved tunnelling through the bottom of the lake and then blasting a gigantic hole upward — somewhat like pulling the plug on an immense bathtub. The lake was then to drain through the tunnel into another stream bed. Even if the blasting were successful, there was always the possibility that the rush of water would drag obstructions with it to block up the tunnel repeatedly. The lake drained itself with dispatch and Eaton's second $100 million received a strong boost.

As part of the overall plan, Eaton had established his own sales organization, Premium Ores, Ltd., of Canada, which contracted to purchase ten million tons of ore over a ten-year period and to provide additional financing if needed. In return Premium received 1,437,500 shares of Steep Rock at a penny a share. Steep Rock was earning forty-eight cents a share ten years later. The government sued Eaton in 1956 for $10 million of back personal income taxes, penalties and interest, claiming among other things taxes on the difference between a penny a share and the government's estimate of $1.67 a share as "fair market value" at the time of the awarding of the stock to Premium, of which Eaton owned seventy-four percent. As usual Eaton won the case. If there were any taxes at all, he claimed, they were owed to Canada, which had been kind enough to waive in advance both corporate and personal income tax for Steep Rock for the first three years of its operation.

In 1958 Eaton invested further in Canadian iron ore, this time in subarctic Ungava Bay, Quebec, in association with Alfried Krupp and four other West German steelmen. If this seems inconsistent with his friendship for the Russians, Eaton could point out that he believes in trading with all nations and that Russia for some time has been a substantial customer for West German steel. The loss of all this good business made no sense to Ernest T. Weir, president of National Steel and a great conservative in domestic affairs, who surprisingly called for trade with the Russians shortly before he died in 1957. Ungava is one of the few Eaton ventures that has not worked out and is presently inactive.

XI

While Harry S. Truman was registering a stunning upset victory in 1948, his friend Cyrus Eaton was involved in the fight of his life and appeared to be losing it. Is it "Taps for Cyrus?" asked *Fortune* magazine while *Time* called back "Curtains for Eaton?"

It was to say the least a sensational affair, involving charges of dishonesty, hypocrisy and fraud along with a welter of lawsuits and government investigations. Suing Otis & Co. was none other than Henry J. Kaiser, Eaton's partner in Portsmouth Steel and like Eaton regarded as a friend of labor and of Washington. It was a case of the People's Industrialist versus the People's Financier.

Henry Kaiser had gained fame as a liberty-ship builder in World War II and with Joseph W. Frazer of the Graham-Paige Corporation had bravely engaged in auto manufacturing. They had taken over Ford's gigantic Willow Run bomber assembly plant after the war and gone into business with a $17 million common stock issue headed by Otis & Co. In addition, they had guaranteed their vital source for steel by becoming partners in Eaton's Portsmouth Steel.

On the surface Kaiser and Eaton appeared to share considerable affection for each other but some conflicts quickly appeared over the price of Portsmouth steel to K-F. With the bland statement that K-F, being a twenty-five per cent stockholder as well as a major customer of Portsmouth, should escalate its price paid for steel to offset Portsmouth's rising costs, Portsmouth tacked on three increases adding $5 million to K-F's costs. Kaiser became hopping mad at "this first exhibition of Cyrus Eaton's true nature" and was hardly mollified by the claim of Harold Ruttenberg, the former labor economist, that K-F was "insisting on the letter of an unconscionable contract."

Now in 1948 it was time to come back in the market again and K-F was advised that it was no time for the speculative new auto company to be changing underwriters. Eaton later claimed that he was disturbed about K-F having shifted valuable aluminum holdings to another Kaiser company, but he agreed to float 1,500,000 K-F shares in conjunction with the First California Company and Allen & Co. The issue was filed with the SEC on January 6, 1948, to be effective on January 26. Meanwhile K-F stock drifted from a high of $15 in December to a low of $11 and the date of issue was hectically postponed. On February 3, the new issue day, K-F prepared to "stabilize" the market in accordance with previous arrangements. Stabilization is the practise of maintaining the price of a stock at a selected level just before the new issue is thrown on the market. It is done under tight limitations permitted by the SEC. K-F thought 15,000 or 20,000 of its own shares might have to be purchased to stabilize the price but orders to sell poured in and by the afternoon they had been forced to buy in a staggering 186,000 shares at a cost of $2,500,000 to maintain the desired price.

At this point, William Daley, president of Otis & Co., announced the deal was off. Since the contract had not been signed, it was possible for the underwriters to pull out although lawsuits would surely follow. Faced with Kaiser's outraged reaction, Eaton then directed Otis & Co. to sign an amended contract. The contract now called for guaranteeing the sale of only 900,000 shares involving about $11 million instead of the original 1,500,000 shares. By February 4, only a portion of the stock had been sold in spite of further stabilization efforts and the offering was withdrawn from the market for sale at a later date.

On February 9, the day of the formal closing and exchange of documents, one of Eaton's lawyers, according to a K-F lawyer, said in an aside, "Well, I guess we better let them have it," and announced to the assembled attorneys and company officers that the deal was cancelled. The reason given was the filing of a stockholder's suit against K-F that morning in Detroit by one James F. Masterson, identified with grim humor as a "Philadelphia lawyer." Since underwriting contracts specify that there may be no "material litigation" pending against the company beyond that revealed in the prospectus, such a suit, if material, was grounds for cancellation. First California concurred with Eaton's attorney that the suit was material and withdrew. Allen & Co. demurred and stated it was willing to go through with its part of the deal. The thunder had struck and the weary attorneys and executives went home to sleep after a hard day's work. "It is for the courts to decide," smirked *Fortune*, using an unfortunate noun sometimes found in financial slang, "if he (Eaton) pulled the biggest welsh in financial history."

K-F sued in the Federal Court of the Southern District of New York for breach of contract and damages of $17,419,819 plus $1,856,250 for wrongfully inducing First California to break its contract. "They are suing us there among our ancient enemies," Eaton cried to the press. "They are our enemies because we advocated competition in finance and establishment of financial centers outside New York." He was correct in assuming no mercy from the K-F attorneys. They were led by Wendell Willkie's own law firm in New York, Willkie, Owen, Otis & Bailey, supplemented by the Newton D. Baker firm in Cleveland and the Taft firm in Cincinnati.

On July 2, 1951, Federal Judge John W. Clancy finally ruled against Otis & Co. and entered a judgment for the plaintiff in the amount of $3,120,743.

The judge ruled that Masterson's last-minute litigation against K-F was a phony stockholder's suit:

> This action was instituted as a result of a plot to establish an excuse to breach the contract conceived by Eaton, approved by Daley, and executed by Bulkley who procured Masterson as a dummy plaintiff and Harrison who supplied Martin as the attorney. What Bulkley and Harrison did was done by them in response to directions given to them by Eaton and as Eaton's agents and what

Martin and Masterson did was done by them with full understanding by each that they were operating on defendant's behalf and in performance of a common scheme participated in by all.

As for Otis & Co.'s other defense, that the K-F prospectus contained false and misleading statements of earnings, Judge Clancy ruled that it was only a question of two different systems of accounting, both of which produced the same total of earnings.

In July the Cleveland federal court ordered Otis & Co. to tell its customers that it would be insolvent if it had to pay the judgment and Otis & Co. went into bankruptcy proceedings under Chapter 10 of the federal bankruptcy law, inasmuch as the judgment exceeded its capital of $2 million. All of its branch offices had been closed during the stormy controversy, and the personnel in its main office shrank from 100 down to eight.

Meanwhile the SEC had pursued Otis & Co. with a vengeance, being prodded by Eaton's ridiculing and threatening of the government agency. In 5,219 pages of testimony, the SEC claimed "information which tends, if true, to show that" Eaton was behind the Masterson protest which looked like a case of "fraud and deceit." As a result of the SEC hearings, Otis & Co. had already received a temporary injunction from engaging in the securities business at the time of Judge Clancy's decision. The National Association of Securities Dealers, the investment bankers' own trade association, had also suspended Otis & Co. until 1954, which meant no other NASD member could do business with it, a virtual deathblow in the securities business.

In the United States Court of Appeals, Justice Augustus N. Hand rendered a decision on April 7, 1952 that snatched victory from K-F and bestowed it on Eaton. K-F tried to take the case to the United States Supreme Court unsuccessfully and the Court of Appeals decision prevailed. In reviewing the suit, Justice Hand's court disregarded the Masterson portion of the Otis & Co. defense. "We need only discuss one of the alleged errors: Namely, whether the district court was correct in finding that the plaintiff had not misrepresented but had adequately disclosed its profit for the month of December 1947 in the statement of earnings in the prospectus."

The court pointed out that while it was true a strong seller's market was being experienced at the time of stock issue, a new competitor like K-F was still subject to great pressures and risks. Thus its record of sales and earnings on a month to month basis would be a matter of extreme importance, revealing whether any significant trends were taking place. K-F had chosen an accounting system which overstated the December 1947 earnings by $3,100,-000. This substantially affected the final quarter's earnings, even though earnings for the year as a whole were not overstated. This was less than the full disclosure of facts required by the Securities Act and even though Otis & Co. was probably sophisticated enough to discern this accounting device in the prospectus it had helped prepare, such a contract was unenforceable and could be breached.

The SEC's charges were also rebuffed in the courts. On August 24, 1954 the SEC declared Otis & Co. innocent of charges that it had violated the anti-fraud and registration rules of the Securities Act. Finally on October 20, 1954 the NASD dismissed its complaints against Otis & Co. By then Otis & Co. was through with public underwriting and was continuing as a private investment corporation.

When all the smoke had cleared, the financial community was still incredulous as to why Otis & Co. had broken the contract. Its portion of the underwriting was only 337,500 shares at $11.50 a share to K-F. Surely Eaton could easily have added to Otis & Co.'s capital, picked up the shares and held them on the shelf until the market was acceptable for their sale to the public. Even if Otis & Co. had to sell the shares at a loss of a million dollars or so, it would be tax deductible and certainly a better choice than four years in court with all the attendant expense and notoriety. It is true that K-F eventually went out of business and 30,000 stockholders suffered losses but that could not have been anticipated at the time and the underwriters would not be held responsible anyway. Allen & Co., with equal knowledge about K-F, had been prepared to pick up its share of the deal from the beginning. If Eaton's decision was activated by pride — by just not being able to stand being taken in by old Henry J. — then it was one of the grandest and most reckless gestures in financial history. Whatever one may say about Cyrus Eaton, for sheer survival talent he is, as John O'Hara grudgingly used to say of Ernest Hemingway, "a champ."

XI

Still another facet of Eaton's controversial life is of interest — his relationship with John L. Lewis, the fiery "lion of labor," a gigantic figure in the revolutionary accommodation of American business to its labor unions.

As prideful as Cyrus Eaton ever was, Lewis ran the gamut of human virtues and frailties. As a result he has been loved, despised, feared and respected in a long life that shaped and influenced labor's modern history. Today's union leaders often appear to be solid and content citizens. They are easily mistaken for their counterparts in corporations whom they resemble in their conservative appearance and dress. When offenders are occasionally sentenced for racketeering or mishandling of union funds, they disturbingly call to mind business executives who have gone astray rather than the romantic firebrands of only thirty years ago. Among these romantic leaders, Lewis was a natural to speak for labor's cause. His workers descended into the pits to make their living underground, subject to the terrors and grime that most Americans experienced only in the movies about Welsh miners. Beetle-browed under a mane of wild hair, he is a consummate actor given to Biblical prose and wrathful scorn. Brash enough to berate both Roosevelt and Truman in times of national emergency, this supreme egotist was also candid enough to state: "He that tooteth not his own horn, the same shall not be tooteth." He is endowed with the same flexibility of mind that allowed Eaton to embrace traditional enemies under new circumstances. It is not surprising that the two men became bosom friends, sharing a common interest in Greek poetry, and, as it turns out, the use of the union's treasury.

The horn that called Lewis to action was the New Deal and its famous Section 7a of the National Industrial Recovery Act, or NRA as it was known. When the early New Deal passed the NRA legislation to stimulate employment and purchasing power, it decided that since management would be given the right to organize without violating antitrust laws for the purpose of preventing "cutthroat competition," labor should also have the right under 7a to organize and bargain collectively. This tremendous spur to unionism expired when the Supreme Court declared NRA unconstitutional in May 1935 but Congress immediately passed the Wagner Labor Relations Act which restored the right and also created the National Labor Relations Board, empowered to supervise union elections.

Lewis had been one of the old-time labor bosses in the moribund labor movement preceding the New Deal. A staunch Republican, he was admired by Herbert Hoover and autocratically ran a tired but loyal union in an industry racked by a previous history of bloody repression. Recognizing the great charter to labor implicit in the new legislation, the fifty-five year old Lewis gained a new lease on life and dreamed of huge industrial unions organized on an industry-wide basis rather than the smaller craft units sponsored by the traditional AFL leadership. The new movement would enlist the great mass of unorganized and unskilled workers into a powerful social force, somewhat along the line once proposed by Thorstein Veblen and the old IWW leaders.

Lewis and other AFL visionaries such as Sidney Hillman formed their own organization, the Committee for Industrial Organization, and split off from the AFL leadership in 1936. They swept through the textile industry and heavy industries such as steel, autos and rubber as total union membership increased remarkably from four million in 1936 to over fifteen million by 1947. Their critical fight with General Motors culminated in the forty-four day sit-down strike, illegal but effective, in the GM plant in Flint, Michigan, before the CIO's United Auto Workers were finally recognized. It did not help the cause of the nation's largest employer when the Senate's La Follette Committee released in January 1937 verified reports that GM had spent $995,000 for strike-breakers, labor spies and the purchase of machine-guns, ammunition and tear-gas shells. By comparison the alleged persecution of Ralph Nader, the auto safety man, thirty years later, was mild indeed.

Meanwhile Lewis scored another personal triumph by quietly breakfasting with Myron C. Taylor, the head of U.S. Steel, and negotiating the recognition of the CIO's steelworker's unit in this stronghold of fifty years of anti-unionism. In a few years, big unions had suddenly become established as an integral part of American capitalism. Although it may be charged that they have become inflationary as well as respectable and stodgy now that labor's rights have been well-secured, their chronic demands for a larger supply of the rewards have shaped as much as anything else America's fabulous middle-class purchasing power. Ideally they also serve to counter-balance the forces of both big business and big government, acting as an economic counterpart to the government's political system of checks and balances. This balance has been helped by the union members' frequent refusal to vote as they are told to vote, as Lewis soon learned.

The man who helped to make such history was also a trial to his country. Roosevelt distrusted and feared the headstrong Lewis in spite of the huge financial support provided by the United Mine Workers in the 1936 elections. "A plague on both your houses," was FDR's answer when Lewis demanded action against the steel companies. Lewis thereupon supported Republican candidates with a vengeance. So sure of his popularity against Roosevelt's, he pledged to resign as head of the CIO if Willkie did not win. He kept his word and thereafter concentrated on an exasperating series of UMW walkouts, generally ordered as cold weather approached, which caused Roosevelt in war-time 1943 and Truman in 1946 to federalize the mines temporarily. There were news reports that Cyrus Eaton attempted to negotiate between Lewis and the operators in 1946. Eaton's published comment on the 1946 episode was as follows:

The nation was driven from one fit of madness to another by ranting oratory on the radio and by blazing headlines, inflammatory editorials, and brutal cartoons in the press, until civil war would have been inevitable, had it not been for the wisdom and the restraint of the miners' leader. Throughout the entire time, John L. Lewis never uttered a syllable of complaint and never issued a statement criticizing anybody.

In 1947 Lewis was talking strike again. This time Secretary of the Treasury George Humphrey and Benjamin Fairless of U.S. Steel showed a new flexibility on the business side that must have pleased Eaton. They met with John L. Lewis for private talks and brought about a settlement largely on Lewis's terms. Many industrialists and members of Congress objected indignantly but Humphrey defended the move on practical grounds and stated that Lewis's demands were quite reasonable.

In time, Eaton decided to go into the coal-mining business himself. He began buying into West Kentucky Coal Company, one of the country's largest independent producers of bituminous coal, in 1951. By 1954, it was announced that he had successfully gained control and he assumed chairmanship of the company. One of the first orders of business was the signing up by the UMW of West Kentucky's approximate three thousand non-union miners. In 1955, Eaton negotiated the purchase of the Nashville Coal Company from Jet Potter, one of the most belligerently anti-union employers in the country, who bought full-page ads in the *Chicago Tribune* to call the TVA, one of his major customers, a "Communist rathole." As a result of the purchase, fourteen hundred more miners became union men and Nashville Coal was merged into West Kentucky. Meanwhile West Kentucky continued to convert into a highly mechanized operation.

When John L. Lewis became President Emeritus of the UMW in 1959 he seemed to be on excellent terms with those coal operators who had survived his incessant demands as well as the more devastating requirements of mechanization. They expressed their sincere regrets on his retirement and presented him with a rare set of Shakespeare, from whom Lewis had borrowed a good deal of his blasts against them. The man who had once been vilified as a menace for his single-minded obsession with wage and welfare improvements has been raised to the level of labor statesman. The reason for this has been his realistic appraisal of the fact that coal would become obsolete as a competitive fuel without the ruthless mechanization of the mines. As a result, the present membership of the UMW is about 50,000 compared with a post-war peak of 400,000 and areas such as Appalachia are poverty pockets for unrelocated miners. Since royalties to the UMW Welfare Fund are paid by the mine operators per ton, this Fund, as well as the UMW's own assets, are considered extremely healthy for a sick industry.

On September 14, 1959, the Landrum-Griffin Act was passed, requiring unions such as the UMW to file financial reports for public knowledge. Meanwhile, some independent non-mechanized mine operators in Tennessee, having been sued by the UMW for delinquent royalty payments to the Welfare Fund, counter-sued in the Tennessee federal court on the grounds that the UMW and the Welfare Fund trustees were conspiring against them to put them out of business. Of interest here is the fact that the UMW financial report as well as the sworn testimony of Lewis and Eaton confirmed what had often been rumored, a significant financial relationship between the capitalist and the labor leader. As reported by Nathan G. Caldwell, an honored staff writer on the *Nashville Tennessean* who has been reporting TVA news for over twenty-five years, the transactions included a loan of several millions secured by C & O railroad stock to help Robert Young gain control of the New York Central as well as direct ownership by the UMW of $16 million of C & O stock. It was also revealed that West Kentucky Coal Company had been purchased by Eaton with the aid of UMW funds. In 1960 the UMW owned or held as collateral against Eaton borrowings West Kentucky Coal common and preferred stock then valued at $10 million.[13] In 1963 Eaton sold his 63½ per cent interest in West Kentucky Coal to a Cleveland group headed by the former chairman of the board of the Cleveland Trust Company and was presumably out of the coal business. In a sense the financial interest between Lewis and Eaton, completely legal, spoils the image of the two octogenarians meeting for the simpler joys of Greek poetry and Shakespearean prose. Inevitably invidious conclusions would be drawn as to their motives as there have been to Eaton's mission to the Russians. But as capitalism has transformed itself in the twentieth century, the roles of labor leader and management representative often seem to blur. As a matter of fact, so does the old distinction between capitalist and commissar. "He's a clean desk man," is how Cyrus Eaton once described Nikita Khrushchev.

PART II

I

The State Department may have itself to blame for Cyrus Eaton's establishment as an unofficial ambassador to the U.S.S.R. In 1955 Frank Kluckhohn was escorting a visiting team of Russian journalists on a reciprocal friendship tour. They had come to Cleveland among other things to watch a pro football game between the Cleveland Browns and the Pittsburgh Steelers. The Russians said they would prefer to see a live capitalist instead of the game and Kluckhohn had the inspired thought of taking them to Eaton at his Acadia Farms.

Until this time Eaton had advanced no particular views about American foreign policy, although he had graciously started a series of international intellectual retreats at his summer home in Pugwash in 1955. Quite unconnected with Pugwash and perhaps in response to the visit of the journalists, he sent in 1955 a prize Scotch Shorthorn bull to the Russians from his world-famous Acadian herd.

Even sending a bull to the Russians was a controversial peace offering in 1955. America in the mid-fifties was in a bitter mood, having won World War II and then finding itself in an endless cold war against an expanding Communist threat both in Europe and Asia. A revolutionary foreign policy concept known as "containment" and "coexistence" had to be digested and accepted by a nation used to simpler solutions. The common sense on which the policy was based was apparent to most people. It was the best of three choices, the other two being either a war to eliminate the Russian threat or an isolationism that would abandon the field to them. The seventeen billion dollars being spent on the Marshall Plan and other aid proved to be the most satisfactory containment action of all since it generously helped rebuild a fallen and friendly Europe and bolstered our own economy at the same time. But Korea proved that a war could break out again. A pained nation in August 1953 reviewed the war that was never officially a war and had cost 25,000 dead, 115,000 other casualties and $22 billion. The ugly blot of McCarthyism, covering the same time span as the Korean war and preying on American fears and uncertainties, was a symptom of the strains inherent in the containment-coexistence policy. Yet gradually, through the leadership of Truman and Eisenhower, most Americans were beginning to realize that the social and economic revolutions in Russia, China and other countries throughout the world were not necessarily going to produce "democracies" in the foreseeable future and they generally supported this appeasing, bi-partisan foreign policy. They reluctantly recognized the limitations imposed on foreign policy in a world where one quarter of the earth's surface and over one quarter of its people were under Communist leadership.

At least three new elements had to be considered in the mid-fifties. Stalin died in March 1953, hastening the end of the Korean war. Instead of violent disorder, Russia showed itself capable of calmly transferring leadership to a much less fierce Malenkov and then to Khrushchev early in 1955. The latter, with his grinning countenance, corny humor and courageous exorcism of Stalin, stirred cautious hopes for the wisdom of our policy.

A second element was the explosion of the H-Bomb on November 1, 1952 revealing a capacity for ultimate destruction in World War III. This was apparent also to the Russians who followed our belated announcement of the H-Bomb in March 1954 by proclaiming they also had one. The balance of terror had arrived. The cover of the *Bulletin of Atomic Scientists* showed the clock at two minutes before twelve. President Eisenhower expressed the spreading American awareness when he said: "We have arrived at the point . . . where there is just no real alternative to peace."

The third element, subject to considerably more divergent opinions than the others, was Secretary of State John Foster Dulles's change in the containment policy when he announced the decision to rely on "the deterrent of massive retaliatory power" on January 12, 1954. The new policy reflected less willingness on the Republican Administration's part to maintain the huge expenditures for armaments and foreign aid of the Truman Administration, an admirable decision in relation to disarmament at least. There was also skepticism about the desirability of adjusting so readily to unfriendly social revolutions throughout the world. Dulles, a particularly strong Secretary of State, took the lead in hardening the idea of containment by referring to "liberation" of satellite countries and calling for a "crusading spirit" to instill American values and hence peace in the world. This was received by the Communist world as a threat of "peace or else" on American terms and the cold war was intensified. Since then of course the trend of foreign policy has been tremendously complicated by the escalation of the war in Viet Nam, but these were in general the conditions of the 1950's when thinking men, all equally high-minded and devoted to peace, took differing stands on foreign policy. Among them was Cyrus Eaton, who achieved prominence for his views solely because he was a capitalist and a very rich one. To dismiss him as a fellow traveller or as a man looking only for business advantages or publicity would do him an injustice.

II

It was an easy step for the Pugwash conferences to switch from Aristotle in 1955 to nuclear disarmament in 1957. Intellectuals and scientists could not help gravitating towards these themes. The immediate impetus to Eaton's imagination was the appeal by nine eminent scientists in July 1955, including Einstein and Lord Russell, calling on the nations to give up war because the H-Bomb threatened the existence of mankind.

Unable to call his conference of nuclear scientists at his home in Ohio because the Soviets would not be permitted by the United States to attend, Eaton held it at Pugwash after assuring the Canadian government that the meeting would not be turned into a platform for anti-western propaganda. A top-echelon international group of scientists attended and established the Pugwash Conference of Nuclear Scientists on July 6, 1957. The second meeting, held at Lac Beauport in Canada in 1958, brought Eaton a warm letter of congratulations from Khrushchev which led Eaton to announce that "Premier Khrushchev's reply provides full evidence that Russia wants to meet us half way." The conferences have continued intermittently in Austria, Moscow and London. Although Eaton picked up the bill for the earlier conferences, the scientists soon declared their financial independence of him. They nostalgically retained the name "Pugwash" for their meetings, but the American wing at least made it clear that the recent recipient of the Lenin Peace Prize was now something of a liability. In a letter to the *Bulletin of Atomic Scientists*, they stated:

> However, as Mr. Eaton has come to play an increasingly active and controversial role in political affairs, the scientists felt that his exclusive support of their conferences may place them in the wrong light. The Continuing Committee therefore solicited and obtained the greater part of funds for the conference of Kitzbuhel from other individuals and foundations, and did not ask for support from Mr. Eaton in the organization of the conference in Baden, Austria, in September, 1959 . . .[14]

Eaton was already moving on his own, however, and in 1958 he announced he was going to Russia to talk to Khrushchev. Congressman Walter brought up the Logan Act which forbids U. S. citizens from communicating with foreign governments to influence U. S. foreign policy. The law perpetuates the memory of the good Dr. Logan's negotiations with Talleyrand in 1798 by forbidding others to follow his example. Eaton has never been prosecuted under the Act, perhaps because to do so would admit he is influencing U. S. policy.

The 1958 visit was a great success for Eaton and he received red carpet treatment for the ten days he spent in Russia. Khrushchev flew up from a vacation in Yalta to receive him in the Kremlin and they talked for an hour and a half. When he returned, Eaton attacked American foreign policy in relation to Russia, intemperately calling Dulles an "insane fanatic" and charging that the majority of American politicians, generals and journalists were driving the country to war. The speech was delivered at the Cleveland City Club but was widely reported. "I found the Russian people friendly and eager for peace," he said, "and I came away convinced that peace can be obtained if there are concessions on both sides. The Soviets have accomplished prodigious feats of industrial and intellectual progress. I, a confirmed capitalist, could never subscribe to their system, but neither could I shut my eyes to the obvious fact that the Russian people are thoroughly sold on it." A month later Mikoyan delivered Khrushchev's gift of the troika and three white horses to Eaton at Acadia Farms.

In 1959 after Vice President Nixon called on Khrushchev in Russia and argued the merits of capitalism and communism in the famous "kitchen conference," the irrepressible Khrushchev made his first visit to America. He visited Los Angeles, a movie set, a farmer friend in Iowa and Eisenhower at Camp David, omitting Eaton from his busy schedule. The "spirit of Camp David" was a warm one, giving the cold war the greatest thaw in its history. The world looked forward hopefully to the Big Four summit conference in Paris in May 1960. A relaxed Eisenhower even wrote a pleasant letter to Eaton in March 1960 stating that the United

States was "prepared to explore every possible avenue to find a way towards disarmament."

Meanwhile early in May Eaton received notice that he was being awarded the Lenin Peace Prize, joining Paul Robeson, Dr. W. E. Du Bois, Howard Fast and Andrew W. Moulton, the retired Episcopal bishop of Utah, who were previous American recipients of the recently renamed award. He graciously accepted the honor and donated the $35,000 cash accompanying it to the Pugwash conferences. Now a world-famous figure, he announced plans to visit the satellite countries and by chance soon met Khrushchev once again.

Khrushchev had scuttled the summit conference in a display of vitriolic anger at the shooting down of Gary Power's U-2 spy plane over Russia on May 1. Curt and rude, Khrushchev insulted Eisenhower at the conference and cancelled his invitation to visit Russia. He continued his insults at a Parisian press conference after the meeting, calling Eisenhower a thief and suggesting his head be dipped in milk. The spirit of Camp David was in shreds.

It was under these circumstances that Cyrus Eaton deliberately arrived at Orly Airport in Paris on May 19. Khrushchev was being given a farewell by the French government at Orly when Eaton arrived. For colossal nerve, Eaton's embrace of his Russian friend at a time when his President had been so astonishingly vilified must have set some kind of record for audacity on the part of a private citizen. It also illustrates in a remarkable way the privilege of being an American citizen. There was a twenty minute chat, after which Khrushchev went off to Moscow and Eaton went on to accept an honorary degree from Charles University in Prague. He announced to the press: "Certainly a very vigorous speech, hardly in the Harvard University style, but one must remember Khrushchev was a coal miner. While I always regret the use of bitter phrases, I can understand quite well that Khrushchev in my judgment has had a great amount of provocation in his attempts to deal sincerely with disarmament." In the U. S. Senate, Senator Thomas J. Dodd of Connecticut denounced Eaton as a "materialistic, meddlesome, evil old man . . . a useful tool of the Communist movement."

III

In September of 1960 Khrushchev returned to the United States, having appointed himself head of his country's United Nations delegation in order to appear before that body. It was the session in which television viewers witnessed Fidel Castro hugging Khrushchev and giving a four-hour speech. Then the scene of Khrushchev taking off his shoe and shaking it at the speaker and finally the demand for Dag Hammarskjold's resignation. In the midst of all this the imperturbable Eaton entertained Khrushchev for lunch with one hundred fifty guests at the Hotel Biltmore. Eaton's after-luncheon remarks were phrased in the business metaphors with which he is most convincing. Asking for more Soviet-American trade, he stated:

> The lesson of business history is that the success of a great industrial corporation does not derive from impeding or retarding its competitors. When two or more rival enterprises prosper simultaneously, it is one of the highest benefits not only of the companies themselves, but also of the entire national economy.

> Similarly, in an expanding world economy, any nation with natural resources and energetic people can and should prosper without hindrance to other nations, but with benefit to all nations and to all mankind.

Those who expected or hoped that Eaton's pipeline to the Kremlin would vanish when Khrushchev was deposed were disappointed. Mikoyan was still the Soviet President and his son spent the following Thanksgiving as Eaton's house guest. Premier Kosygin held long conversations with Cyrus Eaton and his wife in Moscow on May 20, 1965 and used the occasion to warn the U.S. of increased Soviet involvement in Viet Nam, an unofficial rebuttal at the time to official sources in Washington that had expressed doubts about Russian willingness to increase its involvement in the war. Eaton had already advocated U.S. withdrawal from Viet Nam. On

June 30, 1967 Kosygin visited Castro in Havana and stopped over in Newfoundland on his way back to visit Cyrus Eaton for a lobster dinner and more hints to the press. In May 1968 Eaton visited Castro and praised him as a bold, clever leader.

The new breed of cool Soviet leadership seems to acknowledge Eaton as a legitimate inheritance but not with the warmth Khrushchev showered on his favorite capitalist. Eaton's relationship with the colorful Khrushchev was a highly personal one, underscored by Khrushchev's robust sense of humor and theatricality, qualities which are presently at a premium in the Kremlin. Eaton's credibility as a Soviet expert would be enhanced if he chose to comment openly on his old friend or to criticise the new leaders for apparently making Khrushchev a non-person in Soviet television programs and news releases. Like many enthusiasts, Eaton suffers from the intensity of his convictions and exasperatingly finds little wrong with the Russians. He accepts their domination of the Soviet bloc countries dispassionately and had no criticism to offer for the billion dollars of Soviet arms poured into Arab countries against Israel, let alone the transparent charges made against Israel by Federenko in the United Nations. Although urged by Cleveland Jewish leaders to take a stand as an important friend of Russia, he has also been silent on the periodic outbursts of anti-Semitism in that country, unlike his admired Lord Russell, who has repeatedly lent his name to such protests including direct appeals to Khrushchev. On the other hand, he has served usefully in advancing the view that Communist rhetoric need not be taken too seriously or as a basis for U. S. foreign policy. With a businessman's pragmatic approach, he separates the economic determinism and conspiratorial framework of Marxism from the self-interest and motivations of a Soviet Russia now over fifty years old and a century away from Marx. As a representative capitalist he speaks with authority in reminding us of the value of "bulls over bullets" and of how futile it is for Russia and the U. S. to be spending $100 billion a year on armaments even before Viet Nam became a major war. As a citizen he has been eloquent in warning industrialists as well as statesmen about the razor's edge his scientific friends have proved to him we are traversing. Even his home-town newspaper, the Cleveland *Plain Dealer*, decided to take a second look at him in 1964:

> Being a tycoon was unpopular enough, but making friends with the Russians these past ten years is something of which the public has taken a dim view.
>
> All this performance has given Eaton a very "bad press."
>
> He has been pretty much vilified by usually responsible critics who have implied that he is a rich eccentric rather flamboyantly off base.
>
> But has he really been off base?
>
> In the last year the relations between Russia and the United States have changed rather remarkably.
>
> We have a nuclear test-ban treaty.
>
> We are opening up trade with Russia.
>
> Cultural exchange programs between the two super powers are increasing, not decreasing.
>
> All along the line, in spite of occasional setbacks, we are moving toward more agreeable relations with the Soviet Union.
>
> This is the approach on a political level which Mr. Eaton has been pursuing on a more intellectual level.
>
> While he certainly will never be kissed on both cheeks by the old-guard established business community of Cleveland, it could be that the white-haired charmer of Acadia Farms, as he passes his eightieth birthday, may yet be vindicated by future events.

V

"It is a very wise policy," Cyrus Eaton, Jr. recently said about Cyrus Eaton Sr.'s belief that a wealthy man should not give his wealth to his children. "No one in the family will get a penny on my father's death. As kids this was spelled out to us by my father. He told each of us: 'I'll live my life and you live yours.'"[15]

One way Cyrus Eaton, Jr. hopes to make it on his own is through his Tower International Inc., which is in the business of developing trade relations with the Communist world. Tower made front page news in 1967 when it announced it was taking in the International Basic Economy Corporation, controlled by the Rockefeller brothers, on a 50-50 basis for iron curtain country enterprise, such as hotels and films in Hungary and an aluminum plant in Yugoslavia. IBEC was organized in 1947 and heretofore had been specializing in enterprises in 29 underdeveloped countries, none of them in the Communist bloc. There is a storybook aspect to this partnership between the son of John D.'s office clerk and John D.'s grandsons sixty years later. The affiliation of the prestigious, socially-conscious Rockefeller clan with Tower is a tacit endorsement of Cyrus Eaton and his plea for American business to support coexistence. It is another victory for the irascible old man who always seems to land on his feet.

Footnotes

CHAPTER 5

Cyrus Eaton:

Khrushchev's Favorite Capitalist

Cyrus Eaton's twin careers of businessman and self-appointed statesman have been duly reported in the press and business journals. Marcus Gleisser, a prize-winning staff member of the Cleveland *Plain Dealer*, wrote *The World of Cyrus Eaton* (New York, 1965), a valuable first full-length biography of his fellow Clevelander. Though objective in the sense he did not intend "to portray the subject either as a hero or as a villain," Gleisser seems to reveal the dominating presence of the litigious old charmer breathing down his neck. Journalists have generally found direct interviews with Eaton unsatisfactory. Similarly members of the Cleveland Establishment spoken to by the author are not quite sure about Cyrus Eaton except that they do not want to tangle with him.

Robert Sheehan's "The Man From Pugwash" in *Fortune* of March 1961 is an excellent article which includes an analysis of Eaton's philosophical detachment from the threats of Communism in terms of Eaton's intellectual heroes. "The Kaiser-Eaton Feud" in *Fortune* of October 1948 is an exciting tale of the great conflict. An excellent criticism of Eaton from the right is John Chamberlain's "Cyrus Eaton: An Old Man Goes East," in the *National Review* (June 6, 1959); and for an equally cogent approval from the left there is John Barden's "Cyrus Eaton: Merchant of Peace," in *The Nation* of January 31, 1959.

[1] Marcus Gleisser, *The World of Cyrus Eaton* (New York, 1965), p. 244.

[2] *Newsweek*, October 1, 1965, p. 65.

[3] Marcus Gleisser, *op. cit.*, p. 65.

[4] *Finance*, "Cyrus Eaton," April, 1966, p. 9.

[5] Thomas M. Girdler, *Boot Straps* (New York, 1943), pp. 193-194.

[6] Cyrus Eaton, "A Capitalist Looks at Labor," *University of Chicago Law Review*, April, 1947, pp. 331 ff.

[7] *Business Week*, February 17, 1968, p. 123.

[8] *National Review*, November 19, 1960, p. 300.

[9] Matthew Josephson, *Infidel in the Temple* (New York, 1967), pp. 339-344.

[10] *Ibid.*, pp. 53 ff.

[11] Cyrus Eaton, "A Capitalist Looks at Labor," *op. cit.*

[12] *Fortune*, March, 1961, p. 230.

[13] Nat Caldwell and Gene S. Graham, "The Strange Romance between John L. Lewis and Cyrus Eaton," *Harper's Magazine*, December, 1961, pp. 24 ff.

[14] *Bulletin of Atomic Scientists*, October, 1960, p. 16.

[15] *New York Times*, January 22, 1967, p. 61.

ADOLF BERLE:

Keeper of the Corporate Conscience

A. A. Berle, Jr. is a man of many talents who has spent a lifetime studying and writing about the American big business corporation. Whenever experts analyze the direction or significance of the modern corporation, they automatically acknowledge Berle's concepts. He has been at his task so long and faithfully as a seminal thinker in this field that no treatise on corporations is likely to appear without a string of references to Berle in footnotes and index. As evidence of his stature, a large literature has already appeared which gleefully takes exception to his predictions and positions, much as Berle himself impaled the myths and beliefs of the pre-New Deal economists and business spokesmen. Now in his seventies, the former Brain Truster of FDR must face the fate reserved for most of yesterday's radicals — the label of conservative bestowed by a new left. A truly philosophical and cultivated man, Berle can take such criticism with grace. Accustomed to viewing history and man's fate with sweeping vision, he undoubtedly appreciates the irony of his situation. Perhaps it would be too much to expect two intellectual revolts within the lifetime of one man.

As a critic of business, he appears in retrospect to have been a loving admirer, if not an outright seduced one, of reformed capitalism. Reformation versus orthodoxy may be a key to Berle's character and style. He believes in the capacity of people to reform themselves and to make their institutions just and humane. He also believes in the capacity of the law, his first love, to put teeth in reforms, aided by high-minded commissions, courts and administrative tribunals as needed. These are the premises which an experimental, trial-and-error New Deal used to launch a political and economic structure so different from its predecessor. Thirty years later, Berle fondly calls the result "The American Economic Republic," seeking a national, noble name for the alliance between state and business which has given us our unsurpassed standard of living. J. K. Galbraith, in a more cynical frame of mind, calls it "The New Industrial State," revealing overtones of internationalism and a dominant technology in his choice of title.

Galbraith, incidentally, expresses affection and admiration for Adolf Berle, his equal in versatility and national importance. Galbraith includes an irreverent reference to Berle in the cast of his novel, *The Triumph:*

> The ambassador's (to the Organization of the American States) long political and public career was behind him. This career and his years and modest wealth entitled him to a certain consideration. But he had always shown an inclination to the premature position. Before they had become popular or even commonplace, he had been for the CIO, migrant workers, Social Security, the TVA, modern painting, birth control, Averell Harriman, Herbert Lehman, Fiorello La Guardia, Norman Thomas, Luis Muñoz Marin, and Negro rights. In advancing years, he still showed a predisposition to change. If a policy seemed wrong, he would propose revision regardless of consequences.

Berle in turn is an admirer of Galbraith. Of Galbraith's recent *The New Industrial State*, he wrote that the book was long overdue and would make economic history. He also noted that practically everything Galbraith said had already been advanced by himself in his own books.[1] Of the two critics, Berle is the better one for sharpening our historical comprehension of twentieth century American business. Berle is a born teacher and more tolerant of dissent. With him we can examine the underlying theory and significant trends. As his colleagues do, we can also use his ideas as a convenient point of departure for conflicting views.

II

First a glance at the man himself, more for human interest than for an explanation of his beliefs. He was born in Boston in 1895, was educated at Harvard and is presently Professor Emeritus of Law at Columbia University. Few people have lived such an exemplary and active long life: New Dealer (and outliner of the Securities and Exchange Act), Treasurer of the City of New York from 1936 to 1938, Assistant Secretary of State of the United States from 1938 to 1944, Ambassador to Brazil from 1945 to 1946, Chairman of President Kennedy's Task Force on Latin-American policy and in 1961 special assistant to the Secretary of State. Presently he is Chairman of the Board of the Twentieth Century Fund. In between, he has written books, practised corporation law and taught at Harvard Business School and at Columbia Law. He has also gained some experience in the business world as Chairman of the Board of American Molasses Company. A Republican when his fellow professor at Columbia, Raymond Moley, brought him into FDR's 1932 campaign, he was saluted as a leader of the New York State Liberal Party on his seventieth birthday, confirming his disposition towards change. At this banquet, he must have chagrined many of his audience by strongly backing President Johnson's Viet Nam policy and warning, as so many of his fellow elder statesmen have done, of the dangers of appeasement.[2]

If Berle has one bias that could be construed in some quarters a weakness, it is his militant anti-Communism. On the economic front, it often leads him to extolling the American system because of its superiority to the Russian system rather than concentrating on the defects of the home product. Although he acknowledges that the American system has consigned classical capitalism to its historical nineteenth century museum, he will not willingly grant the Russians similar custody of classical Communism. His claim that "the number of prisoners in concentration camps in the Soviet Union has steadily been greater than the entire number of men and women unemployed in the United States save perhaps for one brief period of the Great Depression"[3] calls for proof and is a somewhat irrelevant commentary on our unemployment. Similarly, the statement that "an unemployed workman (in the U. S.) drawing insurance pay is better supplied with goods and services than a fully employed and paid workman in the Soviet Union or Czechoslovakia"[4] would bring no cheers from either workman.

Unlike many corporation executives, Berle opposed in 1963 the lifting of trade barriers, including the sale of wheat, to a hungry Russia.[5] Senator Fulbright in turn called such an attitude a step towards isolating the U. S. from its allies.[6] Fulbright and Berle had previously disagreed on a more painful issue, the Bay of Pigs invasion of Cuba. President Kennedy later gave Senator Fulbright alone of all his advisors credit for forthrightly opposing this discredited maneuver. Berle, as the Latin-American authority in the group that met in the Cabinet Room to advise Kennedy, consistently advocated placing the invaders in Cuba "but did not insist on a major production," according to Arthur M. Schlesinger, Jr., who was there.[7] In spite of his strong commitment to social reform rather than reactionary government in Cuba and his familiarity with the country and its problems (one of his first assignments for FDR was to Cuba during its revolutionary crisis in 1933), Berle's performance was necessarily a disappointment to Kennedy. As Berle has stated elsewhere, public service for corporation executives as well as professors is rewarded more in "brickbats than halfpennies" in Washington. After performing valuable service in organizing the

Alliance for Progress at Punta del Este, Uruguay, in August 1961, he retired from government service. Noting a possible error of judgment in our guide to the business system is not meant to discredit him. On the contrary, discovery of any flaw in this admirable man can make him more credible for having a human weakness.

Among his colleagues in his younger days, such a search would be exasperatingly in vain. Adolf Berle was a child prodigy. In fact, for years he was regarded as a child prodigy who never ceased being a prodigy. Descended from the ancient line of von Berlebergs of Germany, Berle's grandfather was a colorful artist who fled Europe in the 1850's and died at Vicksburg at thirty-two, serving with the Union Army. His son, Adolf, Sr., on the other hand, lived to a ripe old age and saw Adolf, Jr. rise to eminence via the intellectual route he had plotted for him. This planning for genius was implemented by the father's marriage to the daughter of G. Frederick Wright, clergyman and geologist at Oberlin. Berle's mother, a graduate of Oberlin, had a strong intellect and social conscience. She worked among the Sioux Indians before settling down with her husband as he assumed a Congregationalist pastorate in Boston.

Berle père had a speed-up system for the training of his progeny that would have horrified Dr. Spock. Before they could read, the Berle children recited Homer, Virgil, Dante and Goethe from memory. Like the father of John Stuart Mill, Adolf, Sr. "harnessed" the children to the cart of utility, extending the discipline even to the games children play. Digging in the garden became a lesson in soil erosion and sandpiles evoked Caesar's fortifications. Their dolls and pets bore classical names. The children were tutored practically the year around by both parents and each emerged a prodigy on time.

Although Adolf, Jr.'s childhood was comfortable enough, the parents instilled in him a concern for the poor that made him a natural reformer. He vividly remembers, at age eight, "stumbling over bodies of men dead of starvation or exposure, or both, in Chicago during the depression year 1903."[8] By the same token, he reaches no further than his own ancestry for an understanding of the Protestant ethic which he so typifies in service and duty and which, according to Max Weber and R. H. Tawney, helped create the new institution of capitalism:

> In describing the "Protestant ethic," I have discarded secondary statements. I have drawn heavily on the statements to me personally by my grandfather, G. Frederick Wright, whose memoirs perhaps give a fair picture of the economic as well as the theological doctrine . . . From him and my father (also a Congregationalist clergyman) and from familiarity with Protestant colleges established straight across the northern tier of the United States, one can perhaps reach a rather deeper understanding of the scope of the Protestant ethic than from the familiar statements of economists and secondary students. They, naturally, give greatest weight to the fact that the Protestant Reformation eliminated many restrictive Catholic rules carried down from medieval thinking. The Reformation permitted lending money at interest, whereas medieval Catholic doctrine considered any interest as sinful "usury." Protestant doctrine did not attempt to control prices by maintaining the conception of a "just price," as Catholic schoolmen had done. Unquestionably, the Reformation played a great part in bringing into existence the "free-market" conception dominant in the nineteenth century. But it also set up moral limitations on its operation, and those have been largely ignored.[9]

Berle graciously adds that the Jewish ethic and the Catholic ethic are equally important to American business ethics. He notes precisely, however, that their influence was not felt until the twentieth century, so the term Protestant ethic is historically correct for preceding centuries.

The boy prodigy entered Harvard at fourteen. He completed his courses in three years and spent a year in graduate school picking up a Master's Degree while waiting for his classmates to catch up with him. He entered the law school at eighteen and when he was awarded his degree three years later became the youngest graduate in law school history.

Berle's classmates recall him as a youth in short pants who would tag along with eminent students such as John Reed, like Berle destined to write about revolutions. By the time he was in law school, he had attained long pants and was by no means shy about using his precocious mind to hold his own. He became a favorite of William Z. Ripley, Harvard's famous authority on trusts, whose studies provided the groundwork for Berle's early investigations of the modern corporation. In turn he was obnoxious in the eyes of Felix Frankfurter, who often found himself being cornered in classroom argument by the bright lad who had boned up for the express purpose of goading him. Their mutual dislike is said to have survived their service in the New Deal.

After graduating he became an apprentice in the Boston law office of Louis D. Brandeis, whose views on the evils of corporate size he was to repudiate effectively. Berle had a deep regard for Brandeis and feels that in the 1960's Brandeis would finally have come around to seeing the other side of bigness.[10] After brief service in World War I, Berle was attached to a staff of experts on Russia, Poland and the Baltic nations with the American delegation to the Paris Peace Conference in 1919. Like several other idealistic young delegates, including John M. Keynes and William C. Bullitt, he resigned in protest against the Treaty of Versailles, an action hardly noticed by the men in charge.

Moving to New York, Berle began his teaching career and produced with Gardiner C. Means the book that would launch his national reputation, *The Modern Corporation and Private Property*, in 1932. This elaborate study emphasized the independence of corporations from their stockholders and their headlong rush towards concentrations of great size. The book was Berle's passport to the New Deal which already had cast business in a villain's role. Berle was captivated by FDR and gladly joined the "Brains Trust" with his fellow Columbia professors, Rexford Tugwell and Raymond Moley. Legend has it that the term was originated by James Kieran of the *New York Times*. Soon it was renamed the Brain Trust and Berle, five feet six, high-domed and bursting with theories, was known as The Brain.

Berle's tour with the Brain Trust lasted only a few years, as he cautiously refused to take a full-time position in the Administration, although he had been highly productive and influential as a technician and theorist in Washington. His concern with the problem of size in American business helps us understand some of the basic changes in the first years of the New Deal.

There is a convenient generalization which classifies Moley, Tugwell and Berle as the "First New Deal," men whose theories were sympathetic to centralized power but who also favored large units of production, regulated by the state in cooperation with business. They shared the feeling of Berle that America could no longer be a nation of small businessmen and that the free market as governor of the economy was not only obsolete but unworkable. Berle added his own moral dimension to the discussions by proposing that responsible businessmen were capable of self-restraints in the public interest and thus could diminish regulation. He had commenced his lifelong probe for the corporate conscience.

The generalization associates the "Second New Deal," from about 1935 on, with a reaction against the recalcitrant business interests, marked by tax increases, tougher regulations and a resurgence of "trust-busting" fervor. The large corporations, which Berle and Means had exposed as a power equal to the state in many areas, became a special target of the Temporary National Economic Committee hearings in 1938. The mood was exaggerated by the appearance of Ferdinand Lundberg's first book on "America's Sixty Families." The Committee asked Berle for a memorandum of suggestions for the investigation. Berle set aside his duties as Assistant Secretary of State and dashed off a 12,000 word, twenty-three page document that made him the sudden favorite of *Time* and *Business Week* among all New Dealers. In it he called for an investigation of business organizations and practises in which business could logically cooperate rather than feel harassed. It cautioned against the notion that bigness was badness and advocated a pluralistic system involving competitive smaller units, oligopolies and quasi-public ownership, according to which worked best in a given field. Lundberg's charge of irresponsible fortunes was brushed aside as irrelevant to the control of power. The memorandum called for repeal of the unpopular undistributed profits tax and elimination of proposals for federal licensing of corporations. As a final heresy he stated that "a fair criticism of the technique of the New Deal has been that it indulged in shotgun imposition of regulations without adequate definition of standards."[11]

The business community, already shorn of much of its old power, was of course correct in looking at the offer of a return to a free market, small enterprise system by way of the TNEC with a beady eye. TNEC in turn reached no clear-cut conclusions and terminated as the country approached the brink of war. Henceforth antitrust activities would continue as a highly important restraint against monopoly but bigness was here to stay.

Looking back at the New Deal in 1964, Berle is incredulous at the charges of socialism levelled at FDR as well as himself by right-wing forces of business, finance and political power:

> In a broad sense the New Deal was an institutional revolution. It shifted the major center of economic power from private to public institutions. President Roosevelt and his intellectual as well as political cohorts quite consciously chose not to make it a socialist revolution. . . . We certainly refused to take advantage of the economic collapse to set up state socialism (let alone Communism) or to intrigue within the government to prepare for such a development. We did undertake through democratically adopted measures to redistribute the national income, steering more of it towards the least favored among the population. We hoped for a better distribution of wealth. We did intend that the federal government should take over the ultimate controls of currency and credit (as it did), and the power, where necessary, to allocate capital resources as well. We did hope for the location of residual power over the economic system in the hands of the democratically-elected Congress and the United States government, while maintaining non-statist enterprise as the major method of production. . . . For once in history, the pragmatic, socially-minded reformists won . . .[12]

Behind every man one searches for a woman. Berle married Beatrice Bishop, the daughter of the wealthy Courtlandt Field Bishop, in 1927. Mr. Bishop, something of a testy, real estate-rich patroon, was not enthusiastic over his ·new son-in-law, who was busily engaged in volunteer social work at the Henry Street Settlement House in New York at the time. The feelings were exacerbated by a dispute with his daughter over the Bishop estate. Under the terms of the will, Beatrice had become the potential heiress of a considerable fortune from her grandfather Bishop. The father had resisted the will's directions to share his trusteeship with the New York Life Insurance & Trust Company. The trust company took the case to court. Mr. Bishop lost, further alienating him from his daughter.

It was a marriage almost as cerebral as that of Beatrice and Sydney Webb and an extremely happy one. Beatrice was a Vassar Graduate who went on to accumulate degrees at the Sorbonne and Columbia and to become a psychiatric social worker. While raising a family, she decided to go to medical school and has since become a leading international public health specialist in her own right. An early recognizer of her husband's genius, she earned what must be unique among book dedications in *The American Economic Republic:*

> To Beatrice Berle, Baccalaureate of the University of Paris, Master of Arts in History, Doctor and Teacher of Medicine, Ambassadress of the United States, whose skill and hearth and heart have been open alike to the high and humble of many lands, this book is dedicated, in admiration, friendship and love.

III

Back to the classroom, then, with Adolf Berle. Our mentor is an extremely rational man with an optimistic faith in the capacity of American democracy and business to bring the good life to the greatest number of people. He has been at the seat of power both in domestic and foreign affairs. For a lifetime he has considered our political and economic condition as a student, philosopher and seer. He is a hard-working, driven man who expresses his thoughts in lucid prose. A one hundred per cent pragmatist, he still holds to his ideals. One reservation: Perhaps the serenity of his rich life prevents him from expressing the doom and outrage associated with less poised and balanced social critics. This should not be a handicap.

Our course with Berle starts with property, fundamental to economic systems. Next to power, eternal problem found in all systems and organizations. On to capital, since we are examining capitalism. Then to markets as the regulator of capitalist enterprise. Finally the matter of responsibility. This is an offshoot of power. It provides an opportunity for the exercise of conscience, a corporate specialty of Berle. All in all, hardly an outline for traditional economics, but Berle starts on the assumption that how we make our living is a social and political matter, even a philosophical matter, quite as much as an economic one.

Property

"Property is theft!" Can it be the voice of Thorstein Veblen once again? It is Pierre Joseph Proudhon, summonsed up by Berle to help stretch our minds about property.[13] The famous French philosopher and anarchist (1809-1865) uttered his paradox somewhat in the manner of today's "God is dead!" At any rate, he created a similar sensation.

Berle reminds us that the concept of property has changed in the course of history. Except for personal possessions, widespread ownership of property hardly existed in feudal society or even under the Tudors of England. "Few of us in the twentieth century remember that private property, except as a favor of the state, hardly existed until the middle of the eighteenth century."[14]

In turn, ownership of productive property was recognized as a balance against too powerful a state. This was one of the daring points made by some primitive economists known as "the physio-crats," led by François Quesnay, a physician to Louis XV at the Court of Versailles, a century before Proudhon. Proudhon reluc-tantly endorsed these sentiments, disliking the illegal powers of the state quite as much as the illegal powers of the rich. Working away in the British Museum, Karl Marx agreed about the theft but urged in his *Manifesto* that property be expropriated altogether from individual ownership.

In America, removed by geography, history and the Protestant ethic from class struggles, the new nation recognized property as an inalienable right, drawing inspiration from the natural rights philosophers such as Locke and the progress of the industrial revo-lution in the mother country England. Thomas Jefferson empha-sized it was not just an economic matter. His hope for a society of small and relatively equal property owners was based on the moral and character-building qualities of private ownership. Such men, he felt, would be capable of self-government and able to resist the power of church and state.

From considerations such as these, Berle spins a typically imaginative and bold theory in a paper prepared for the Center for the Study of Democratic Institutions. From his promontory, he sees a "kind of rhythm of history."[15] It starts with the downbeat of the feudal system, wherein property is owned only by the power systems of nobles and prelates. As the king-state succeeds feudal-ism, the revolutionary doctrine that there should be widespread private property asserts itself, for example, among the physiocrats. The private property system then reaches its peak of moral and political sanctification in the eighteenth and nineteenth centuries, only to yield to a new power system once again.

This time the agent is a strange animal called the "corporation," not Karl Marx as one might expect, at least not for the Western world.

The new corporation promoters had a checkered career. In part-nership with kings and queens they plundered the seas and rendered other profitable services. When Adam Smith wrote in the 1770's, the corporation had been outlawed for fifty years as a result of the

South Sea Bubble fraud. In *The Wealth of Nations*, Smith dismissed the corporation as a major force in economics because it required men to work for other men and obviously no man would pay as much attention to other men's affairs as he would to his own. As a collective enterprise, it would be inefficient. Its inefficiency would then eliminate it under the "invisible hand" of the free market.

It was only a matter of time before the corporation flourished mightily, despite attempts by state and national governments to restrict it. The control of property reverted once again to a new power system, the corporate managers. The property owners still maintained legal title to their property as evidenced by their engraved stock certificates. But it was property without power. For the most part, it was also without responsibility. Hardly the source of moral and political invigoration that Jefferson prescribed.

Robert Heilbroner notes a similar rhythm in economic history and adds a new agitator in his book, *The Limits of American Capitalism*. Would an observer in thirteenth century France, for example, possibly recognize the limits of feudalism? More particularly, could he recognize a coming change in the feudal economy, tied as it was to the manor, established customs and rigid classes? Not unless he anticipated a totally different form of social organization. Just such a subverting influence was at work, the evolution of cash markets which would critically undermine the power of the lords and elevate out of all proportion the upstart merchants.[16] The rhythmic aspect is that possibly another force has already limited the future of capitalism, in this case the inevitable triumph of non-capitalist technology.

Thus the intellectuals shake the businessmen out of their complacency, or at least make them think harder about property. Berle has some other points for us to consider. If property is now largely "paper property" (close to one-half of all individually held property in the United States is such), it is rather essential that it be "liquid" paper. A share of American Telephone & Telegraph would have little attraction, even for the late Billy Rose, who was for a time its largest stockholder, if it weren't convertible into money as against telephones. Liquidity depends on the adequate functioning of the banking and currency system. This, in turn, Berle can state with authority, depends on the state running an effective central banking system, as it has for the past three decades. With such a system, it is possible to maintain supporting institutions for liquidity like the New York Stock Exchange. "It shocks the American financial community to be told that the New York Stock Exchange is one of the most highly developed statist institutions that we have. But there is no escape from the fact."[17]

J. K. Galbraith carries the thrust one step further, using a stock exchange metaphor. Emphasizing the fraternal relationship and interdependence of the "mature corporation" (i.e., General Motors, General Electric) with the state, he notes that the latter, through military and other technical purchases, "underwrites" the corporation's largest capital commitments in its area of most advanced technology.[18]

Berle has some final observations about these stock certificates, which he calls "passive" property. Aside from the vagaries of the stock market, the real value of the certificates reflects the going organization of staff and personnel as well as plant and equipment. It even represents strategic considerations beyond the control of management, for example, a favored tax position for the oil companies. If this is property, he asks, "What quality of it can fairly be called private?"

IV

Power

Berle has always been fascinated by power. Equally this peaceful man has been fascinated by revolution, one of the dynamics of power. In 1954, he described the modern corporation as the end result of "The Twentieth Century Capitalist Revolution" in his book of that title. His most recent book, *The Three Faces of Power*, (1967) heralds "The Supreme Court's New Revolution" in its subtitle. Clearly this advocate of gradual change has witnessed revolutions in his lifetime.

It *is* a revolutionary century. In fact its revolutionary qualities
in science, psychology, population growth, politics, economics,
racism, morals and what not must make many yearn for the next
century. Berle, of course, is drawn to the non-shooting kind. His
choice of revolution rather than evolution to describe what has happened is an expression of his tendency towards romanticism, as one
may discern in his search for the conscience.

Granted a revolution in capitalism, instead of a plain maturing
process, the specifics are first of all an overwhelming concentration
of power in America's two hundred largest corporations. If not two
hundred, *Fortune's* annual five hundred will do. The principle is
the same:

> Today approximately 50 per cent of American manu-
> facturing — that is, everything other than financial and
> transportation — is held by about 100 corporations, reck-
> oned, at least, by asset values . . . But in terms of power
> without regard to asset positions, not only do 500 cor-
> porations control two-thirds of the non-farm economy
> but within each of that 500 a still smaller group has the
> ultimate decision-making power. This is, I think, the
> highest concentration of economic power in recorded his-
> tory. Since the United States carries on not quite half of
> the manufacturing production of the entire world today,
> these 500 groupings — each with its own little dominat-
> ing pyramid within it — represent a concentration of
> power over economics which makes the medieval feudal
> system look like a Sunday school party. In sheer economic
> power this has gone far beyond anything we have yet
> seen.[19]

"Exaggerated for effect!" is Harvard Business School Professor
John E. Lintner's response:

> The evidence is clear that concentration ratios in other
> Western nations (let alone the areas behind the Iron
> Curtain) are substantially higher than those in the United
> States. Moreover, on the measures Berle uses, the concen-

tration in manufacturing is substantially the same in 1955 as in 1947 and 1931, and the overall concentration of assets, and still more of economic power, within the entire non-financial corporate sector is unquestionably lower than it was thirty years ago — noticeably as the result of SEC action under the death-sentence clause of the Public Utility Holding Company Act and the general economic disabilities of the railroad industry.[20]

Berle is not easily dislodged. He has long admitted — with relief — that the trend he and Means feared in 1932 has levelled off to a stable ratio. To conclude that the present situation equates to the situation in the thirties or even earlier, however, is decidedly wrong. It ignores the results of absolute size. A corporation with $400 million has one set of characteristics. That same corporation expanding to $4 billion is not the same. The pressures, stresses, power, potential and impact have shifted all along the line. As for proportions staying the same, Berle reminds us that forty years ago a much larger proportion of workers were agricultural. With the great bulk of Americans in industry today, the power factor of the corporations has increased proportionately as well as absolutely.[21] Most observers would agree that the tiresome statistics about concentration are unassailable and the question of power must be faced.

The reason is because of the powerful and uncontrolled choices left to the "self-perpetuating oligarchy," Berle's unkind name for the top management in the five hundred (Galbraith's "technostructure"). When General Motors decided to spend $1 billion on capital expansion in 1954, it may have headed off a pending recession. It could just as easily have increased its dividends and wages by the same billion. On the other hand, when General Motors led the auto industry in an all out race for an eight million car sales year in 1955, it accomplished a good deal of its objective by relaxing instalment sale terms. But the next year saw sales of only six million and a closely related recession. GM's control over its dealers and suppliers contributes similar questions of tremendous power, not to mention the effect on our public information media of its over

$100 million advertising budget. There is both truth and consequence in the unfortunate claim that "what's good for General Motors is good for the country." Similarly, the recurring negotiations between the steel industry and labor — and lately the government — over prices and wages have reverberating effects on all of us.

There is not much help in relating this condition to lack of stockholder responsibility, easily demonstrated by the ritual of annual meetings. Every schoolboy knows they are a farce and the critics need not belabor the point. *Fortune* occasionally makes the claim that management is responsive to shareholders since the jobs of those on the firing line at least are at stake. That would assign profitability as the sole function of management, however, since happy stockholders are quiet stockholders. Management itself scoffs at the idea of its independence from stockholders, pointing out the threat of tenders by raiders against weak management. In the present rash of raids, it is worth noting that the raids are more likely to be for the healthiest rather than the sickest companies. Often the tender or the forced merger is for the express purpose of satisfying the ambitions of new growth companies armed with unexpected resources in a churning investment atmosphere. Whether they are rationalizing industry, as they claim, or simply overpaying and thus overcapitalizing as the investment trusts did in the 1920's, remains to be seen. As always, statutory reforms will arise from the abuses. Meanwhile, Berle's theory of corporate independence from stockholders remains unchallenged by this weird wooing of stockholders to sell their atrophied power to the highest bidder.

* * *

Always ready to bring his theory up to date, Berle returns to the problem of business power in *The Three Faces of Power*, the revolution in the Supreme Court.

The three extraordinary examples of overt legislative power assumed by the Supreme Court, as cited by Berle, are *Brown* v. *Topeka* (the 1954 school segregation cases), *Baker* v. *Carr* (the 1962 one man-one vote ruling) and *Federal Trade Commission* v. *Procter & Gamble* (the order to P & G to "unmerge" Clorox in April 1967).

The third case is relevant to our study of business but one should note beforehand that none of these cases impels Berle to call for Chief Justice Warren's impeachment. On the contrary, he makes it very clear that:

> When Chief Justice Warren grasped the nettle in *Brown* v. *Topeka* and thereafter, he was entitled not to a call for his impeachment, as some extremists have done but to the public thanks of the United States. The Chief Justice was revolutionary. But he was right . . .[22]

In brief, Berle feels the Court could not have acted otherwise than it did:

> Far from arrogating to itself powers it did not have, the Court's latent constitutional powers granted it by the Fourteenth Amendment (in the first two cases) were activated by the pace of technical and social change. When this history is written, it will probably be found that the Supreme Court's action saved the country from a far more dangerous and disorderly change . . .[23]

Nevertheless, Berle feels the Court is stretching things a bit, following the tendency of power to aggrandize itself or to step into a vacuum left by others. The reaction of thirty-four irritated states to date having passed laws calling for a national constitutional convention to upset *Baker* v. *Carr* is an example of what he means. To avoid a constitutional crisis, Berle advises the Supreme Court to slow down its "legislative" activities. He advocates that advisory commissions be established by Congress with power to dispose of most of these problems by decrees or, when legislation is clearly needed, to refer it to Congress, leaving the Court as a last resort.

In the antitrust cases, such as *FTC* v. *Procter & Gamble*, this agency would be an enhanced Federal Trade Commission working in conjunction with the President's Council of Economic Advisers. Since it is unlikely that the nation will heed Berle's advice in the near future, interesting though his proposals are, we can turn to the practical effects of the Clorox case.

The Court's antitrust decisions are based on the quasi-constitutional status of the Sherman Antitrust Act and the Clayton Act. The Court's expanding interpretation of the mandates of these Acts beyond the usual "restraint of trade" or "substantially lessening of competition" is what annoys big business and Max Ways, editor of *Fortune*, as we have previously noted. In the *Brown Shoe Company* v. *United States* case in 1962, the Court flexed its muscles by ordering Brown Shoe to divest itself of the Kinney Shoe chain even though the diminished competition was found to be less than 3%. In the Clorox case, the Court broke new ground. Since P & G was not in the bleach business, its merger with Clorox could hardly lessen competition. The Court ruled, however, that since Clorox already had 48.8% of the bleach market, joining forces with the giant P & G would not only eliminate P & G as a potential competitor of Clorox but would also frighten off any future competition after the merger. Undue market power capable of forestalling *future* competition became the test. P & G proceeded to spin off Clorox. In 1968, P & G also meekly consented, without going to court, to dispose of its previously acquired J. F. Folger & Co. coffee business within five years and to stop acquiring consumer product companies altogether for seven years.

Those who wonder what became of antitrust had better take another look at the list of divestitures ordered or agreed to in the past few years alone, many of them years after the mergers or acquisitions had been effected. On the basis of the above decisions, it would be quite easy for the Court to attack conglomerate mergers in unrelated fields or corporations whose excessive advertising power, for example, may affect competition now or in the future.

No one can study the structure of American business without considering antitrust activities as a countervailing force in the giant corporate world which has become our heritage. Yet policy, even theory, in this field is a hodgepodge, probably to the great delight of the antitrust lawyers. One thing is clear. Both the executive and the judicial branches of government regard corporate size (more than competition) as a political and social problem as much as an economic one. Antitrust activity has been a bi-partisan, generally vigorous effort since World War II and undoubtedly represents a consensus of what the nation wants. Neither stockholders nor consumers picketed the Brown Shoe and Clorox decisions or wrote letters to the editor. Americans like big business, but they also prefer their corporate giants, like their pro football teams, to be as evenly matched as possible and subject to the referee's whistle as well as a few new rules.

Before leaving power, one can pay respects to Berle's liberal concern with the Bill of Rights as it may be eroded by the modern corporation in its role of giant bureaucracy. In *The 20th Century Capitalist Revolution* (1954), Berle criticizes Ralph Cordiner, General Electric's president, who in 1953 announced that refusal to answer questions by a Senate Investigating Committee would result in immediate suspension from employment. Among the few dissenters was an outstanding Republican newspaper, the *Berkshire Eagle*, in Pittsfield, Mass., a General Electric city. It loudly raised the question of individual rights, which were being so painfully abrogated at that time. Although Berle sympathised with GE's predicament as a defense contractor for having to make rules where the government had failed to make them itself, he agreed with the newspaper and asserted a principle that may yet find itself become a law.

This is simply the proposition that corporation employees should be subject to the Fourteenth Amendment, with "due process of the law" to protect them against arbitrary acts of their employers.[24] Presently, of course, the business corporation has discretionary power (subject to state Fair Employment Practises Acts, federal contract provisions and union agreements) to select and reject employees at will. This may have been suitable for a time of small employers but does it suffice for giants who are the largest employers in communities throughout the country? Ironically, the Fourteenth Amendment, by which we noted Justice Field granted refuge from the state to corporations in the nineteenth century, may be needed to grant persecuted employees refuge from the corporation in the twentieth century.

Yesterday's victims of the corporate world included the conformists in William H. Whyte, Jr.'s *The Organization Man*. There is a
new school of thought that these executives really aren't so badly off
after all. They are beginning to love their corporations and the
younger ones, according to Walter Guzzardi, Jr.'s *The Young
Executives*, a serious interview study for *Fortune* in 1964, actually
find a challenge and excitement they wouldn't otherwise experience.
They say they are stimulated by jobs that bring them responsibility,
authority and the opportunity to exercise their potentials to the
limit.[25] Be that as it may, perhaps the concern should have been
directed to the labor force all along. Its liberties can subtly be
abridged in new ways by the bureaucratic corporation. Pension
trusts, for example, may bind a man tyrannically to his job. Should
they not be transferable at full value to another employer's fund?
In an age of consumer credit, might not a capricious denial of credit,
key-punched into a national credit data bank, interfere with a man's
right to life, liberty and property? Who shall wear miniskirts and
beards on the job?

V

Capital

"Get capital!" William Graham Sumner urged upon his students
at the turn of the century. Capital is used to produce goods and
services and is essential for industrial progress. It arises from that
portion of production which is not consumed but saved for use in
current or future production. One could say it consists of plant,
equipment, inventory and, as Berle points out, "incorporeal capital."
This ghostly addition is the whole deposit of technical ability and
research accumulated through the years. As with property, Berle
believes that such capital can hardly be considered private. Actually,
socialists and Communists believe in capital, if not in capitalism,
quite as much as we do. They simply choose to do without the
capitalist in the control or in the rewards of capital resources.

Berle sees the formation of capital in twentieth century America as a parallel to his theory of property. The ownership of capital is now substantially separated from the power or control over capital.

Sumner's "hero of civilization," the savings bank depositor, is small fry indeed in the new formation process. The greatest source of capital in America — about 60% — comes from retained earnings and depreciation allowances generated by the corporations themselves. Investors are not asked to provide this money. It is included in the price at which the products are sold. As a result, the corporation managements are quite independent of the investment and banking fraternity and decide for themselves how billions of dollars will be spent for plant expansion and modernization each year.

Next consider the state as a great collector of capital, again by conscription rather than voluntary savings. One of the marvels of modern capitalism is that the state is really a one-for-one partner in the profits of business. Since taxes run at least 50%, half goes to the state and half is kept by business for its dividends and retained earnings. The taxes flow back as capital investment in the form of great capital projects the state undertakes, such as dams, space projects, roads and public buildings. In addition, a tremendous boost is given by the state to incorporeal capital, since two-thirds of all research in the United States is now paid for by the federal government out of its tax income.

A third major source of capital formation is the involuntary collection of Social Security and unemployment insurance funds by the state and federal governments from both employers and employees. As with insurance companies, tremendous reserves are accumulated in these accounts against future payments and a good deal of these reserves are employed as capital. Finally, consider pension trust funds, which are acquiring compulsory status for more and more employers and have grown in a short time to approximately $80 billion available for investment. They absorb about one-third of new stock issues. In the unique case of Sears Roebuck, its pension trust fund bought so much of its own stock it has a controlling interest in the company.

That leaves the individual voluntary saver. In an affluent society

— even in a depressed society — the hope is he doesn't save too much. His function is to spend and consume and if much more than 5% of total personal income is saved, the danger signals of recession are generally seen. Still, personal savings (over half of them from the upper 5% income bracket) are approximately $30 billion annually and a fair portion enters the capital stream, largely through the investments of financial and insurance institutions. The average American need not feel obliged to supply capital for production. He does quite well for the system by investing his extra money in personal capital, such as home and equipment, life insurance, education and a modest investment program. It is true that 25 million Americans own securities. To call this "people's capitalism" has a nice connotation but is somewhat irrelevant when we are told that industry, with the aid of bank credit, obtains 90% of its capital funds from sources other than new stock issues. (The Japanese, by the way, have already reached the point where 25% of their citizens are corporation shareholders against our 12%.)

The significance of these sources of capital comes back to control. Both Berle and Galbraith assume their readers will be quite surprised at how capital is formed. They enjoy ridding us of preconceived myths about the process. In the case of capital, this is an unnecessary assumption. Few people still believe that great enterprises are being fueled by capitalist entrepreneurs of the type that agitated Karl Marx. We are all extremely conscious participants in taxes, pension funds, stockholdings with earned surplus entries and personal savings accounts. What we are not sure of is who should control allocations of capital after it is formed. We can be sure that both Berle and Galbraith recognize this as a political problem in that it involves the state just as avoiding depressions finally involved the state. For them it is also a philosophical problem in that it involves the quality of our lives.

"The capital is there; and so is capitalism; the waning fact is the capitalist," concludes Berle.[26] If the owner-capitalist no longer makes private sector investment decisions and the investment banker's influence has been reduced, then the small group of self-perpetuating management men and their directors hold the power. Galbraith agrees. The shift of power is "one from capital to organized intelligence."[27]

The financial community is still important, of course, as sellers of securities, administrators of savings and credit-granting institutions and as trustees of pension funds. In fact, it might be amused at the reports of its impotence. Mutual funds have acquired important positions in practically all of Berle's 200 largest corporations and could easily begin to challenge management at annual meetings. The bank trustees of pension funds and other employee benefit accounts hold over $250 billion in assets, heavily invested in corporation stocks, and have been under attack for possible antitrust conflicts of interest because of large competitive holdings in their portfolios. Investment bankers may not impress General Motors but they can point out that their risk capital decisions have launched dozens of giant growth companies, such as Litton Industries, Polaroid and Xerox, in recent years. If there is a particular crack in Berle's theory, it is in underestimating the resurgence of stockholder power in the hands of the various financial institutions, assuming these are reasonably critical of corporate management. As a general rule, one would find their ideology to be the equivalent of management's.

The fact is Berle does not have to prove his case in terms of capital formation or separation of ownership from control. It is clear that these corporations are a force for tremendous good and tremendous harm. Power has been concentrated in management. For Berle, as for Galbraith, there must always be checks and balances against undue power. Traditionally this balance is supposed to be found in the free market.

VI

Free Markets

Readers of Berle and Galbraith know that "free markets" are a straw man which they set up as a countervailing force to corporate power and then thoroughly demolish. As the years go on, the un-reality of this nineteenth century — actually eighteenth century — concept increases. One is tempted to see if it really is set forth as applicable to large corporations in "classical" textbooks still in use.

This ambiguous phrase constantly reappears to complicate the use of English in economic discussions. It is confused with free enterprise which in turn is confused with the profit system. The profit system in turn is confused with freedom, completing the circle.

Congress added to the confusion by hammering out the Employment Act of 1946 in language which could only be written by a committee:

> The Congress hereby declares that it is the continuing policy and responsibility of the Federal Government to use all practicable means . . . for the purpose of creating and maintaining, in a manner calculated to foster and promote free competitive enterprise and the general welfare, conditions under which there will be afforded useful employment, for those able, willing, and seeking work, and to promote maximum employment, production and purchasing power.

This is a milestone law of the land. It already seems archaic when the poor march on the Capitol with more stringent demands which are likely to be granted. Berle, of course, warmly approves of the objectives in the Act of providing employment and promoting maximum employment, production and purchasing power. He adds:

> As economic development proceeds, it may appear (or may be true now) that "free competitive enterprise" may be inconsistent with either or both of these objectives. This fact has not yet been taken into account by politicians, and few economists (J. K. Galbraith excepted) have been willing to deal with it.[28]

Berle is consistent in the sense that "free competitive enterprise" embraces free markets, which we don't have in the most important sectors of our economy. He claims that as much as two-thirds of our economy has been removed from free market forces. Briefly, no twentieth century state could afford to submit to the miseries that can be brought about by uncontrolled competition for goods or labor, just as no depression will ever be allowed to "wring itself" out again in an extension of free market theory.

Whenever possible free market competition is pursued as the simplest way to equate supply with demand for the great variety of goods and services suitable to it. But the forces of the free market have been abridged to serve the economic system rather than stand as the goal of the system. Transportation, communications and public utilities are areas where free markets have been removed completely in favor of fixed pricing. The banking and insurance industries are substantially removed from price competition. Agriculture has survived disaster as a result of "parity prices" to maintain reasonably orderly marketing conditions. The aircraft and shipping industries are in effect subsidized. In other areas, prices are not regulated or fixed, but measures are taken by the state to adjust supply to demand, as in the oil and sugar industries. Non-ferrous metals are often stockpiled by the government to prevent gluts in the market. Finally, there is the typical structure operating in most of America's largest corporations, the "administered prices" set by the leaders in those industries known as oligopolies, such as autos, electrical appliances and tobacco. Granted competition is fierce, sometimes with limited price wars, in these industries. They would each tend towards monopoly and cartelization in short order if not policed by the antitrust acts, fair trade acts and regulatory commissions. Berle states that one of the greatest interventions of the state in the economy has been its distinguished service in the cause of maintaining the so-called free market as much as it does.[29] In the national value system, free opportunity to "rise through the ranks" or to engage in enterprise are regarded as more important than buying and selling at the very lowest prices. Big business does not rejoice in the extinction (except by acquisition) of its competitors.

The freezing of the market system through rigid state planning is another matter. Free market advocates can point to the miracle of West German production and the complaints of the Czechoslovakian economists as evidence that the free market-profit system works very well. But these countries are simply approaching the modified American business system in such endeavors.

At any rate it is time to dispose of the straw man. The large corporation is not subject to the iron law of the market place. This statement would offer little comfort to the designer and the sales manager of the Edsel, which reportedly cost Ford $250 million because the consumer didn't like the car, even at close-out prices. Galbraith jauntily regards the Edsel case as an exception to the rule, which should not have occurred in a large corporation capable of precision long-range planning.[30] This leads to one of Galbraith's more controversial ideas, that the big corporations can — and do — manipulate their own demand through market analysis, market power and consumer conditioning. Let us grant that the consumer, powerful or drugged as he is, does not adequately balance the power of the corporation.

VII

Responsibility and Conscience

It takes a special kind of nerve to talk about conscience on the part of business. Even President Kennedy expressed incredulity on the subject after Roger Blough, United States Steel Chairman, advised him that his principality was raising the price of steel after the Steelworkers' Union had negotiated a non-inflationary contract at the government's request. "My father always told me," Kennedy said, "that all businessmen were sons-of-bitches, but I never believed it till now."

Adolf Berle has imperturbably advanced the theory of conscience for thirty years. In *The 20th Century Capitalist Revolution*, he announces a straightforward proposition. If checks on corporate power such as the financial community and the free market no longer are valid, what force other than the state itself can do the job? Berle makes it clear that he does not want the state to take over industry. It is enough that it stands up to industry when public opinion will not tolerate unreasonable situations, as Presidents have done in coal and steel crises. He acknowledges Galbraith's concept of countervailing power, that big unions will stand off big business, but he is not satisfied with that alone. Bravely he advances two other major forces. The first is public opinion which translates itself into political action when sufficiently aroused. Corporations must pay attention to it for their own good. The second is the developing corporate conscience. One might say corporations will act properly because they are good.

Though this appears naïve, Berle is far too sophisticated a reformer to be blasted with such a charge. What he is talking about is a process, which he expects to grow and mature after getting off to a good start in recent years. Nor does he expect it to flourish without continued prodding from the state. When Professor Lintner, a specialist in modifying Berle's theses, observed that Berle must have "had his vision somewhere on the road to Damascus, and now regards the concentrated authority of the nucleus of corporate management as being not merely inevitable but positively beneficent in important ways,"[31] Berle replied:

> I suggest that the administrators of corporations may have seen some light (possibly somewhere on the road to the Pecora Investigation or the Securities & Exchange Commission) since 1933. The principles and practise of big business in 1959 seem to me considerably more responsible, more perceptive and (in plain English) more honest than they were in 1929.[32]

There is, of course, an elaborate theory of "managerialism," derived from corporate statesmen, managerial consultants, businessmen's councils of ethics (including one sponsored by the U.S. Department of Commerce) and the graduate schools of business administration. In general, they claim that the enlightened business manager no longer seeks only to maximize profits, but instead does his best to serve the community, the labor force, the consumers and the nation as well. Harvard's Graduate School of Business Administration, where Berle has taught, is a hotbed of this activity. The story goes that at one commencement Harvard's president saluted the school as "the youngest of the arts and oldest of the professions."

Berle's corporate conscience is always included in what has been called "the apologetics of managerialism,"[33] but it is unique enough to stand examination on its own. Well prepared to spin a theory on a broad frame, Berle, like Shakespeare, first considers the conscience of the king.

*   *   *

The old Duke's body was about to be lowered into the tomb. An obscure man ran to the fore, interrupted the burial of William the Conqueror, Duke of Normandy, and cried "Haro!"

He had a complaint. The land belonged to his family and had been forcibly taken away by William. The bishops consulted and made their move. They paid the man and interred the Conqueror.

What happened to the man immediately thereafter is mercifully veiled by history. Berle does trace back the cry. Duke Rollo, William's predecessor, had a keen sense of justice and ordered that any man who called out "Ha! Rollo!" was entitled to state his grievance. As with many court terms, this was abbreviated.

Although the king could do no wrong, he had a lively conscience. It was finally invested in the Chancellor, who became a keeper of the conscience. The King's Court, attended by the Chancellor, eventually became institutionalized as a result of the meeting at Runnymede. The resulting rules placed the Court in Westminster and there British courts with equity jurisdiction sit to this day.

Thus, perhaps, Harvard business students learned that although sovereigns had power, there were also conceptions of morality and justice that stopped even kings in their tracks, at least in Western civilization.

It seems a far cry from Norman dukes to corporation managements but Berle easily makes it. Meanwhile the managers might find the association with kings quite pleasing, far better than the usual allusion to barons.

In the corporate world, Berle expects substantial checks on business power to emerge as law. Yet it is conscientious action short of the law which really intrigues him. Without such self-control, he finds a gap in the system of power, an "institutional failure."

As an example of corporate conscience on the working level, he describes in *Twentieth Century* the General Motors dealer grievance board. This is offered as a case of power (the cancellable dealer contract) submitting to review. It was hardly a good choice. Earl Latham, one of the many professors who keep an eye on corporate power, studied the *Hearings* of the Senate Subcommittee on Antitrust and Monopoly and came up with a highly skeptical view of the quality of justice dispensed by this private judiciary.[34] Berle himself noted approvingly that legislation was about to appear in at least one state. As discussed in a previous chapter, federal legislation pre-empted the field in 1956. Abram Chayes, an authority on corporation law, finds that a highly improved GM grievance board now seems preferable to recourse to the law by the dealers after all,[35] a welcome sign of the possibilities of self-government in technology-land. Thus Berle is confirmed by the passage of time, though the forces of conscience seems less important in this ameliorative process than the give and take of reform and the brooding presence of the law.

The planning function of the corporation, states Berle, accelerates the need for a conscience. He urges that we overcome our suspicions of "planning" and face up to the fact that large production is essentially a planning operation. Galbraith, in *The New Industrial State*, implies that planning is so indispensable for giant technology that corporation managements would cherish planning more than monopoly, if given a choice. The logistics, the time lag from research to product and the enormity of the resources involved all make it essential that the plans work out.[36] Governments and consumers have wisely accommodated the needs of our private planners, who seem more like commissars than captains of industry in Galbraith's world.

Both men hold management accountable to society but Berle probes for the conscience. The planning requirements have long-range effects on the community at large. Influences are set in motion which are not easily reversed. The result is a different kind of responsibility from the mere maximizing of profits. Like it or not, "the really great corporation managements have reached a position for the first time in their history in which they must consciously take account of philosophical considerations."[37]

Philosophers are generally found on the campus and one feels that Berle would be happiest if executives would return for frequent refresher courses rather than donate buildings and help run the real estate. He does note approvingly that corporations are now allowed to contribute generously to charities and to education. It was not just a matter of tax deductibility. For a while there was a question of whether stockholders' funds could legally be used for non-business purposes. The Supreme Court said yes, confirming the social role of the corporation, not to mention the Court. Still the alternatives should be weighed. If corporations keep the money, one-half would end up in taxes. These would flow back more or less beneficially into the economy, including a handsome share for education. At best, corporation executives might object to such a circuitous routing of their money. At worst, others might object to corporations supporting so heavily institutions such as Harding College in Searcy, Arkansas, a right-wing propaganda mill.[38] This philosophical question is not adequately met by Berle; nor is the collateral question of political contributions disguised as advertising in journals.

*   *   *

The late Walter Paepcke of the Container Corporation of America assembled business tycoons annually at Aspen and dressed them in togas while they studied humanism. Unkind critics may comment that the cowl does not make the monk. In one of his most remarkable flights, Berle used the monk to make the businessman.

Augustine, Bishop of Hippo in North Africa in the fifth century A.D., sat in his study and reflected on power. The Pax Romana had broken up. It was a time of disintegration and troubles. He thereupon wrote *The City of God*, in which he stated an important political hypothesis. Underlying all human organizations there is a final arbiter of power, the moral and philosophical element. This also gives permanence or legitimacy to institutions. He christened this moral authority "The City of God." Worldly power had to be shared with moral power.

Berle bids adieu to St. Augustine and makes a fifteen century leap. Modern capitalism, having delivered power to the management of a few hundred corporations, will in turn be delivered to the state if management is not beholden to some moral authority.

Many observers would be willing to regard the state, with its growing body of laws resting firmly in a sea of ethics, as the true conscience of the corporation. Personal morality is all to the good but no substitute for the Securities & Exchange Commission. The state may in the long run take over capitalism. We would then have socialism but not necessarily a lapse in moral authority. Meanwhile, neither the state nor the people want to own or run production, except in the politest and most indirect manner. It works much better the present way and we have enough bureaucracy as it is. Should not conscience have a more positive motivation?

Undoubtedly Berle today feels less concerned with the preventive or negative aspects of the corporation conscience than he did when discussing "The City of God" in 1954. It was then that he also wrote that corporations were exhibiting something "surprisingly like a collective soul,"[39] a line which inevitably suffered the fate of Defense Secretary Wilson's famous remark, even if true. Pursuing the point, he expressed confidence that America would soon begin to honor spiritual, philosophical and intellectual leaders as never before and that these men would gravitate to corporation boards and offices in good measure. If not inside business, they would be outside, leading and shaping the public consensus towards elevated standards. In 1959, in *Power Without Property*, Berle gave them a title. They would be the "Lords Spiritual" set against the "Lords Temporal." They would serve "not merely a need for the times, but also as a need for businessmen."[40] Not since Thorstein Veblen's call for a "Soviet of technicians" to arise from the engineering class and take over corporation management has such an unlikely title appeared on the American business scene. Berle has had to live it down with his unfailing good humor.

VIII

One more step in economic theory, related to conscience, is still to be explored. In *The American Economic Republic* (1963), Berle proposes an explanation for the American success. Our political and economic system is not just a practical blend of responsible democracy and limited capitalism. An ethical graft has made an impact on it. There is an extra margin which Berle calls the "Transcendental Margin."

As a concept, it is hardly a catchy one. It will not be found in Presidential addresses or in popular economics. Yet coming from Adolf Berle, it must be given attention.

In spite of its mystical name, it is basically our old friend the Protestant ethic. The impulse to work hard and to be charitable was a real force in the making of America. Without it, the eighteenth and nineteenth centuries might have succumbed completely to the official concept of the "economic man," a person eagerly pursuing his own selfish interests in a mad scheme that would somehow produce the efficiencies of a truly free market. Some critics called Adam Smith's theory "deified greed" but it was modified by this ethic. To take less than what one can get at any time is a kind of altruism. Not even to try to take it with you, but to give it away with abandon, as Andrew Carnegie did, is philanthropic. Long before the state entered the economic picture, altruism and philanthropy gave an added moral dimension to the laying up of wealth. "It conscripted income and profits in a fashion rarely equalled in history,"[41] claims Berle, in words that require a quick second look to make sure he is praising and not attacking our ancestors.

It is arguable that the ethic went underground from about 1890 to 1910 when, as Henry Adams observed, wealth was the supreme value in America, but none can gainsay the ultimate philanthropy of that gaudy age. The institutions endowed by its famous names helped produce, with poetic justice, a generation of reformers. The reformers added still another margin, the organized social devices of the welfare state, such as the Social Security program. This added dimension brought an unexpected dividend. Businessmen and economists alike began to realize that bread cast upon the waters comes back enriched. Far better than philanthropy — for business — is full employment and a higher standard of living for all. The selfless aspect of the ethic presently seems blurred by association with self-interest, as in our foreign aid program or in the need to cure our central cities. The underlying ethical drive, however, should not be underestimated.

Structuring his theory, Berle points out that Utah does better than Nevada, and Israel better than Syria, because of their own versions of the Protestant ethic. It is even possible, he states, to strike a mathematical coefficient of productivity for countries with the right inner drive, where the value system leads to effort beyond personal gain. Of course, there is a hitch to this theory, which Berle sadly admits. Under the evil goals and prodding of a Hitler, Germany too produced miracles of productivity.

IX

A bad seed abroad does not destroy Berle's vision of America. He sings its praises as strongly as Walt Whitman and with cold facts to prove it. Yet even before the younger generation denounced the old New Dealers, there were thankless critics both on Berle's right and on his left.

Business spokesmen have never embraced Berle as their champion, even though no one of similar intellect and standing has done so well by them. They don't want to be constitutionalized with a bill of rights for their masses of employees or federalized with impartial surrogates sitting on their boards. They are probably uneasy about the moralizing from secular quarters. They resent the implication of their concentrated power. All in all, they wear a tipsy crown, considering the harassment of labor, stockholders, the arts, government, foreign and domestic competitors, neglected families, alienated children and corporate raiders.

Nevertheless, big business has absorbed a good deal of the preaching of Berle and the taunting of Galbraith. Both of these critics seem to have had a twofold mission towards business. First, to get it to realize that government intervention was not only good for business but indispensable for business as well as the health of the nation. This was not an easy task, considering the implacable conservative ideology voiced so anachronistically by business leaders and trade associations well into the fifties. When big business mounted its massive campaign, tax deductible, to sell a Barry Goldwater type of "Free Enterprise" in the late forties and fifties, it was the last of such efforts. William H. Whyte, Jr. and the editors of *Fortune* summed it up, in Whyte's appropriately entitled *Is Anybody Listening?* as a $100 million failure.[42] Goldwater's defeat confirmed its lack of appeal among the voters.

Though business, especially its liberal leadership, such as the Committee for Economic Development, has gladly accepted the stabilizing intervention of the government, there is no such receptivity towards the second goal of the Berle-Galbraith mission. The second goal calls for more direct planning as against the earlier technique of indirect stimulation and guarantees. The reasons for direct planning are qualitative and philosophical. They cannot be measured in terms of increased Gross National Product. If we have such a wonderful economic machine, how can we possibly let it produce such mediocrity, so much tail-fins and gimmicks, air pollution and billboards, waste and shoddiness?

In more specific areas, shall the control of allocation of goods and products by management allow overproduction of autos in one year followed by a recession in the next? Shall capital expansion versus dividends for giant corporations be a management or quasi-public decision? Should the urgent needs of the central cities and hard-core unemployed depend so greatly on private enterprise decisions? Shall the giant industrial and Defense Department trade become so self-propelling and self-perpetuating? Shall oligopolistic corporations collaborate with labor in price increases producing "cost-push" inflation? Are thirty million relatively poor and hungry evidence of failure of the system after all?

Here business draws the line. It does not appreciate the croaking voice heard at the very time of unparalleled abundance and reasonably good behavior on its part. Carried to its logical conclusions, control of such decisions could mean creeping socialism, although Berle wanly observes it would only be "galloping capitalism."[43]

Actually Berle and Galbraith have never proposed socialism and are quite disinterested in its claims, tied in as these claims are with questionable political power. For all their compelling demonstrations of how our economy really works and their dispelling of economic myths, neither critic has yet proposed — nor perhaps do they intend to propose — grand solutions. They still believe in gradualism and pragmatic experiment. They rest their hopes for more quality, more beauty and more effective allocation of resources on continued social legislation plus one visionary ingredient. This would be the emergence of a class of élite, educated, all-around men, humanists with briefcases, Medicis with social consciences. Coming from the scientific and academic establishments, their influence would prevail as technology itself becomes too complicated for the comprehension of ordinary men. Hardly the full-blooded capitalists Professor Schumpeter eulogized — and slightly resembling Berle and Galbraith themselves — such men indeed would be industrial assets.

The seminal critics do not have to be on target. The thrust of their opinions, backed by the authority of their eminence and intellect, carries forward to ultimate change. The critics on Berle's right may reject him but business will never abandon its new sense of responsibility and conscience. There are dissenting professors who urge that business should stick to its last and perform the invaluable task of maximizing profits as the most efficient use of capital. Eugene

Rostow, former Yale Law School Dean, votes against the concept of a conscience-ridden "managerialism." The new corporate morality may result in prices and wages which sabotage the market mechanism and systematically distort the allocation of resources — something like rent control carried on for too long a time. From Veblen to Berle, Rostow maintains, no criteria to replace profit-maximizing as a standard for establishing wages and prices have yet been produced.[44]

Professor Milton Friedman, the conservative economist who surprisingly advocates a "negative income tax" (a form of guaranteed annual income for the poor), offers a critique of management's social responsibility that would thrill Ayn Rand:

> . . . fundamentally subversive . . . Few trends could so thoroughly undermine the very foundations of our free society as the acceptance by corporate officials of a social responsibility other than to make as much money for the stockholders as possible.[45]

The dissenters' cause is all but lost. All sections of America are undergoing self-examination in the violent sixties. Take for example the enthusiastic line-up of Berle's 500 corporations behind Henry Ford II and his National Alliance of Businessmen, enlisted by a welfare-style President to produce 100,000 jobs for hard-core unemployed by July 1, 1969 at a considerable expense to stockholders. Other corporations such as Chase Manhattan Bank, Alcoa and Avco are deliberately investing in ventures more related to social problems than short-run profits. Henry Ford II almost redefined profits in a 1966 speech:

> There is no longer anything to reconcile — if ever there was — between the social conscience and the profit motive . . . It seems clear to me that improving the quality of society . . . is nothing more than another step in the evolutionary process of taking a more farsighted view of return on investment.[46]

R. A. Peterson, president of the Bank of America, made an
equally unconventional proposition in 1968. Perhaps sensing that
volunteerism such as the NAB cannot survive a drop in profits (or a
lack of conviction about such feather-bedding on the part of business), he has called for an outright coalition between government
and business to cope with the current crises. The private sector,
he maintains, works best and most efficiently when goaded by the
desire for profit. The new partnership will pay business a fair profit.
It would be somewhat similar to the Federal Housing Administration's pioneering guarantee of risks business wouldn't ordinarily
undertake, in order to create the historic housing boom. Peterson
acknowledges all kinds of political and accounting problems but he
feels Congress can establish satisfactory ground-rules for success.[47]
Giant corporations would become poverty contractors just as they
are defense contractors. Their corporate consciences, which tell
them they cannot avoid these social problems, would receive the
added balm of profits, though not the maximized kind.

X

If Berle can take satisfaction from results on the right, regardless
of recognition, how does he fare on the left?

A review of *The American Economic Republic* by Philip Green
in *The New Republic* is typically harsh:

> Surely this kind of America-mongering with its clarion
> note of national self-congratulation, has virtually become
> the preserve of the mindless in our society . . . Is the
> American economy *really*, without question, "the most
> successful in the world"? . . . Berle has gradually gone
> from the destruction of old myths to the creation of new
> ones . . . He is still attacking the free enterprise, private
> property myth . . . But the purpose of this myth-breaking
> now seems to be to lull us to sleep with the fairy-tale of
> the welfare state and the affluent society, whose "defi-
> ciencies, omissions and problems" are steadily being

solved by the application of the "transcendental margin"
and American know-how; there is really nothing left to
worry about seriously.[48]

Strangely this excessive criticism seems less blatant as the sixties
draw to a close. Berle himself would share in the current distress.
He must be judged in the total context of his illustrious works and
piercing intellect. A comparison is suggested with another moralist,
the liberal theologian, Reinhold Niebuhr, rather than with the
worldly Galbraith, as we close this chapter.

Berle and Niebuhr both celebrate what Niebuhr calls the "triumph
of common sense over both the business oligarchy and the deter-
minist theorists"[49] — in other words, over both Commodore Vanderbilt and Karl Marx. The clergyman, however, has more lingering
doubts than the clergyman's son. Perhaps it is Niebuhr's sensitivity
to the irony of America's success, or his greater receptivity to the
haunting merits of the Marxist challenge, which makes him less
complacent than Berle. Strangely, neither of these models of modern
liberalism adequately sensed the magnitude of the passions that
would tear America apart in the 1960's — a misguided international role culminating in a lost war, racism run wild and unper-
ceived millions living in poverty. While they celebrated common
sense, a young minister named Martin Luther King, Jr. emerged
as a secular saint by prophesying the common peril, rather than
the great hopes, facing the nation.

Footnotes

CHAPTER 6

Adolf Berle:

Keeper of the Corporate Conscience

Adolf A. Berle's books cover economics, law and diplomacy. They are, of course, the key to his developing thought and extend from 1932 through 1967. J. K. Galbraith's classics provide a convenient and stimulating comparison with those of Berle.

An excellent selection of articles on the corporation is found in *The Corporation in Modern Society* (New York, 1966) edited by Edward S. Mason, with foreword by Adolf A. Berle. Berle states that it is "the best body of material on the American corporate system yet offered." *The Corporation Take-Over* (New York, 1965), edited by Andrew Hacker, emanated from the think-tank at the Center for the Study of Democratic Institutions, and is predictably stimulating. It contains a key Berle essay: "Economic Power in the Free Society." Also included are Scott Buchanan's suggestions for enfranchising workers and other groups in corporations along the lines of a constitutional organization, and W. H. Ferry's plea for more criticism of "metrocorporation." *The Annals* of the American Academy of Political Science devoted its September 1962 issue to "The Ethics of Corporate Enterprise" with the dullness that imposition of ethics generates. *Corporate Accountability* (New York, 1964) by Paul O. Gaddis is dedicated to Alfred P. Sloan and is a reasonable antidote to the impatience with corporations expressed by the academic writers. Peter F. Drucker's books are all enlightened essays in managerialism. He was among the first (1949) to suggest that stockholders simply shouldn't have the vote in large corporations, forcing the board of directors to be more responsible in a trustee's capacity.

Fortune is a magazine which continually wrestles with the conscience of businessmen. Few of the managements that authorize the handsome ads producing *Fortune*'s profit would want to be judged negatively in *Fortune*'s pages. Two *Fortune* books, selected from articles, are essential reading: *The Regulated Businessman* (New York, 1966) and *The Responsible Businessman* (New York, 1966).

1 Adolf A. Berle, "Analyzing the Corporate-Complex," *Saturday Review of Literature* (June 24, 1967), pp. 29-30.

2 *New York Times*, April 11, 1965, p. 5.

3 Adolf A. Berle, *The American Economic Republic* (New York, 1963), pp. 6-7.

4 *Ibid.*, p. 179.

5 *New York Times*, October 20, 1963, Part VI, p. 9.

6 *Ibid.*, November 22, 1963, p. 12.

7 Arthur M. Schlesinger, Jr., *A Thousand Days* (Boston, 1965), p. 252.

8 Adolf A. Berle, *op. cit.*, p. 195.

9 *Ibid.*, pp. 235-236.

10 Edward S. Mason, editor, *The Corporation in Modern Society*, (New York, 1966), Preface, p. x.

11 *Business Week*, September 3, 1938, p. 10.

12 Adolf A. Berle, "Intellectuals and New Deals," *The New Republic*, March 7, 1964, p. 21.

13 Adolf A. Berle, *The American Economic Republic*, *op. cit.*, p. 19.

14 *Ibid.*, p. 21.

15 Adolf A. Berle, "Economic Power and the Free Society," in *The Corporation Take-Over* (New York, 1964), edited by Andrew Hacker, Anchor edition, 1965, p. 86.

[16] Robert L. Heilbroner, *The Limits of American Capitalism* (New York, 1965), p. 56.

[17] Adolf A. Berle, *The American Economic Republic*, *op. cit.*, p. 28.

[18] J. K. Galbraith, *The New Industrial State* (Boston, 1967), pp. 308-309.

[19] Adolf A. Berle, "Economic Power and the Free Society," *op. cit.*, pp. 96-97.

[20] Edward S. Mason, *op. cit.*, p. 311.

[21] *Ibid.*, Foreword, pp. xiv-xv.

[22] Adolf A. Berle, *The Three Faces of Power* (New York, 1967), p. 13.

[23] *Ibid.*, Foreword, pp. vii-viii.

[24] Adolf A. Berle, *The 20th Century Capitalist Revolution* (New York, 1954), pp. 94 ff. Also, *The Corporation Take-Over*, *op. cit.*, p. 100.

[25] Walter Guzzardi, Jr., *The Young Executives* (New York, 1966), pp. 43 ff.

[26] Adolf A. Berle, *op. cit.*, p. 39.

[27] J. K. Galbraith, *op. cit.*, p. 57.

[28] Adolf A. Berle, *The Three Faces of Power*, *op. cit.*, p. 76, fn.

[29] Adolf A. Berle, *The American Economic Republic*, *op. cit.*, p. 146.

[30] J. K. Galbraith, *op. cit.*, p. 12.

[31] Edward S. Mason, *op. cit.*, p. 170.

[32] *Ibid.*, Foreword, p. xiii.

[33] Edward S. Mason, "The Apologetics of 'Managerialism'" *The Journal of Business*, XXXI (January 1958), pp. 1-11.

[34] Edward S. Mason, *The Corporation in Modern Society*, *op. cit.*, p. 322.

35 *Ibid.*, p. 44.

36 J. K. Galbraith, *op. cit.*, p. 76.

37 Adolf A. Berle, *The 20th Century Capitalist Revolution, op. cit.*, p. 166.

38 Arnold Forster and Benjamin Epstein, *Danger on the Right*, (New York, 1964), pp. 92-97 and 277-278.

39 Adolf A. Berle, *op. cit.*, p. 183.

40 Adolf A. Berle, *Power Without Property* (New York, 1959), Harvest edition, pp. 6-7.

41 Adolf A. Berle, *The American Economic Republic, op. cit.*, p. 191.

42 William H. Whyte, Jr. and the Editors of *Fortune, Is Anyone Listening?* (New York, 1952), pp. 4-10.

43 Adolf A. Berle, *The 20th Century Capitalist Revolution, op cit.*, p. 109.

44 Edward S. Mason, *op. cit.*, p. 64; p. 67.

45 Milton Friedman, *Capitalism and Freedom* (Chicago, 1962), p. 163.

46 *Fortune*, August 1968, p. 90.

47 R. A. Peterson, "A New Business-Government Coalition?" *The Conference Board Record*, July, 1968, pp. 10-12.

48 Philip Green, "A. A. Berle—New Myths for Old," *The New Republic*, June 22, 1963, pp. 21-23.

49 Reinhold Niebuhr, *The Irony of American History* (New York, 1952), p. 34.

Chapter 7

MICHAEL HARRINGTON and
HERBERT MARCUSE:
Critics of the Left

"I disagree," states Michael Harrington.

The author of *The Other America* — the America of built-in, often hopeless poverty — takes exception to the position of Adolf Berle and J. K. Galbraith. He disagrees that the great American corporations, even under the management of enlightened, organized intelligence, can fulfill their responsibilities if subjected only to the indirect pressures of Washington. They can but they won't.

In selecting our critics and heretics of American business, we have been careful, just as Veblen was, and Berle and Galbraith are, not to slide into the socialist camp. Karl Marx is certainly an indis-

275

pensable critic of capitalism but he has been treated here mainly as a point of reference. In fact, he is a very satisfactory reference, inasmuch as we can see, from our safe harbor, how wrong he was. Those who believe he was right must by deduction be Marxists. They would surely lose an audience interested in constructive criticism of our business system, since for Marxists the game is over, beyond repair. It is one thing to talk about business at bay, and another to pursue the idea of business, as Khrushchev boasted, buried.

Why, then, do we include a young man who is an avowed socialist and an old man who is an avowed Marxist? First of all, there is a certain intellectual objective to be gained from exploring the spectrum several degrees to the left. It reminds us how things get to be in the center over a period of time. Secondly, Harrington is a special kind of socialist and Marcuse is a special kind of Marxist. Both men are very much in the news and have interesting things to say about business.

Michael Harrington at forty is acknowledged as one of America's foremost social critics. Educated at Holy Cross, followed by some time at Yale Law and a Master's degree at the University of Chicago, he first tasted the pleasures of crusading in print as an associate editor of Dorothy Day's maverick *The Catholic Worker*, from 1951 to 1953. Touched with the social impulse that has made the Catholic Church a living rebuttal to the old charges of conservatism, he participated — participatory democracy is one of his cries — in the real world by ministering to Bowery derelicts in the Catholic Worker House in New York. It was a sobering experience. He learned what poverty was about when all his clothes were stolen and he resolved never again to call a victim of society a "bum." An avid reader of government statistics and the *Wall Street Journal*, he found proof in these fine publications that there were somewhere between thirty and fifty million Americans living below the poverty line in an affluent society.

The wheel of fortune turned his way when his newly published *The Other America* caught the attention of another young Irish-American in the White House. It strongly influenced President

Kennedy's call for a war on poverty only three days before his assassination. The Johnson Administration then invited him to help Sargent Shriver start the struggling program, which Harrington deplores as having been all but lost to the competing war in Viet Nam.

That both Presidents should have welcomed one of the few politically active socialists (he is Chairman of the League for Industrial Democracy) into their Administrations is a testimonial to Harrington's irrefutable idealism and conscience. Like his predecessor Norman Thomas, the soft-spoken, poetic-looking Harrington is one of those rare controversial persons whom society generally admires even while in disagreement.

For Harrington there is still a time for political ideology in America. He does not find it in the Democratic party, which is too tame for his visionary, rebellious soul. No longer a Catholic, he has retained an undiminished secular fervor for the ethical and democratic values of his personally defined socialism. As discussed in his second book, an intellectual feat entitled *The Accidental Century* (1965), very few socialist countries measure up to the Harrington version. Russia is out for obvious reasons and so are the hard-nosed emerging nations. The Social Democratic countries of Western Europe (Sweden and Denmark are leading contenders) have too often "equated their vision with a welfare state rather than with a new civilization." Here is the apocalyptic element of Harrington's vision, no less than a new civilization, a "City of God" but not with Berle's deacons.

Even the traditional state ownership of the means of production would be only a technique to insure freedom, not a goal in itself. More important would be an intangible, moral objective, "making democratic and free choice the principle of social and economic life," an attainment apparently not possible in a non-socialist system. In addition, there is a new urgency for transforming the United States into a highly planned society. This is because the overwhelming forces of technology have tumbled upon us *accidentally*. Their effects, from air pollution to sick cities to loss of individuality are, in Harrington's view, pointing us straight towards doom. Alternatively, these forces can be directed towards producing a humanist, emotionally satisfying life on a scale never before possible.

The objectives are upright enough to please Dr. Billy Graham but the prescription would hardly attract those men in Washington who are grounded in their function as power brokers between the White House and a traditionally conservative Congress. Remembering the realistic, fact-laden analysis of poverty that two Presidents were able to translate into a call for action, Harrington has returned to the fray with a new book, *Toward a Democratic Left* (1968). Bowing to the idea that the art of politics is the art of the possible, he has disarmingly checked his socialism at the door and offered an in-between program to combat the awesome crises of racism, poverty and urban violence he anticipated in *The Other America* six years earlier.

II

First of all, he finishes off Keynesianism, perhaps to the dismay of those who had just about caught up with the master. Galbraith had already spotted Keynes as a conservative and Robert Lekachman, Keynes's distinguished American biographer, has labelled the mixed system "commercial Keynesianism." To Harrington, what we have is "Adam Smith-Keynesianism."

If he is correct, this is a remarkable dialectic. Adam Smith, symbol of free enterprise, provokes a reaction in the form of John Maynard Keynes, symbol of government intervention. The synthesis is American capitalism, which Harrington says "doesn't work any more."

It doesn't work because it favors business too much and thus is an inadequate model for the great social needs of the sixties. It was all right to zig and zag through the Great Depression and the post World War II period in a series of pragmatic reforms and experiments that finally led us to the brink of a trillion dollar Gross National Product. Now there are new expectations and levels of accomplishment that demand over-all direct planning rather than a harmonizing of countervailing forces. Keynesians and corporate businessmen, however, resist federal planning because they think it is overly bureaucratic and leads to socialism.

Yet how, Harrington asks, will 500,000 homes a year for the lowest income group and five million jobs for the jobless and under-employed be created without the heavy hand of planning? The figures are there, he challenges, brandishing the government's own Department of Labor statistics and official Manpower, Crime, Automation and Civil Disorder Commission reports (which are, in their way, as embarrassing as the *Communist Manifesto*) before us. When will America redeem its pledges — FDR's of 1944 advocating the right to useful employment, the great intentions of the Employment Act of 1946 and the pledge of Senator Robert Taft in 1949 of decent housing for the poor?

One would expect his wrath to fall upon the "vested interests," but the shopworn phrase is not even raised by this seemingly reasonable man. He acknowledges that powerful, organized forces are stalling off sweeping social changes but "they are not the bloated Wall Street plutocracy of Leftist myth and that is why it is all the more difficult and all the more imperative to recognize them."

As the book closes, he does recognize them. The resistance is none other than the majority of American voters. Good democrat that he is, Harrington vows to change the majority point of view in due time. The new majority will consist of the old liberals, the voters among the 30 million poor and the fast-growing, educated, scientific and intellectual élite of the nation. They will join forces to create a "democratic left." Curiously this overworked élite has been called up by Veblen, Berle, Galbraith, Heilbroner and now Harrington. Will it ever appear in any kind of solidarity? Perhaps its members are only the "new men" of a new technocracy, happy in their suburbs, multiversities and metrocorporations, more interested in solving problems than in joining parties.

Polemics and virtue aside, Harrington's confrontation with the giant corporations adds another opinion to the debate over the function of this most important section of our business system.

He parts company with Berle and Galbraith over the profit motive. On the assumption that business must maximize profits, Harrington states it will only make a hit and run mess of social spending generated in the usual way by subsidies, guarantees and tax benefits from Washington, no matter how generously funded. The corporation will either be guided from start to finish in its efforts or it will play the dominant role, and the latter doesn't work. The idea that the corporation, comprising a neutral association of qualified experts, will for a reasonable profit promote the public good, in an impartial and scientific way, is wishful thinking. Social problems such as the elimination of poverty are too important to have their fate entrusted to profit-minded organizations.

There is a touch of Veblen here, with his separation of money-minded instincts as being incompatible with the machine or social process. Indeed Harrington draws up a list of infirmities. When the chips are down, management remains self-interested and even anti-social. There are, besides the economic reasons, sociological and even psychological reasons (the compulsion to make more money as a power reflex, even if it is all taxed away), that keep management beyond the pale. Harrington hardly has time for the corporate conscience. He also seems to forget that the élite technostructure, so instinctually amoral, is an important part of his voting constituency on the proposed majority democratic left.

Harrington admits that big business really no longer fights Washington and has accepted the welfare state. The welfare state, however, is equally concerned with helping business maximize its profits, even while employing it. He quotes Gardner Ackley, then Chairman of the President's Council of Economic Advisers, as stating in 1967 that, in most instances, industry's decisions are consistent with the welfare of the country. In Harrington's view, this mutual esteem results in state programs of intervention, using business as the contractor, turning out to be "more on behalf of the rich than of the poor." There is no class conflict in Harrington's phrase, as it is assumed the number of poor he has helped publicize makes their amelioration a matter of common concern. Nor is a conspiracy involved. It is simply a natural tendency when the government insists that private sector values be applied to economic priorities. In this sense, Harrington seems to say that history is being repeated: The old trusts that dominated the Congress in the nineteenth century, having been thoroughly reshaped and reformed, are subtly corrupting the government once again.

His bill of particulars is random and subjective, the type of argument that is too doctrinaire to be resolved but which deserves its day in court. Thus, the great highway programs have been carried out at the expense of the transit systems, helping suburbanites and creating traffic jams in the cities, as well as an immobile population in the Watts ghetto area of Los Angeles. Federal housing policy has been geared almost exclusively to the more profitable market of middle-class families, who live in the suburbs, at the expense of the Negroes and poor in the cities. Federal food programs (including school lunches which reach only one-third of the children in need of them) are not designed to serve the needs of the intended beneficiaries. Influenced by the farm lobby and "agribusiness," national agricultural policy is dominated by a concern for maximizing farm income.

The Federal Highway Act of 1962, the Housing and Urban Development Act of 1965 and the Demonstration Cities Act of 1966 all required coordination of spending at the state and city levels. This was accomplished by a "one mayor-one vote" procedure within the area, which ends up favoring suburbs against central cities. The Air Quality Act of 1967 commenced the war against pollution at the state level, playing into the hands of the dominant industrial groups, such as the coal producers, which caused the pollution in the first place.

These angry charges, well-documented and undoubtedly perceptive, are scarcely an indictment of the business system. It is one of Harrington's weaknesses that in his frustration over the irrationalities of give-and-take reform, compared with the Utopian symmetry of an all-knowing state, he often confuses business with government. Each of these programs is the end result of hundreds of pressure groups leaning to their own advantage, a democratic play of forces that is admittedly not the most efficient procedure. Yet they are expressions of a government constantly expanding its social concern and hopefully dedicated to the evolving art of city and regional planning.

When he writes of the "social-industrial complex," Harrington draws closer to accurate business criticism, as here he finds business and government already embraced. His title, of course, derives from the "military-industrial complex" which most citizens, following the lead of President Eisenhower, view as a fearsome growth which is excused, if at all, by the necessities of defense. An example of the social-industrial complex cited by Harrington concerns a major corporation overselling advanced educational equipment to an Indian reservation school system in Wisconsin, purportedly on behalf of the Office of Education. Conflicts of interest inevitably arise in government purchasing, and, as Adolf Berle has well pointed out, the American record of exposure and punishment is quite noteworthy, reaching into Cabinet positions. Since the federal government purchases about 20% of the Gross National Product, presumably it is able to watch out for its end of the bargain. What it buys is ultimately based on a political decision that cannot reasonably be laid at the door of business. Unless, of course, the business spirit subverts government, which is what Harrington implies.

In the end, it appears that Harrington barely wants government to contract with the big corporations at all, although he came with intentions of massive spending subject to massive planning:

> America cannot sell its social conscience to the highest corporate bidder. It must build new institutions of democratic planning which can make the uneconomic, commercially wasteful and humane decisions . . . this society so desperately needs.

III

What a pity this high-minded critic cannot consummate his deal without reservations that would probably cancel it, at least for the time being. He is correct in asserting that massive public spending, in the form of housing, job-creation and some form of negative income tax, as a replacement for the old welfare system, is needed. To this, big businessmen would readily agree, especially once the burden of war is removed. Imagine the change of attitude that has taken place when the negative income tax (desperately searching for a better name) has already been endorsed in principle by an illustrious cross-section of American industrialists. It is a pragmatic, quick response to Martin Luther King, Jr.'s economic bill of rights which asks for either a job or income for the one-third black and two-thirds white in this country who are considered poor. It is a program, incidentally, which Harrington heartily endorses.

Harrington grants that real socialism is many years down the road and he is willing to keep his version of it on reserve in the face of the present catastrophe. He would find most businessmen equally ready to acknowledge that we already are living with substantial socialism, if they could but mention the word. Regarding a major turn towards planning, businessmen are far ahead of administrators and Congress in this respect. All they want is to be included in the planning. They also have an understandable desire to decentralize this planning towards their sector as well as towards regional levels. This sentiment is shared by two outstanding liberals, the late Senator Robert F. Kennedy and Senator Eugene McCarthy, both of whom sensed a need for a revision of the traditional bias in favor of bureaucracy.

Indeed Harrington quotes Galbraith correctly to the effect that the giant corporations are planners *par excellence*, able to teach the state itself how it is done. Some of them, like Litton Industries, have already contracted to build entire cities for foreign governments, probably creating a new set of problems for America in the process. Amid such enthusiasm and expertise, it is reasonable to assume that America is even ready for some of the advanced "indicative planning" which the French government has worked out with French industry. Countenanced by a benign President who cares as little for capitalism as he does for socialism, it involves conscious direction of the use of a good portion of the country's resources. To round out the tale, 500,000 Frenchmen have recently bought Jean-J.

Servan-Schreiber's *The American Challenge*, which tells them they should be more interested in absorbing some of our organizational genius and managerial aggressiveness than in expanding their planning.

Surely Harrington realizes that big business pays only lip service to maximized profits. As defense contractors, businessmen have been subject to contract renegotiations to take away excessive profits, which already are taxed at approximately fifty per cent. As a supplicant for public approval, business avoids monopoly and has been known to hold prices down, for example, on the new autos appearing during the shortage after World War II. Businessmen can afford to take government business at less profits because risk is reduced. The present goals of major corporations emphasize increased sales and continuity of the enterprise as much as profits. Peacetime federal contracts, directly or indirectly stimulated, will be welcomed by business with open arms, as R. A. Peterson of Bank of America suggested in the previous chapter. For a good portion of big industry, the change in product from defense to social needs, at restrained prices, will seem the height of reason, in more ways than one.

The quality of our economic life is still another matter. As much as anything else, it will reflect the quality of our elected leadership. It will also reflect the moral fervor of our social critics. Harrington performs an invaluable public service in holding us all accountable for the "other America" — and in goading the business system to meet its responsibilities.

IV

Herbert Marcuse, now in his seventies, is as typically European as Harrington is native American. One of the intellectual geniuses contemporary with Einstein who were washed to our shores in the wake of Hitlerism, he operates in the realm of philosophy rather than advanced physics. The bomb which Einstein helped to create

understandably colors the views of philosophers. As full-time thinkers, the older sages, from Bertrand Russell to Herbert Marcuse,
bear the twin horrors of Hiroshima and the concentration camps
indelibly branded on their minds. The one horror gives them an
innate revulsion for the dark side of the machine; the other for the
dark side of man.

It stands to reason that the mature philosophers of the Western
world are not going to celebrate, as William Graham Sumner did,
the virtues of a business civilization. Probably Sumner himself
would today view it with suspicion. In the businessman's own language, the system has been spoiled by success. After confounding
the ancient forebodings of Marx, that it would only result in the
rich getting richer and the immiserated poor rising in revolt, the
system faces new forebodings. One of these is the pervading materialism of the "people of plenty," as David Potter calls us. The
system has succeeded fantastically as a producer and there is little
doubt that even poverty can be abolished in America. But Marcuse
goes so far as to call it a "hell on earth," for the poverty-stricken,
at least, in some of his darker moments.

Why should we listen to this Jeremiah in our midst when there
are so many others, from Galbraith to Arnold Toynbee, who patiently upbraid us — often with a sense of humor, or at least satire —
for being gadget-ridden and commercial? Perhaps Marcuse does not
belong in these pages. It would probably infuriate him to know the
company he is keeping in what hopefully has been a pro-business
seminar. One of his most fascinating indictments of our society is
that there is no chance for a critic or a heretic. It is not a matter of
the Establishment preventing them from speaking out. On the contrary, our society is more likely to embrace them — as it did pop
artists and Norman Mailer — and make them celebrities. This rein-
forces the *illusion* of criticism and "multiple dimensions," Marcuse
claims, while taking away the cutting edge. Ironically, Marcuse has
become a celebrity himself, fully exploited in *The New York Times
Magazine*, *Time* and educational television.

On the political spectrum, he goes beyond Harrington's "democratic left" to take his position on the "new left," where he is one

of the spiritual leaders. Since the new left has enlisted a really remarkable and spontaneous support of bright and idealistic youth throughout the world, open-minded adults — or at least parents — ought to hear him out. His influence as a new left leader should not be underestimated. It is a canon of the new left, however, to avoid the cult of personality, not to idolize leaders or supermen who have so often turned out to be false. If anything, the new left is an emotional response rather than an organized political response against the status quo. It has an economic element which is perhaps unique in history. This economic protest is not for more of society's dividends for youth as much as it is for less. Inheritors of an affluent society, they clearly reject the mass consumption ethic. Many see it as spoiling the values of the culture they are studying for a brief and final period before joining it. In a variety of ways, ranging from obstructing the nearest institution at hand to actually "dropping out," they are registering a desire to avoid integration into the existing society. This society, in their view, is dominated by large economic interests that are impersonal monopolies. They sense these interests are allied with political institutions and marketing forces that manipulate man and turn him into an acquisitive more than a human being. Marcuse can hardly be credited with bringing about such an accumulation of converging ideas throughout the world, let alone the United States, where the revelations of poverty and the Viet Nam war add to the unrest. Yet his writings provide a ready handbook and erudite reinforcement for such an outlook. He is thus legitimately the "professor of the new left."

Marcuse rejects servile adherence to ideologies. Certainly the new left movement is closer to anarchism than traditional ideologies in its improvised subversion of authority on the campus. Marcuse readily admits that the students who rioted at Columbia were apparently influenced by his writings (although they contain no such programs) and he does not deny that the siege of the Sorbonne which almost overthrew de Gaulle, or the riots in Rome, may have been similarly inspired. There were no tactics or directions, however, emanating from his headquarters on the San Diego campus of the University of California.

Commenting on these activities, Marcuse says that he deplores violence against people but not necessarily against "things." (In his writings, he deplores the "reification" of our life, which would certainly indispose one from enjoying twentieth century progress.) Like Veblen, however, he accepts technology and simply wants the Frankenstein kept in its place. He also states in relation to the campus disturbances that they are justified only if democratic action first fails. Since he has a weak enthusiasm for democracy, this reservation is somewhat less than acceptable. One of the most daring and disturbing ideas of Marcuse is the limitations he places on democracy. Followed to its logical conclusions, it would mean that freedom of speech and assembly could as easily be denied as granted, depending on the merits of the case. Marcuse's answer that Hitlerism could thus have been prevented and that democracy isn't really democratic does not satisfy believers in the democratic process.

Just as Harrington finds the old New Deal too entrenched for the times, the new left finds Communism too dogmatic. Its rigid imposition of doctrine insults their intelligence and they wonder how some of their parents could have travelled with it back in the thirties, assuming they are now paying that much attention to their parents. Marcuse, who admits he is a Marxist to the extent it helps him analyse the sickness of society, has attacked the conformity of thought in Russia just as much as in the United States. Those who have struggled through his books can readily understand why they have been denounced and sometimes banned in the Soviet. The tyranny of mind is a symptom of advanced industrial states, he maintains, and in Russia's case he commits the additional offense of castigating its working class for having lost its principles. This, in highly simplified terms, makes him a "humanist Marxist." There is a school of thought which finds evidence of an earlier, humane Marx behind the beard of the incredible man who married the daughter of a German baron and caused so great a train of events with his pen. It would be easy enough for Marcuse to say he is not a Marxist — just as Marx once did himself — but this white-haired Socrates does not bend.

V

The book that brings the students to the barricades is *One-Dimensional Man*, as frightening and pessimistic a portrait of modern society as one is likely to find. For the record — and to expose business to the full spectrum of criticism — a brief summary, subject to the glaring faults of all summaries, will be attempted.

Marcuse's technique is the familiar one of "things are not what they seem to be." *One-Dimensional Man* is a series of paradoxes. Though we seem to be having endless debates over business power, labor rights and domestic and foreign policy, for example, there is really only one side to the discussion, the acceptance of the status quo. A true opposition demands consideration of what Marcuse calls a "transcending" choice, a choice that logic and rationality tell us should be made, or at the very least debated with great heat. These are the "historical alternatives which haunt the society as subversive tendencies and forces," the subversion presumably being of the constructive kind. Although Marcuse chooses to offer practically no historic parallels in his book, perhaps the need for the alternative of Judaism and Christianity in the all-powerful Roman world of paganism would be a case in point for another era. Marcuse is firmly grounded in the present. His present transcending alternatives would include an end to war, an end to capitalism, the elimination of poverty and the raising of man to some vaguely described new levels of freedom and self-expression. The words used are "autonomous" as against "heteronomous," another version of David Riesman's better-known inner-directed rather than outer-directed man.

As with most passionate critics, Marcuse is stronger in conducting us through his inferno than in leading us out of it. What we have in our society is "integration of opposites" which restrains social change. The underlying population, which by all logic should cast off onerous work and employer domination by demanding new institutions, is too beguiled by the immense consumer production of technology to roll over and fight. Business and labor have integrated. Pluralism has declined throughout the country due to such agents as mass media and homogenized Main Streets. The immense production for war goes on endlessly, sustained by the unanimous fear of destruction by the very weapons we produce for defense. Meanwhile, the industrial system becomes bigger and better, stimulated by wasteful production and defense budgets. Life becomes easier for increasing numbers of people, space is explored, science is mastered and we all submit to a totally irrational scheme of things without a whimper.

Thus we live under a new kind of dictatorship, not one of terror but one of technology and total administration. No government forces are needed to keep us in line. We shape up in gratitude for our rising standard of living. We even think what we are doing is the height of reason, when in fact it is apparently sheer madness. Man, with all his glory and potential for complexity, is a cardboard man, one-dimensional.

In fairness to Marcuse, this seemingly absurd summary glosses over his intent to focus on "tendencies" in the advanced societies. There are obviously large areas, he grants, where even the tendencies do not prevail. The universities, for example, have been noted by Marcuse as being frequent oases in this open asylum. "I am offering these tendencies," he cautions in *One-Dimensional Man*, "and I offer some hypotheses, nothing more."

By now Marcuse's kinship with Thorstein Veblen, with whom our journey started, may be apparent. Both men describe the "drift" or "tendency" of things and scorn the "vested interests" and "underlying population" alike. They are resistant to ideology, fascinated and repelled by technology and able to see human folly with X-ray eyes. Both share a healthy disrespect for the business spirit, including a Puritanical downgrading of material possessions.

In *One-Dimensional Man*, Marcuse refers the reader to Berle's 1932 exposé of corporate bigness as background material. As for the merits of Berle's corporate conscience, the very idea receives summary treatment. "Is it still necessary to denounce the ideology of the managerial revolution?" Marcuse asks incredulously. The image of the managers not even denounced, perhaps before being marched away, is rather frightening. One wonders whether Marcuse, given the opportunity, would be a Robespierre after all. The possibility heightens when it is noted that Marcuse, unlike Veblen, does not have a sense of humor.

Marcuse makes it clear that the employees of advanced industrial societies are manipulated, administered slaves, even though they don't know it. Lack of awareness does not change the condition of servitude, just as apparent freedom can be unfreedom. There is no hatred for the technocrat bosses in this structure. The latter can't very well be identified, busy as they are with their scientist and government colleagues in the search for efficiency behind "the veil of technology." The Soviet system is granted equally rough treatment. In 1968, *Pravda* paid back in kind. Marcuse it stated, was a werewolf, blaspheming the name of Marx and leading youth away from the working class struggle.

Serious though Marcuse is, he need not be taken seriously based on the exaggerations of *One-Dimensional Man*. In his "Political Preface 1966" (to *Eros and Civilization*, a revision of Freud), he shows no signs of mellowing. In the affluent society, the authorities "deliver the goods." The opposition is effectively and democratically "contained." The master and slave relationship continues with television sets going full blast, although "it is not a bad life for those who comply and repress." Automation will eventually "explode" the system by creating so much free time a new and better order will have to be established. Finally, like Veblen in *The Engineers and the Price System*, Marcuse unexpectedly makes a direct call for political action. As might be expected, he summons first the scientific and intellectual élite. If they will kindly refuse to cooperate with the authorities . . .

One is tempted to dismiss Marcuse in bewilderment and chagrin, at least as a business critic. It is hardly a brain-washed, neutralized society of non-debaters that forces a President to forego renomination. The youth movement itself, even the hippies, contradicts his gloomy diagnosis of a nation of walking zombies. Still the impact of this philosopher runs deep and the brief summary is quite superficial. One should take time to think. How far along the road is Ray Bradbury's *Fahrenheit 451?* George Orwell's *1984?*

The forces of repression that Marcuse describes as being "sub-limated" have ominously come out in the open to harass the man himself. He has received anonymous letters threatening his life from people who don't like his views and probably haven't read his books. A veteran's post has gratuitously offered to buy up his teaching contract, as if it were for sale. Some state legislators have called for his removal. His students support him. His fellow faculty members endorse him overwhelmingly, praising him as "the preeminent contemporary political and social philosopher . . . in the age-old quest to find truth."

If they all gathered on this page, Thorstein Veblen would light a cigar and indulge in some choice dialogue with Herbert Marcuse. Sinclair Lewis and Babbitt might see in him the image of Professor Brockbank marching in the telephone girls' strike amidst the dark mutterings of Vergil Gunch and the Good Citizens League. Marriner Eccles might be reminded of his own intellectual daring. Could a man change a complete set of political and economic beliefs in his fortieth year? Cyrus Eaton would muse upon the protection a great fortune lends to unpopular ideas. T. K. Quinn would reflect on the two faces of business he had come to see in a courageous lifetime. Adolf Berle would glory in the strength and resiliency of a country that can tolerate the very marrow of dissent. Michael Harrington would receive inspiration to pursue a life of independent thought. Businessmen, large and small, might be reminded that business itself is always searching for the new and the untried; and that it is just as important to be a man as a businessman.

INDEX